The Wives' Room

A Look Behind the NFL Curtain

Sally Gardocki

MASTERS PRESS

A Division of Howard W. Sams & Company

Published by Masters Press
A Division of Howard W. Sams & Company
2647 Waterfront Pkwy E. Dr, Suite 100
Indianapolis, IN 46214

Printed in the United States of America.

96 97 98 99 00 01   10 9 8 7 6 5 4 3 2 1

Library of Congress Cataloging-in-Publication Data
Gardocki, Sally
    The wives' room : a look behind the NFL curtain / Sally
Gardocki.
        p. cm.
    ISBN 1-57028-158-0 (pbk.)
    1. Football players' spouses -- United States. 2. Wives -- Effect
of husband's employment on -- United States. 3. Football players
-- United States -- Family relationships. 4. National Football
League. I. Title.
GV959.5.G37 1997   97-26790
796.332'086'55--dc21   CIP

To the love and inspiration of my life,
Chris,
Without your support none of this would have been possible.
To my son,
Cole,
Who teaches me something new every day.
Finally, to my parents,
Who never told me I couldn't fly.
I love you all.
Thank you for everything.

Author Sally Gardocki and her husband, Indianapolis Colts' punter, Chris

Table of Contents

Acknowledgements

Many thanks to Eldon Ham, my literary agent and friend, for his never-ending encouragement.

Many thanks to the people at Masters Press for taking a chance on me. And a very special thanks to Holly Kondras, my editor, for her friendship, patience and guidance.

Many special heartfelt thanks to all NFL players and their wives.

To Stacy, Cathy, Kim, and countless other wives who are my friends, I will never forget what we have all shared or what your friendships mean to me.

To everyone who shared their stories with me, I sincerely appreciate it. This book wouldn't have been possible without you.

To Troy, I hope this book becomes a "must" on your recommended reading list.

Thanks also to my friends at Colleton River Plantation for your support.

And finally, to MCO, who watches over and protects me from above, thank you for all the years of wonderful stories. You were, and always will be, the master story-teller.

Although there are people in this book who are real people – friends and acquaintances made through our years in the NFL – there are some who are pure make-believe. Most notably the characters in the stories of Ricki, Grace, McKenna and Sloane are not walking, talking human beings. Although their stories are based on actual events, the characters are purely fictional and were invented by the author to entertain her readers.

Credits:

Cover design: Suzanne Lincoln
Cover Photography: Chris Smith
Hand Model: Debra Delk
Back cover and interior photographs are from
the collection of Chris and Sally Gardocki

The Wives' Room

The choice was mine and mine completely.
I could have any prize that I desired.
I could burn with the splendor of the brightest fire,
Or else, or else I could chose time.
Remember, I was very young then;
And a year was forever and a day.
So what years could fifty, sixty, seventy be?
I saw the lights and I was on my way.
And how I lived! How they shone!
But how soon the lights were gone.

Andrew Lloyd Webber, from "Evita"

Prologue

The Wives' Room, n.   1. An area in most football stadiums reserved solely for players' families.

2. A television room where wives can watch the game together, escaping fans and extreme temperatures.

3. The place where a wife is initiated into the customs of the National Football League, endures the highs and lows of her husband's career while finding herself, and finally passes her baton of knowledge to an eager rookie's wife.

The wives' room is the common denominator between all National Football League wives. Their pilgrimage through professional football begins and ends in this room. From the excited cheers of a wife watching her husband's first professional game to the tears she sheds while enduring his last play, the wives' room witnesses all and becomes a part of her life. It can be the best seat in the house, even though the only view of the game is from a television stuck in the corner. It is a place of joy and a place of sorrow, and it is the keeper of many, many secrets.

I am an NFL wife and my journey through the wives' room has not ended. It will not be over until my husband turns in his jock for the last washing. With a little luck and blessing from the football gods, my personal odyssey will continue a few more years. But I have witnessed partial and entire journeys of many other wives. I have learned from, been inspired by and patterned my own life after the lessons taught in the wives' room. And Pigskin 101 has been the toughest course I've ever taken.

◆ ◆ ◆ ◆ ◆

My grandmother died at the age of 86 in the summer of 1996. She left behind many pictures and journals, yellowed and frayed with age to tell her life's story. As they had been hidden in her attic, these journals had never been seen by my family. My dad found them when he was looking for some of the personal belongings with which she wanted to be buried. As I sat in my jeans, cross-legged on the floor of her sun porch hours after her funeral, I learned who my grandmother really was. I read each page diligently and examined each picture. Like a character in a book, her whole persona slowly took shape. My grandmother had once been beautiful, vibrant and full of life. She had travelled throughout the country with her friends, dressed to the nines, in fancy-looking automobiles, smoking those elegant, long cigarillos.

She hadn't always been ancient and wrinkled, smelling of Worth perfume, like I remembered her. The grandmother who dyed Easter eggs for me couldn't have been the twenty-year old woman who had an affair with a man named Teddy and penned the long-kept love letters that I now read. She couldn't have been the woman laughing with abandon, head thrown back, at the World's Fair in Saint Louis in the 1930s. But this spontaneous and sprightly woman with an immense joie de vivre was my grandmother. And she was gone. I could never ask her about her other, younger life, or what she had most longed for, and if she had been satisfied with her life at its end.

As I sifted through her past, I began pondering my own life and wondered how I would one day be perceived from my photo albums with hand-scribbled notes in the margins. My most interesting experiences, the ones that had taught me about life, involved my years as a wife in the NFL. There were so many stories behind the smiling faces of my photo collection. I determined that I didn't want my future grandchildren to have to piece together and guess what kind of person I had been, what type of friends I had surrounded myself with, or what I had learned in life. I decided that I wanted to preserve and share my life journey in more detail than had my grandmother. That day on her porch, I decided to write this book and tell the whole story behind the pictures, programs, ticket stubs and newspaper articles stuffed in my albums.

Who am I to write this book? I sing loudly off-key to Alanis Morissette when I am alone in my car. I cry when the little girl in the Kodak commercial grows up, gets married and tells her father goodbye. I wear baseball caps because I am too lazy to fix my hair everyday. I am addicted to MAC lipstick. I belly-laugh at "Seinfeld," and wish I had hair like Jennifer Anniston. I have been divorced and learned the hard way what love isn't. I think Brad Pitt and Sean Connery are sexy. I am moved by the writings of Pat Conroy and aspire to own an original oil by Alexandra Nichita. I think fake eyelashes are fun. I have to yell "fatso" at myself to run more than two miles. I would die for my husband or son. I love the serenity and peacefulness of South Carolina marshlands and pink-red sunsettings over the Intracoastal Waterway. I am impressed by people who sacrifice for others, like my mother... I am probably a lot like you.

So, in this book, I will be your guide, like Virgil in Dante's *Inferno*, helping you explore a foreign land. NFL wives, to this point in time, have been an enigma to the public. Usually overshadowed by our famous husbands, the knights of autumn, we are often misjudged or ignored. Our roles as wives and mothers have been relegated to small blurbs in large articles about our husbands. We have been the smiling face behind the laurel-wreathed victor. But I want to show you the whole picture, the image the camera *didn't* catch.

This book is *not* a "tell-all" about who succeeded and who failed in living up to an unrealistic image. This book is about people; normal people living abnormal lives with no dress rehearsals. This book is my view of the NFL from the wives' room.

Pre-kickoff, the Bears prepare to meet the Saints.
Chris is number 17.

First Game

Afoot and lighthearted I take to the open road
Healthy, free, the world before me,
The long brown path before me leading wherever I choose.
　　　　— Walt Whitman, *Song of the Open Road*

Even from one mile away, I could hear the roar of the fans and smell the bratwursts grilling as I stepped from my car on my way to Soldier Field. I had parked at McCormick Place, a mile away from the lakefront facility, because underling rookies weren't granted stadium parking passes for pre-season games. I quickly realized that I should have worn my J. Peterman urban hiking boots instead of my fashionable Nine West heeled clogs.

The parking lots between Soldier Field and McCormick Place were a sea of orange and blue. Bears flags were waving from the antennas of minivans whose horns played a staccato version of what I later learned was the Bears fight song. I cautiously made my way to the stadium, through throngs of beer-gutted, boisterous fans arguing over the point spread of Bear victory. Acutely aware that I was alone, I was thankful to be dressed in clothing that identified me neither as friend nor foe to the ticket-deprived die-hard fans listening to the game on radios from the parking lots.

It was Chris' national debut as a professional football player, and I was late. Hell, I wasn't just late; I'd missed the whole first quarter! Chris' childhood dream had been realized during the National Anthem and I hadn't been there to see it. And if that wasn't bad enough, I'd also missed his first kickoff!

This was so typical of my goofy life. Although I had been a Chicago resident only 48 hours, I had thought I could master the thirty mile drive downtown from the suburbs where Chris and I had our first apartment. I had left Lake Bluff one hour before kickoff, at 6:30 p.m., without a map, thinking there would be numerous signs on the Kennedy Expressway to guide me to Soldier Field. "Just head south," I told myself, "Only a moron couldn't find a landmark as large as Soldier Field."

About thirty-five minutes into my excursion, at the Congress Parkway off-ramp (which I later learned was the Soldier Field exit), a naked, smiling man in a dirty Ford pickup passed me and half saluted, half waved. I almost drove into the Marlboro man's chaps on the large billboard along Interstate 94. I immediately thought of my parents and friends from my small southern hometown who had warned my about the "criminal element" of big city life, and I wondered if this was it: a happy, naked guy. While I was ogling his corpulent flesh, I missed the exit sign for Soldier Field and was heading for Saint Louis. I was still laughing hysterically when I alarmingly noticed that the lights of the large skyscrapers were far behind me and I was on Interstate 55, *not* Interstate 94. I quit laughing, realized I was a moron, and started looking for an off-ramp.

It was dark, I was lost and I was missing one of the most important nights in Chris' life. By the time I turned around in Timbuktu Bolingbrook, about ten miles from the stadium, I knew I wasn't going to see the coin toss. After I finally corrected my bearings, found the stadium and parked, it was the middle of the second quarter.

Making my way to my seat, I noticed every detail about the fans I passed. Since this was my first professional football game, I stared at everything with the wide-eyed wonder of a child. Professional football fans already seemed very different from the mild-mannered college football fans to which I was accustomed. Their game faces were much more serious than those of the Clemson

University fans with whom I had been rubbing shoulders since I was 12.

As I made my way farther into the throng of hot and sweaty enthusiasts who randomly shouted "Go Bears," I was nonsensically reminded of a Monet painting: bold flashes of color were strikingly contrasted against a canvas of muted neutrals. The muted neutrals were dressed in faded Jim McMahon jerseys and Zubaz sweatpants, while the bold flashes were just painted: Bear logos and player numbers were on their heads, necks, chests, faces and any other epidermal area that was visible and un-clothed. Many drank expensive, watered-down tap beer and one group I passed was handing around a "funny-looking" cigarette. Although the appearance of the many fans was as diverse as a combo pack of Jelly Bellys, the Bear aficionados were joined in a common cause — Bear victory. I would later learn that their cause was one of the biggest differences between fans and wives. Wives always want the team to win, but most importantly, we want our husbands to have a good game. Any wife worth her weight in shoulder pads will admit to this.

On that beautiful summer night in August of 1991, the team was still spearheaded by a player's coach, and the Bears were on top of the NFL world. As I gratefully found Section 115, I savored the universe George Halas had created so many years before my birth. I felt there was no better game in the world than football, and I was thankful for Chris' turn under the roving spotlight of fame. Life really couldn't have been better. I wanted to frame this moment in my mind, a snapshot memory to share later with our grandchildren.

When I finally reached my seat, I looked around at the awe-some structure of the stadium itself. It was so impressive upon first glance, the strong, noble columns stood guard over the lakefront field, daring competitors to dream of victory, that I didn't notice the old concrete stairs were unevenly poured until a drunk man fell *up* the aisle and landed at my feet! We both laughed.

He ceremoniously took the unoccupied seat beside me, and within ten minutes had vomited on my foot. The close encounter of the strange kind prompted me to find the wives' room, a safe-haven for player families about which Chris had told me.

On my way there, I envisioned a plush, air-conditioned room with overstuffed sofas, big screen televisions, catered food and beautifully appointed restrooms. Since the Bears were one of the top revenue producing teams in the League, I imagined the wives' room would be palatial. My mouth watered at the thought of the fresh shrimp and hors de'oeuvres I felt sure would be waiting for me on a white tableclothed display.

After locating the wives' room and talking my way in without a pass, I entered a dank, musty room that had, in a different century, been a referee's locker facility. This was apparent from the rusty faced lockers that lined the 30 x 30 room. It now housed two "Goodwill" quality sofas and a small — very small — black and white television with aluminum-foil-laden rabbit ears. People were gathered in front of it, watching the fuzzy game. There wasn't even anywhere for me to sit except on the threadbare floor rug. An attendant guarded Subway sandwiches on a rickety wooden table sans cloth. As the crowd swarmed to snatch them up, I made my way to the restrooms, hoping to find better accommodations. When I entered the women's bathroom, which was identified by a hand-scrawled piece of paper taped to the door, I was stunned to be greeted by a bespattered urinal in the center of the room. I could just picture the naked referees from years ago, peeing at halftime. This was the piece de resistance! I felt like Alice after she fell into the hole.

After carefully using the toilet-paperless facilities, I made my way back to the swarming television area. As women gathered toward the end of the game, a fashion show like no other unfolded before my eyes. One girl with a beautiful face was bedecked in gold lamé. (I think the correct pronunctiation of that word is "lay me" because of what it seems to invite.) If her gold pants, shirt, vest and blazer weren't enough "fashion flair," the golden ten-gallon hat perched atop her blond mane certainly pushed her ensemble past the point of good taste. In another corner, two striking black women were wearing *beaded* evening gowns, which they had accessorized with gloves, hose, and strapless heels. I imagined they were going to an inaugural ball after the game. And holding court on one of the tattered sofas was a bleached blond with the biggest knockers that I had ever seen in person. She was sporting a bikini top, Daisy Duke shorts and cowboy boots. I re-checked my program to see if we were playing Dallas. Perhaps she had gotten lost after her half-time field performance.

I had always dressed pretty middle-of-the-road, not conservative per se, but not lit up like Robert Redford in *The Electric Horseman* either, so I hastily determined that I wasn't ready to mix with the individuals that I had classified as "clothes foreign." I scooted on the floor to the other side of the room where people were dressed more as I was, in trendy "normal" outfits from The Limited, Gap, and Ann Taylor. But my same-tasted sisters didn't approach me to offer a welcoming introduction, so I sat – alone – for the remaining minutes of the game, viturally ignored except for a few stares from a few women across the room, in the Land of Inappropriate Clothes. As I pondered my apparently dismal future with this group of seemingly unfriendly women, I thought to myself "Welcome to Chicago."

I wanted to yell at them, "Hey! I'm fun! I'm friendly! Come over here and talk to me so I don't feel like an idiot!" But, of course, I didn't. Instead, I did the typical "woman" thing and starting comparing myself to them. Most of the women in the room seemed so cosmopolitan and worldly, and had an almost visible air about them that bespoke confidence. I felt like a fish out of water. My fashion sense had been dulled by my years of pouring over legal documents instead of *Vogue*. Even though my outfit was from the same stores as my clothes-similar cohorts, their ensembles seemed brighter and more vibrant than mine. By the end of the game I determined that I needed a new haircut, a pair of *black* jeans, a Chanel purse and a french manicure — a complete overhaul, in other words.

It would take me almost one whole season, ten more visits to the wives' room, to make my own transformation and understand that what I had originally mistaken for unfriendliness was really just indifference to the constant shuffling of personnel into and out of the Bears' organization. The anchored women in the room, the ones who would stay put when the tides of change washed many wives back out into the sea of the NFL, were good people, but they just weren't overly concerned with the well-being of yet another rookie's wife.

And that was who I was: just another rookie's wife. I still had to learn about the customs and habits of NFL wives, but at least, by the end of that first season, I was on my way. I would eventually learn that the wives' room had its own set of rules and newcomers were seldom accepted with open arms. Newcomers meant job changes and that either affected a wife or one of her friends.

The only thing I was sure of that first game was that my journey into the NFL had just begun and I was in the far right-lane, pokin' along, scared to merge into the fast and cocksure left-lane traffic.

The Rules of the Wives' Room

Sisterhood is Powerful.
                    — Robin Morgan

If I have to, I can do anything.
I am Strong, I am Invincible, I am Woman.
                    — Helen Reddy

A s my initiation into the NFL continued, I discovered that most teams had wives' rooms. Some *were* swanky like the one I had pictured in my mind. Some offered babysitting services during the game. Some gave away free game programs. But no matter the size or the amenities, from what I understood, most atmospheres are the same. For the majority of wives, the wives' room is a place to watch the game, talk to friends, go to the bathroom, breast-feed a child, complain about coaches, catch up on gossip, change a diaper, bitch about bad seats, and drink beer.

In the four corners of those rooms scattered across the League, all wives are bound, irrespective of our differences in background and personality, because of our husbands' jobs. Their occupation and the rules of the wives' room are sometimes the only common bonds between us.

The rules were simple: Seniority reigned. Player position defined social hierarchy. Clothing categorized. Jewelry classified. Groupies and mistresses were vilified.

In 1991, as I tried to understand and digest rules and the differences between all of us, I observed that three distinct groups existed within its four walls. In a bizarre way, the factions reminded me of Marx's three divisions of the social classes: the dictators (the aristocrats who had already reached the pinnacle), the proletariat (the calloused laborers who never ceased working), and the bourgeoisie (the respectable commoners who were satisfied with their middle-of-the-road status). In other words, the women could be seen as the Haves, the Have Nots and the Contents.

The Haves comprised the smallest group. They were the veteran wives whose husbands had really made it "big." These players had enjoyed long careers and were multimillionaires. They smiled at you from glossy advertisements and beckoned you to purchase products on television. They usually weren't forced to work post-football, and they often left the game on their own terms because they could afford to.

The most timid group were the Have Nots. They were the wives of the lower draft-round rookies, free agents and younger veterans who earned minimum salaries. Their husbands were always on the "cuts" bubble, moving from team to team every season. The Have Nots desperately sought the job and financial security of the Contents.

My crowd, the Contents, fell in between the other two factions. Our husbands made good money, were either starters or second-stringers who got a lot of playing time and were known to most NFL fans, but would never reach Troy Aikman, Bruce Smith, or Walter Payton status. If we didn't blow the money our husbands earned during their steady careers, there was a chance they wouldn't *have* to work after their football careers were finished. But the odds predicted they would not leave the game willingly and would be gainfully employed after their pigskin years. Our vision of Easy Street was a durable, solid blacktop that would endure for the lifetime of our children, while the Have Nots sought to merely replace a dirt path with low-grade pavement, and the Haves rode on streets lined in twenty-four karat gold.

For the most part, my group was comfortable with our Content status and didn't really care to be Haves. Too much heartache can surround the big problems that big money can bring: mistresses, girlfriends, one-night stands, strip bars, alcohol, drugs, electronic surveillance, private detectives and lies. I quickly learned through others that money does not necessarily bring happiness, and it certainly doesn't defend you against a dick with an attitude who thinks you should consider yourself lucky to be on his arm. This is not to say that all sport superstars have attitude problems or treat their wives poorly, but superstar wives must learn to tolerate celebrity not only in the outside world, but also inside the four walls of their own home.

Of the Haves and Have Nots, it took me more time to understand the Haves. The Haves' perspective of life was so foreign to my own. Their husbands' salaries allowed them to become accustomed to Dom Perignon, get lost in the immense square footage of sprawling homes, and spend tens of thousands of dollars on boutique clothing without putting a dent in their husbands' checkbooks. Never having to worry about their financial futures, those women sometimes forgot how everybody else lived. Their idea of riding coach was an inconvenient middle seat in first class.

The biggest fear of the Haves was that the greenest side of the fence wouldn't always belong to them. With comfort levels and expensive hobbies to match their tax bracket, the Haves realized their after-football income would have to match their playing salaries for them to enjoy the same standard of living to which they had grown accustomed during their careers. And there were few occupations that would enable them to do that. Their NFL salaries were almost a "tease," allowing them to take for granted unplanned weekends in the Bahamas or betting $15,000 a night at a gaming table. The Haves feared that their glamourous lifestyle would probably end once they hung up their shoes, and they would be forced to live in the Contents' world.

The Contents and the Have Nots never feared the inability to maintain the life of Trump. Never experiencing the luxuries, sponteneity and spending habits of the Haves, the Contents and Have Nots remained tethered to reality, where the investment yields from their salaries meant living in a comfortable and mortgage-free home after football, taking yearly vacations and having one car paid off.

The Haves also lived with the knowledge that it was easier to fall from the top than it was to reach the summit by climbing steadily. Whereas the Haves were usually drafted into the pinnacle of the first-string, the Contents battled to be the back-ups and the Have Nots prayed to just make the roster.

The Have Not wives tended to stick together, roaming the stadium and the wives' room as a pack. The Have Not husbands were usually third-stringers and bench warmers, practice dummies waiting for someone else's bad break, whose chances of making it to Content status were slim and to Have status the equivalent of winning the 20 million dollar Lotto. The Have Nots lived their lives out of cardboard boxes, barely unpacking before it was time to move on again. Their existence was a constant juxtaposition of high and low. Cut. Picked up. Cut. Picked up. Their goal was to hold on long enough to qualify for the NFL Pension Fund and be covered under NFL insurance.

Many of us Content wives didn't like the fact that there were three distinct groups. And it wasn't that we weren't all civil to each other, it was just that the tension between the groups could always be felt. So, after one year of coloring inside the lines, a group of us decided to do the unthinkable and mingled. Three or four of us started watching away games together, and, over the course of the season, we slowly expanded our group. We invited and included everyone who wanted to participate, and by the last game of 1992, a friendlier atmosphere had been established — an esprit de corps where there had really been none. By the end of the next year, even most of the hardened veteran wives had relented and we all got to know each other much better. We became friends, not just because of our husbands' membership in the small and exclusive fraternity of the NFL, but because we liked each other.

I learned that *all* of these women were good people. We each just had different perspectives on life, carved from our contrasting backgrounds and colored by our dissimilar upbringings. Even though we didn't always understand each other, we learned to respect and accept one another. We did so partly because no one outside of our football microcosm could really understand the complexion of our lives without living it themselves, without feeling our ever-present stresses and standing-on-top-of-the-world highs. We wives needed each other, for better or worse.

During my four years in the Bears' wives' room, I found myself and learned to discover beauty in the diversity of others' lives. My sisters' legacies carried me to California, Massachusetts, Texas, Georgia, Mississippi, Oklahoma, Nebraska, North Carolina, Florida and Alabama without ever leaving the doorstep of my Illinois townhouse. The friendships forged in those four years are still strong ones, and have been my inspiration in writing this book.

I yearn to tell our stories not to embarrass, ridicule or judge, but rather to educate the public. I want outsiders to come inside, see our world, and understand that the wives they see, if they see us at all, as flat characters are, in truth, multi-dimensional. Most of the wives I have been honored to know are strong, intelligent, courageous and kind. Beauty, the attribute by which most wives are unfortunately judged, does not determine a woman's value or reflect her innerself. I write in the hope that appearance will take a back seat to personality, and that the public will be more empathetic to our lives after they have experienced first-hand our personal revelations, tribulations and victories.

The most enduring lesson I have learned in my years as a player's wife is "judge not lest you be judged." I have travelled halfway around the world to understand the importance of this biblical quotation hammered into my brain as an unwilling child. And I confess that in the beginning of my journey, I did judge some of the people who seemed foreign to my own world. But through their friendships, I learned that so much more can be gained from listening with open ears and an open heart. I learned to celebrate the differences in people. I learned that someone wasn't "bad" or "ignorant" because of a contrasting viewpoint, just different. I learned that people shouldn't be judged by hard-made decisions. And I learned that a beautiful facade can conceal almost anything. In sum, I relay these stories not as judge or tattler, but as defender of the right to be different, the right to be understood, and the right to be accepted for what you are.

To give a more complete picture of our life in the NFL, I have included four fictional wives' stories, the characters composed from the lives of many incredible men and women. The setting is the great city of Chicago, but most of the people behind these characters never played for the Bears. Their life-stories consist of many threads of truth, hearsay and conjecture gathered from seven years of listening, weaved together as an intricate tapestry which links players and their wives all over the League. Back-grounds, positions, names and events have been changed to protect their privacy. But most of their stories are true.

The personalities behind Ricki, Grace, Sloane and McKenna changed my life by broadening my perspective. I think they will also broaden yours.

Yes, see for yourself the decor of the wives' room — as sparse as promised. It was to become known as "The Family Waiting Room" during our tenure in Chicago, but we called it the Wives' Room anyway.

CHICAGO BEARS
Family Waiting Room Pass

Admit _Chris Gardocki_ to Chicago Bears Family Waiting Room. This pass is good for two (2) family members only and is not transferable.

Tim LeFevour
Director of Administration

My NFL Curriculum Vitae

Education is what you have left over after
you have forgotten what you have learned.
— Anonymous

Whenever I am introduced at a cocktail party or strike up a
conversation with someone in the check-out line at the
grocery store and the person I am talking to discovers
what my husband does for a living, I am inevitably asked
the question: "What it is like to be married to a professional football player?" I smile and say, truthfully, that it has
been a wonderful adventure. But my enjoyment of our lives in the
NFL stems from being married to my best friend. I didn't marry
Chris because he's a football player. I married him because I love
him. Kicking a ball is what he does for a living, not who he is.

However, that's not what the inquisitor wants to hear. She
wants to think that my life is different than hers. She wants to
know the everyday goings-on of her heroes. She wants the stories,
the anecdotes and the legends — and I know a million of those.
But it would be impossible for me to share all of this information
in the few minutes surrounding our brief introduction, so I give
her the simple, easy answer.

But I have always wanted the opportunity to answer her
questions fully. I wish that she could *really* feel and see for

herself the responsibility that goes along with the fun of being married to a professional athlete. As you already know through the media, our lives are not always limos, glamour and dancing until dawn. But for me, our years in the NFL have been some of the best of my life. It is with all of the above in mind that I chose the stories on the following pages. I hope they demonstrate the highs and lows of being an NFL wife.

To give you the full picture, I have chosen a wide-ranging variety of topics, from crying in the stands to "mooning" sightseers at Alcatraz in San Francisco. They are an eclectic collection, in random order, and I have tried to write them as if I were telling you stories over a cup of coffee in my kitchen. Actually, that's how I have pictured you, my reader. As a friend to whom I can speak freely. So, pour yourself some coffee and relax. Oh, yeah, please don't mind the dirty dishes in my sink...

Ricki's Story

A mighty pain to love it is,
And 'tis a pain that pain to miss;
But of all pains, the greatest pain
It is to love, but love in vain.
— Abraham Cowley, *Gold*

"Twinkle, Twinkle, little star; How I wonder what you are..." Ricki's voice quavered as she stared blankly at the Winnie the Pooh mobile overhanging her two year old's crib. She chanted the lullaby over and over as she rocked her child in her arms, holding him tightly, to guard him against the evil of the world...and the evil in her own home. She sang to soothe herself also, to keep her mind off the throbbing pain she felt with her every pulse beat.

"The swelling won't be so bad if I put ice on it now," she thought, disgusted. "The game isn't until tomorrow, and I can cover it with makeup then. Nobody will know. Don't panic," Ricki silently assured herself. But as she repeated these words, these same lines she had used so many times before, something inside of her head exploded like a hot-white star. "No, dammit, no. I can't do this anymore. I shouldn't have to do this anymore. Why does this keep happening? Why? I'm a good person, a good mother. Why does he keep doing this to me?" Ricki was sad and scared, her world rapidly spinning out of orbit.

She would have to decide soon. Ricki had conditioned herself to quickly forget the beatings inflicted by her husband Mark, the three-year veteran and star wide receiver of the Chicago Bears, but now her children were getting older and she had to start thinking about them and about what they regularly witnessed. Most parents worried about their children's discoveries outside of a well-protected home, but Ricki worried about the lessons being taught inside her home. She didn't want her children to become silent observers of wickedness. Or worse, to think what happened at home was normal and okay.

Inside her home she was strong for her children. Hiding bruises and stifling screams behind closed doors, she didn't want them to see or know of what their "heroic" father was capable. How strange, she thought, that even here, within the walls of her own house, she had to protect his precious image.

"Image is money," he always told her. "Image means endorsements. We have to look good to the outside world. You enjoy that Jaguar you drive and having two homes, don't you? You just keep your mouth shut if you want to keep it, bitch. One word out of you about what goes on in here, in our house, and you can kiss it all goodbye: the jewelry, the furs, the cars, the houses," he would laugh then, mocking her.

Outside her home, she covered the bruises with thick foundation and sunglasses, her Georgian beauty a perfect, quiet and graceful complement to the much-heralded athlete.

As she looked around little Zachary's beautifully and expensively decorated nursery, she made her decision. The trade-off she had made earlier, favoring material security over happiness, was a sham. Her's was an empty life and she had learned the hard way money didn't buy happiness. She had to leave him for her children and for her own sanity. Tomorrow, the dawn of their new lives, would be the end of Mark's. No one, except herself, knew who he really was. But they would now. She didn't care anymore. No more secrets. Calm in her new-found resolve, she dialed the phone number of the Lake Bluff police.

Ricki Arnold and I met one crisp, fall morning in late September of 1991. I was walking my dogs outside our townhome when her son saw them and came running to play. Ricki followed after, carrying a baby — a tall, attractive woman with sad, knowing eyes

— and we fell into conversation. After a few moments of talk, we discovered that we were both rookie Bears' wives.

I immediately felt a kinship with Ricki. We were from completely different backgrounds, but we were here, far away from our families, because of our husbands' new jobs. The NFL was a fresh and exciting adventure, something we couldn't accurately describe or share with our friends back home, so we talked a lot that first year, becoming stick figure observers of each other's pasts. As we got to know each other, she let me into her world, and told me about her marriage. One of the only places where she could reveal the truth, even to herself, was over hundreds of cups of morning coffee in my kitchen. For the next three years, it became a sanctuary from her real world. But in September of 1991, I was only learning the beginning, the early story of their lives.

She and Mark met when they were in high school. She was fifteen, a stunning flag majorette, and he was seventeen, one of the stars of the football team. "I was so surprised when he asked me out," she confessed, "because I was just a little girl in pigtails and he was being recruited by every major college in America." Mark was fast, tough and could catch anything thrown within five feet of him. "When I told my mama he asked me out, she cried. Everybody in Macon, Georgia knew who Mark was and that he would be famous one day. Mama saved two of her paychecks to buy the yellow, spaghetti-strap dress I wore on our first date. She told me to be nice to Mark, that he could be my 'ticket out' of Macon. Even though I made good grades, she was so afraid that I would wind up flippin' hamburgers like my older sister."

When Mark picked Ricki up in a shiny, new Mazda RX-7 she was stunned. Her parent's car was rusted out and dented and she and her sister were embarrassed to be seen in it. This would be the first time she had ever ridden in a *new* car. Her amazement grew as Mark pulled up to valet park at the most exclusive restaurant in town.

"We're eating *here*?" Ricki asked. "I've read about this place in the paper. It's so expensive! How can you afford it?" she asked, not trying to be nosy, but rather in awe of the unfolding evening.

Ricki had only seen women treated like this in the soap operas she watched after school.

"Oh, I get some money from the colleges who want me to sign with them. Don't worry. I can afford it. Just relax and have fun. This is how *real* people live," Mark told her.

Ricki, who shared a bed with her two siblings, only dreamed of living like this, riding in a nice car and eating fancy food. "Why did you ask *me* out?" she asked Mark when they were seated.

"Because you're sassy, you can dance, and you remind me of Janet Jackson," he smiled. "But, most importantly, your skirt is shorter than the other majorettes!" he laughed, teasing her. She laughed too, and couldn't believe she was here, having this conversation with *the* Mark Arnold. Ricki felt so special.

On Monday, after word got around school that Ricki had dated Mark over the weekend, she became the envy of all the girls at Regis High School. "All the girls at our school wanted to date Mark because they thought he was going to be the next NFL star. I began to like him, not just because he was a star but because he was sweet."

Ricki and Mark dated all during high school. She heard rumors occasionally that he saw some other girls too, but it didn't hurt her. "After all, he was *the man*. I didn't feel like I had a right to be jealous and demand *all* of his attention. We weren't engaged or anything and he always came back to me. I knew he dated some other girls just to impress his friends, especially the white ones. But, I really did feel like he loved me. We understood each other. We had the same upbringing. And his mama *loved* me. A black boy always winds up listenin' to his mama, so I knew I was safe!"

Mark accepted a football scholarship from a large Georgia university on declarations day his senior year. He called Ricki with the good news and told her that he would come by her house after the media left his. She baked his favorite cookies, plaited her hair in a french braid and waited for him until midnight. He never came. "I finally went to bed, devastated that after only one day of securing his future, I had already become a second priority."

The next day at school, Mark apologized for his absence the prior night. "He told me that the university's head coach invited him to dinner and he was there until after midnight. Four years later, I found out that he slept with one of my best friends that night, promising her everything he had promised me. That was just the first of many, many lies. But there was so much I didn't know then. I was so naive and just believed everything he told me."

Mark and Ricki saw each other through Mark's freshman year in college. Their relationship became strained though because Mark quickly became even more of a "Big Man On Campus" than he had been in high school. He hardly had any time for Ricki. And unbeknownst to her, Mark had become a real ladies' man with the reputation of being able to "knock back a few" the night before a Saturday game but still perform like a gladiator on the field. Coaches thought Mark could be even better if he would only discipline himself, but as with most colleges in America, if an athlete is a star, coaches turn their backs to questionable activities.

The weekends were really the only time Mark and Ricki saw each other. He attended most of her Thursday night high school games, and she usually went to see his Saturday home games. "I was so impressed with all of the fanfare surrounding college football. Mark was already the star his freshman year and the school alumni would slip him cash so that he could take me to dinner and buy nice clothes. He kept telling me he wanted for us to be together forever, that I was his 'Little Sunshine.' He said that I always made him happy, like sunshine after a rain. I loved him so much and was so blinded by all of the attention he received that I didn't ever question anything he told me. He had made it out of government housing and everybody respected him and wanted to touch him, as if his magic would rub off on them. I guess I wanted some of that magic, too."

Ricki's senior year in high school started normally. When flag majorette practice began for the upcoming season, Ricki's mama got her uniform out of the closet, washed, ironed it and laid it out on her bed. But when Ricki tried it on, she thought her mama must have accidentally shrunk it. The zipper would only zip halfway and it certainly wouldn't button. "Why doesn't this fit? I know I haven't been eating more than usual. I'm late, but my periods are never regular. No way am I pregnant! *No way.* I only missed *one* birth control pill in my pack. You *cannot* get pregnant from missing one pill!"

Ricki was devastated when the nice lady at the clinic confirmed her worst fears. She was *five months* pregnant. "I wanted to die. Here I was, a seventeen year old honor student with a real future, planning to join Mark at college and get a real education, and I was pregnant. Telling my mama was the second worst experience of my life. The worst was confronting Mark."

The drive to the university was somber. Gone was the usual excitement surrounding a visit to Mark. Instead, Ricki only felt dread and apprehension. She couldn't believe this was happening. How was she going to tell him this? He would surely be angry, maybe even yell at her. He was only beginning his junior year and had such a bright future.

Ricki was so disappointed in herself. Her future was now a question mark, with one of the most important decisions being whether to keep her baby. And she wanted to involve Mark in that decision. She at least owed him that. She just hoped he didn't think she was trying to trap him. Trapping a man into something he didn't want would never work and something she would never do. More than anything, she just wanted to know how Mark really felt about her.

Mark was surprised to see Ricki. Much to her chagrin, he had another girl in his room. Although they were clothed, and even with Mark's explanation that Marlee was only there to study, Ricki understood what was going on by the way Marlee lowered her eyes when Ricki looked at her. This was the last thing Ricki needed to cope with on the worst day of her life. Without much commotion, Marlee left.

Ricki sat down on Mark's roommate's bed, across from Mark, and began to tell him why she was there. Mark kept apologizing for Marlee being in his room until Ricki blurted out, "I don't care about Marlee! Mark, I'm pregnant." Mark sat silently for a moment. Nothing was going right. This was not the way Ricki had practiced breaking the news.

From nowhere, Mark began screaming at Ricki, "How could you? You are trying to force me to marry you and I won't do it. I have too much going for me to throw it away on you. Get rid of the baby and don't come near me or call me again. Get out of my room, now!"

Ricki began sobbing, and running from the room, made one of the most important decisions of her young life. She yelled, "I'm keeping my baby! I wasn't trying to trap you, you bastard. I only wanted to tell you the truth, to see how you felt about me. Now I know. Don't you ever try to visit us. I hate you!"

Despite being pregnant, Ricki returned to high school that fall. "At least," she thought to herself the first day of class, "I'm not the only pregnant twelfth-grader here." She attended all of her classes and even made good grades. School had always been so important to her and she was determined that her pregnancy would not derail her ultimate goal of going to college. In late December, while most university students and alumni were wondering how many points Mark would score in the upcoming Sugar Bowl, Ricki was worrying about giving birth, saving up money to buy a crib, and finding the opportunity to finish high school.

Little Kendall was born the night of the Sugar Bowl. Ricki couldn't believe the irony. Here she was, an indigent black girl giving birth in the emergency room hallway of the local hospital, while the baby's father was being named the Sugar Bowl MVP on the television at the end of the hall. Victorious, dripping with sweat and flashing a million-dollar smile, Mark represented the image that all fathers wished for their sons. She knew that mothers around the country were saying to themselves, "If only he could meet my daughter..." What would all of Mark's fans think if they could see her now and if they knew how much pain he had caused her? He hadn't called or seen her since the day he found out he would be a father. He didn't seem to care at all about his baby. She heard he was dating a rich, white college girl. The thought of him made her sick.

By the time Kendall was six months old, however, much of the bitterness Ricki felt toward Mark had dissipated. She was too busy and tired to worry about Mark. Ricki was juggling the incessant demands of an infant with her studies for night school. She wanted to get her GED so she could apply to the local technical college in the fall. Her goal was to become a paralegal.

Ricki's life was slowly getting back on track, and when she held little Kendall in her arms, she knew that she had made the right decision. She and her family made up for Mark's absent love. Kendall was a beautiful, healthy baby and he was the most important thing in her life. She was getting her education for him, so that he would have a good home and a chance to do better than she had.

Unexpectedly, on a bright June day, Mark dropped by Ricki's house. "Ricki? Mark is here to see you," her mother yelled up the stairs. Ricki dropped Kendall's onesies that she had been folding. She thought her mama must be hallucinating. Why would Mark be showing his face here, *now*? Although she had decided she didn't hate him, she just wanted to move on. She might as well talk to him, though, and tell him that she was getting along fine without his help. She quickly ran her fingers through her hair, glanced in the dresser mirror and then went out to face him.

Mark, who was waiting for her at the bottom of the stairs, started his apology before she had time to react. "Ricki, before you say anything, before you throw me out, I just want to say one thing. I was so wrong, Sunshine. I was so wrong and I'm so sorry. I know that I can't make up for what I've done, and I know that you probably don't even want me here, but I had to come. I have to see Kendall. He's my son and I just want to hold him once. That's all I ask. Just to hold him one time. I'll never come back and bother you again if you don't want me here. Please, just let me see him," Mark had tears in his eyes as he pleaded with her.

Ricki didn't know what to say or do. She was transfixed to the top step like a statue. She heard deep sincerity in Mark's voice that had never been there before. The old Mark could be sweet at times, but he would *never* have come here and admitted that he was wrong. Maybe he had grown up some, enough to realize that she hadn't tried to make him marry her, but she was still leery. He had been so horrible to her and she wasn't ready to forgive him so quickly. She didn't say a word, but led him to the room Kendall shared with her, his small crib wedged between her bed and the wall. As they stood watching over their sleeping son, Mark gently put his arm around Ricki's shoulder and whispered,

"Thank you. He's so beautiful, I don't know what to say."

"You can pick him up. He won't break and he usually sleeps really hard. You won't wake him," she assured him. As Mark held the baby, he realized how shallow his life had become. This baby, this infant, was his and he needed to take responsibility for its young life.

After a few more months of visits and heartfelt talks, Ricki and Mark began to heal their scarred past. Ricki decided that she didn't want to keep Mark from his son. And it seemed like Mark had really changed. He would even drive down to babysit Kendall so Ricki could take her classes two nights a week. As she returned from her technical school one night, Mark took her hand in his, looked her in the eye and said, "'Sunshine, I want us to be together. I know that I was a jerk for doing the things I've done to you, but I've changed. I want to know my son. I don't want him to grow up without a father the way I did. Please think about it. After I make it to the NFL, we'll get married. I promise. I want you to say 'yes' and wear this."

He opened a black box lined in pink silk to reveal a one carat diamond solitaire. Ricki screamed! She had never seen a ring so beautiful. Maybe Mark really had changed. He seemed so differ-ent. She was scared to trust him but she wanted a future for her child. She wanted to be a family. She wanted to believe everything he promised her. He had been so good to her the last few months, even attending church with her on a regular basis. Maybe the Lord had answered all of her prayers. She decided to accept his proposal. Her family was overjoyed.

As expected, Mark became one of the most highly discussed draft picks his senior year. *Sports Illustrated* celebrated him as one of the best wide receivers in the upcoming draft. He hired an agent and started counting greenbacks in his dreams. His life was on the brink of changing dramatically, and he wanted to share his success with those he loved. No more cheap apartments and fast food for his mama. He would buy her a house and make sure that she never had to worry again about street hooligans in the middle of the night. He would also be able to provide for Ricki and Kendall, marrying her and legally making Kendall his son. Mark's agent told him that he could expect a contract with a salary of one and a half to two million dollars a year, topped by a three to four million dollar signing bonus. Nothing could stop him now. He was rounding the curb onto "Easy Street."

The story broke on the AP wire at 3:42 a.m. on April 12, 1991, seven days before the NFL draft. Every newspaper ran it and every sports radio show discussed it. Mark had been named in a drug "sting" operation. One of the arrested men claimed that Mark had purchased cocaine from him on numerous occasions in 1989 and 1990. When Mark's agent called at seven o'clock in the morning to give him the bad news, Mark's heart stopped. As his agent recounted the dispatch, Mark's dreams fell out of the sky and shattered in tiny pieces around his feet. He knew all of the speculation was true. He *had* purchased the cocaine.

He had fooled himself into thinking that he was in control of his life, but now he knew that he had played Russian roulette with every snort and the bullet had just found its way home. Incredibly, he had fooled the NFL drug testers. Mark had taken urine from his straight-arrow roommate and squeezed it into the glass testing vial from a shoe polish bottle concealed in his underwear. The tester was busy filling out the forms and hadn't even noticed. Mark had slid by their standards, but not the desperation of a plea-bargaining snitch.

The hardest part about being caught was that he *had* been trying to turn his life around. Everything he had told Ricki and promised her in the past few months had been true. He wanted to be a good father and a good husband. He wanted to live under the same roof as his son. And he had been contemplating the best way to solve the cocaine problem. He just didn't know where to turn or who to trust. Knowing that any bad press would kill his first-round status in the draft, he had postponed the help he needed. He had promised himself that he would get clean after the draft, before his first training camp began. He hadn't told Ricki earlier because he knew she wouldn't believe him.

Ricki called him dozens of times, looking for answers, but he just couldn't talk to her or anybody else. He was so ashamed and afraid what the future would bring. And within days of the story hitting the paper, Mark's stock dropped from first-round status to tenth- or eleventh-round prospect. Mark's mistakes had cost him millions. Instead of being at the televised draft in New York with the other hot prospects, the new overnight millionaires, Mark watched the draft alone, at home, on ESPN.

For the first time in his life, Mark got down on his knees in the sparsely furnished living room of his mama's apartment. He asked God to forgive and help him. He prayed that he be allowed to run and catch in the NFL like he had always dreamed. He prayed that his son would love him. He prayed that Ricki would stand by him. Finally, he prayed that he be given the strength to conquer his drug addiction.

As if in answer to his prayer, Mark was drafted in the tenth round by the Chicago Bears. His salary would be less than one fourth of what had been expected, but at least he still had a chance to thrive in the NFL. Remarkably, one week after the draft, the drug case that was building against Mark was dropped. For reasons of illegal entrapment, the testimony of the snitch would be discounted, and without the snitch, the police had no case against Mark.

Mark and Ricki quietly married in the small chapel of Ricki's church. "I only agreed because Mark had promised to commit himself to a rehab center before rookie camp started in Platteville, Wisconsin. I couldn't believe he was addicted to cocaine. I never had any idea he had a problem. Even though he had put me through a private hell, I still wanted to help him any way I could. I felt that if I walked away, he would crumble under the pressure to perform and never be able to shake his addiction. After all, we did share a son, and I really did love him.

"My mama had always been the person I listened to most in my life, and she told me that Mark had a good heart and that I shouldn't dwell on his mistakes. She told me I should marry him and give my son a father. She told me I would enjoy life like no one else in my family because of Mark's celebrity. I prayed every day that he would be good to us and that I hadn't made a mistake believing in him. I just wanted to do the right thing."

Ricki and I both had tears in our eyes when she completed this part of her story. I was mesmerized because her life and her decisions were much more complex than my own. I felt the pain in her eyes and voice, and I knew she needed a friend. This chronicle was the first of many shared secrets. At the time, I had no way of knowing Ricki's future would be more painful than her past, that her husband would rise to fame and glory only to face a crossroads in his life, and their subsequent domestic violence would be headlining news. In September of 1991, she was just a new acquaintance with an intriguing past.

◆◆◆◆◆

The Chicago Bears' Wives' Luncheon of 1992 was held in affluent Lake Forest, Illinois at the Deer Path Inn, a quaint little lodge tucked under large, roaming oaks and nestled between carriage lamp-lined streets. Lake Forest, a back drop for several famous movies, was resplendent with off-beat coffee houses, eclectic vintage clothing boutiques and costly antique shops. The long, steely-grey commuter train which ferried hard-working professionals daily to and from the big city was the only reminder of a working world, leisure living being the foremost characteristic of this cash-redolent town.

The Wives' Luncheon was an annual event, usually held in late September after the final cuts. Most of the wives attended the gathering and were treated to an afternoon of Bears' stories and occasionally an in-house speaker, such as the head coach or team owner. The actual luncheon food would be picked over, wasted because a clean plate was equivalent to a public release of gas and would be discussed between the wives long after the luncheon guests exited the building. Wives dressed to impress, and critiqued each other with more scrutinous eyes than those of a *Harper's Bazaar* editor. I always enjoyed the yearly get-together, but at the same time, I always worried about committing a faux pas I didn't even know existed. It made me a little sweaty under the pits just thinking about mingling with everyone, knowing I would be picked apart later that day.

Ricki and I rode together to the luncheon in her new car, a sporty little number that made me laugh when I had to hike my skirt half-way to Cellulite Land to crawl down into the bucket seat. Mark had recently purchased it for her and she was still trying to adjust to the stick shift.

"This is *not* a car for my kids," she laughed. "I can't even fit a car seat in here! Mark said this was *my* car, but I think he really bought it for himself."

"I've only seen these cars in movies. I've never ridden in one," I confessed as we approached the Inn. "It looks great, but can you parallel park it?" I laughed, looking at the small open space in front of the Inn and was reminded of a time when I was sixteen and failed my driving test three times because I couldn't master the art of the parallel park.

"Yeah, the wheels turn so sharply that it's really easy. See that space up front? I can squeeze right in," she assuredly said.

"I'm going to close my eyes because it looks like you only have one inch on either side to spare, but if you think you can do it, go right ahead. If you hit anything, though, I'm not going to be there when you tell Mark that you scratched a $175,000 car!" I teased her.

Impressively, she parked easily and we ran inside. We bordered on being late, but the previous year as rookie wives we had been almost thirty minutes early and had even beaten the hostess to the luncheon. We had stood in heels for an hour before eveyone had been seated for lunch, and we didn't want to make the same mistake. So this year we had planned to arrive at 1:00 p.m. sharp, take our seats, nibble like rabbits on the food, talk to the people at our immediate table, listen to the speaker, and gracefully leave. Since Ricki had a babysitter for the rest of the afternoon, we planned to go shopping after the luncheon.

Our speaker that day was Virginia McKaskey, grande dame of the Bears, and she enchanted us with fascinating tales of Bears lore. Her father, George Halas, was the founder of the first NFL team, and was the reason we all sat there on that sunny day. It was fascinating to hear about the first player contracts and the street-toughness of legends like Bronko Nagurski. The founding players, who weren't paid much, travelled by train across the country and were absent from their families for weeks at a time. As her narrative of the NFL's birth ended, I felt proud to be a small part of its chronicle. As the luncheon came to a close, Ricki and I quickly made our way back to the entrance of the Inn.

The sunlight warmed our faces as we walked toward the car. Smiling, we said in unison, "Northbrook Mall, here we come!" I was about to ask Ricki what she was planning to wear to the Sunday game when I noticed that her mouth was wide open in surprise. She was looking at our parking space. I followed her gaze and realized with a shock that the car was *gone!*

"OhmiGod! OhmiGod! OhmiGod! Where is the car? I know I parked it here! Didn't I, Sally?" Ricki asked me, looking for reassurance that I was too dumbfounded to give.

"Yes," I finally told her, "I *know* you parked it here! I was making fun of the spaces in between the other two cars and these are the same cars! What in the world could have happened to your car?"

I paused. "It's been *stolen*. It *must* have been stolen. I can't believe that *here*, in safe, little Lake Forest, your car was stolen in broad daylight right off this street! I'm going back inside and call the police. Just stay here. I'll be right back. Don't panic, Ricki. We'll fix this before Mark even has to know."

I knew she was thinking how mad and upset he would be with her, maybe even blaming her. Mark was always nice in front of me, but I sensed their relationship lacked balance because she always deferred quickly to his opinion. As Ricki stood crying on the sidewalk and looked for the imaginary giant hole into which her car had been sucked, I walked back into the Inn to use the phone.

The girl at the front desk acted strangely, darting her eyes because she obviously didn't want to meet mine. She acted guilty, as if she already knew the answers to my questions.

"I need to call the Lake Forest police quickly!" I told her. "My friend's car has been stolen, right outside the Inn. We were only here for an hour and a half. I can't believe someone would be able to steal a car like that without being seen! Did you see anything or hear anything suspicious in the last hour or so?"

The young girl didn't move to hand me the phone. Instead, she finally looked me straight in the eyes and said, "How well do you know that woman whose car was taken?"

I said, "What? What did you say?"

Again, she said, "How well do you know her? Her car wasn't stolen. It was repossessed. I saw the whole thing. Two men hooked it up and pulled it right off the street. I wrote down the name on the side of their truck, Helvguard Repossession, just in case anybody had any questions."

I was stunned, like the clerk had open-handedly slapped me across the face. "What? Repossessed? What do you mean repossessed? You mean they just took it? Like he missed *payments* or something? He makes over a half million dollars a year! He can afford that car. This *must* be a mistake. I'm calling the police, anyway. You go out there and tell the lady on the curb what you just told me. We're getting to the bottom of this," I said, trying to sound authoritative.

I was immediately connected with a lieutenant at the Lake Forest police station who had been expecting Ricki's call. Helvguard had notified the police before the repo because of the car's value and the fact that they recognized Mark's name on the title. They also wanted to cover themselves in case they were accused of improperly repossessing the car of a football star. I was still in shock and asked the lieutenant to please come to the Inn, explain this to Ricki and to give us a ride home. He sympathetically agreed to do so.

Ricki was sitting on the curb, her head in her hands, when I approached. The clerk had obviously told her the same story that she had relayed to me, and Ricki was embarrassed.

"Sally, I'm so sorry for all of this. I don't know what is going on. Mark pays all of the bills. I can't believe he would miss a payment on this car. It is new! Mark hasn't told me *anything* about money problems. I can't imagine that a company would repo a car after one missed payment. There must be some mistake. I just don't know what to say."

"Don't worry, Ricki. The police are on their way. We'll figure this out. Just sit tight."

The other wives were leaving, getting into their closely-parked autos and staring at Ricki as they walked past. A couple of wives offered rides, but Ricki declined, explaining that the police would be there momentarily. I knew the situation would provide fat fodder for the next week's gossip. I felt sorry for Ricki.

There were things about Ricki's life I just didn't want to know. I had already learned within one year that it was so much easier to be ignorant of things beyond my control. I couldn't bring her car back, and I didn't want to know why Mark, wealthy star that he was, had missed a simple car payment. Heavy-hearted, I slumped down beside her and put my hand on hers.

"It'll be okay Ricki. I'm sure there is a good explanation for this," I tried to reassure her.

She just looked at me, vacant-eyed as the white police car pulled to the curb, and said, "Yeah. I hope you're right."

The call awoke me at 4:45 a.m. on December 3, 1992. Groggy, I fumbled for the phone. "Hello," my voice scratched.

"May I please speak with Sally Gardocki?" an authoritative male voice resounded in my ear.

"This is she," I replied, waking.

"This is Dr. Craig Jackson from the Lake Bluff hospital. We have just admitted one of your friends, Ricki Arnold, and she asked me to call you. She wants to know if you could get her children and bring them to your house. They are alone at her townhouse and she is very worried about them."

"Of course," I hurriedly replied, "What is wrong with Ricki? Is she sick? Where is Mark?" I asked, alarmed.

"Umm, well, it seems that she has a cracked femur, Sally. She took a very hard blow, one equivalent to being struck by a slowly-moving car, and it has fractured the upper half of her bone. She will be in a cast for a while but will regain full use of her leg. She is in a lot of pain right now, and will be for days, but eventually she should be fine," he told me, textbook-like, without emotion.

"Did you say she was hit by a *car*?" I asked, unsure of what he was telling me.

"No, no," he replied, "I said the blow was equivalent to being hit by a car."

"Then I'm really confused. How did she do this Dr. Jackson?" I asked, even though I was afraid of his answer.

"How well do you know Ricki, Mrs. Gardocki?"

"Very well, doctor. She is one of my closest friends. Why do you ask?"

"Well, I can't comment on someone's condition, unless it is to a family member. It is against the law for me to do so, but I'm concerned about Ricki. Both she and her husband have said that she tripped at the top of their stairs and took a hard fall to the bottom. If that is in fact the case, it is the strangest occurrence I have seen in my sixteen years of practicing medicine. The femur is one of the strongest bones in our body, Mrs. Gardocki, and one of the hardest to break. I could hit you with a hammer and not even crack it. I find it very hard to believe that a fall could do such damage. But both of them have assured me that it is the truth and I'm not going to question it. Especially because of his celebrity. I don't need trouble like that at *this* hospital."

I was paralyzed. As I hung up with Dr. Jackson, Chris awoke and I quietly explained that I had to go to Ricki's and get her children, that she had suffered an accident. I assured Chris that she would be fine and I would be back in a few minutes. He went back to sleep and I put on my sweats and tennis shoes.

Upon entering her townhouse, I found it in complete disarray. Tables were overturned, magazines were strewn on the floor, and lamp shades were askew. It looked like a small-scale war had taken place, and the combatants had left their rubble to be scavenged. I tried to straighten things up, without waking the children, and wondered how in the world a child could sleep through the noise this upheaval must have made. But when I checked on those two little angels, they were still safely asleep.

It was so obvious to me that Ricki and Mark had fought viciously, the result of which must have broken her leg. Tears formed as I began to realize the hell in which she must have existed for the last three years. This was so foreign to me, so Monday Night Movie-ish that I couldn't put it in perspective. I had never even seen a fight where people physically pushed and struck each other until they bled. Although Mark had drug problems in his past, I had never suspected that he might *hit* Ricki. She didn't display any outward signs of abuse. There were never any tell-tale scars or bruises, nor any goofy explanations like this tumble down the stairs. But it was evident that abuse had occurred that night.

What was I doing in the middle of this? My life was normal. I couldn't even imagine Chris raising his fist against me. I didn't know what to do, but Ricki was my friend so I decided to stand by her and help her any way that I could. And right now that meant gathering her children.

Still dazed, Ricki called me the next morning to check on her children. I told her they were fine, that Peepers and Rhett, my two Yorkshire Terriers, were in heaven because they were getting so much attention. I assured her that the children could stay with me as long as she needed.

Mark hadn't stopped by or called me yet, which I thought was odd, but then he must have known that I had cleared away the wreckage from their fray and that I had seen the whole ugly picture for the first time.

When Ricki told me that Mark would pick the children up after Bears' practice and asked if I could keep them during the day for a few days, I told her not to worry, that we would have a great time.

"Ricki, do you want to tell me what happened?" I asked, trying to open the door to the truth.

She quickly slammed it shut with, "Oh, I just fell. You know how clumsy I am. I was running around trying to get the kids bathed and dressed for bed and I just tripped on that oriental runner at the top of my stairs. Thank goodness Mark was there to call 911."

"Yeah, thank goodness," I said flatly. Realizing I was not going to hear the truth, I didn't push it. I didn't say, "Why were you bathing the kids at 2:00 a.m.?" or "Why did your house look like a madman had ransacked it?" I just let it go, leaving her to the story with which she could live. It would be months before those unasked questions would be plainly answered.

Four months after Ricki had broken her leg, I awoke to see underwear hanging in her trees across the street. "Oh, no," I thought, "what now?" The fifteen-foot oak looked like it was decorated for Easter, although many months too late, with her brightly colored panties billowing in the breeze.

I waited until Mark left for practice before I knocked on her front door. Earlier, I had contemplated sneaking across the street, removing the underwear before any of the neighbors awoke to spare Ricki's embarrassment, but Chris told me not to interfere. And he was right, although standing in front of her door, I wished I had taken down the underwear and had the courage to do the right thing. Ricki, holding a bag of ice over her eye, opened the door.

"Did he do this to you?" were my first words. "If he did Ricki, if he did this, by God we are calling the police *now*. This is *wrong*. You know it. And I know what is going on. Don't lie to me anymore. Don't lie to yourself," I said shaking. My heart was stuck in my throat, but I had finally found the strength to ask the difficult questions.

"Sally, it's not that simple. You *don't* live my life. You don't know what I *came* from, where I've *been*. You haven't seen abuse close-up. You don't know what it's like to be poor or hungry. You just don't *know*. I appreciate your friendship, really. And what you say is true. But what am I gonna' do? Walk away from here and work in The Gap? Will a salary from The Gap let me make a mortgage payment on a $650,000 house? No, I don't think so. I am doing this for my kids so that they have a roof over their heads and hot food to eat. One day they can go to college, and break this miserable chain. I endure this for them. I can stand having my husband get mad and throw my underwear out of my bedroom window if it means that my children will eventually live a better life than I did. I appreciate that you want to help, but you don't understand. You never will. If you really want to help, get the ladder out of the garage and pull my damn underwear out of that tree before *everybody* in Chicago sees it," she was crying now and so was I.

Since I had already decided to just support Ricki and not to try and tell her what to do, I didn't respond to her justifications for living the way she did. She had already made her decision to protect Mark. I just hoped it didn't kill her. As I climbed the ladder and threw her underwear down to her, I thanked God that I lived across the street, in a normal house, with a normal husband.

In August of 1993 Ricki told me she was pregnant with their third child. She was happy, seemingly in denial of the unstable environment in which she lived.

"Are you sure this is good?" I asked her.

"Of course. What could be wrong with having a baby?" she responded, not understanding the nature of my question.

"Well, Ricki, I just don't see how all of this stress could be good for a developing baby. I think you should really consider what you are doing, that's all." I wasn't trying to tell her *not* to have the baby, but that maybe she should consider giving it a safer home, away from Mark.

"He never hits me when I am pregnant, Sally. He's sweet and we get along so much better. He takes time to talk to me, and acts like he really loves me. Just yesterday he brought me flowers for the first time in months."

"Ricki, I know that you love him. And I hope that he is good to you when you are pregnant. But you can't have this child just so he will treat you well for the next nine months. He needs *help*," I said, deciding by the look on her face that I had already said too much.

"We tried. And he had agreed to attend one of those player programs, you know, the ones that are supposed to be confidential? Well, a couple of days before our first session, I found out that our counselor was married to Kent Lord, the famous sportswriter. I'm sure his wife is completely trustworthy, but Mark wasn't gonna' risk a little pillow talk when his career depended on it! That's as far as it got. After that, Mark laughed every time I tried to convince him that we needed to see a marriage counselor."

She continued, "Now, he denies that we have a problem. At least the next nine months will be peaceful. I love Mark, Sally. I know you don't see it but deep down he is a good person. He never had a role model to follow and he grew up surrounded by violence. His daddy was never there and his mama was abused by all of her boyfriends. It's *all* he ever saw. He knows the way he treats me is wrong, but he just can't help himself. He is always sorry afterwards. I know, I know. Don't even look at me that way. Just be happy for me today, that I am going to have a new baby. The rest of the problems will solve themselves," her eyes pleaded with me to forget our past secrets and pretend her world was normal.

"Ricki, I am sincerely happy for you. I just want what is best for you and your children. That's all. I'm not trying to tell you what to do. It's your life and only you can lead it. It's just hard for me because I care," I told her, letting the issue die.

A couple of months later, I dropped by to return a purse I had borrowed. She answered the door and I was immediately concerned. "Ricki, what is wrong? You look so tired."

"I'm bleeding. A lot and I can't stop it. I think I might lose the baby," she told me, beginning to cry uncontrollably.

"Oh my God. Let me call the doctor. I'll take you to the hospital," I reached for her phone, but she stopped me.

"No. Don't, Sally. It was Mark. He kicked me in the stomach last night. He was so mad about yesterday's loss. He just took all of his anger out on me. He was so sorry this morning, though. He even offered to call the doctor, but I told him 'no,' that I didn't want him to get in any kind of trouble."

I could feel heat rising to the top of my head. But I had already decided I was not going to interfere. No matter what. "Ricki, you need to see a doctor or at least call a nurse. Something could really be wrong. Just tell them that you fell again. I can't leave here thinking you could be seriously injured," I pleaded with her.

Finally, she made the call and they instructed her to come to her doctor's office. Her injuries were not as severe as I had imagined and the doctor didn't think that the baby was in danger after viewing the sonogram. I don't think he believed her story of another fall, but he let it slide because of her last name. He sent her home for bed rest. I went to the store and picked up some food for her two kids.

When I returned, Mark was standing in their kitchen. "Sally, I want to thank you for helping Ricki. She is just so clumsy sometimes. I don't know what gets into her," he began.

"Look, let me stop you right there. I am not a fool. I know what happens here, not because of what Ricki tells me, but because of what she doesn't say. She is my friend and I will do what she wishes, which is to keep my mouth shut right now. But don't cross me, Mark. Don't you *ever* cross me," I said, placing the grocery bag on their table and slamming the door behind me. I was shaking as I raised my garage door with the remote clutched in my hand. That bastard. He thought he was beyond reproach because of what he did on Sundays. But everybody must face Judgement Day sometime, and I just wanted to be around when Mark Arnold faced his.

After Zachary was born, Ricki's situation worsened. The beatings, the screams, and the slamming doors continued and were whispered about by the gossip-mongers in our small neighborhood. One cold day I looked outside to see her two older children sitting on their doorstep, jacketless against the bone-touching breezes carried in from the North Shore. I opened my door and asked them if they would like to come over and play with Peepers and Rhett. Their little faces brightened as they scurried across the street. I wondered how long they had been sitting there and what they must have been thinking. Surely, they were terrified of what happened in their house. They probably thought that everyone lived that way, that abusive behavior was normal. I prayed every night for those children. And for Ricki to gather the strength she needed to leave.

The following August, Mark threw Ricki down the stairs for what was to be the last time. Kendall called 911, but Ricki got on the line and told them it was a mistake, that Kendall was playing a joke. They didn't come to rescue her, to take her away, but as Mark left the house and she went upstairs to comfort their crying infant, she made her decision. She was tired. Tired of covering up the scars, tired of covering for Mark, tired of feeling fear in her own home, and tired of wasting her life. She called the Lake Bluff police and Mark was arrested within hours. They found him at his mistress' apartment, the address which had been supplied by Ricki. Ricki had failed to include that crumb of information in our chats. She later told me that she was just too embarrassed, the girl was a white waitress and the part of Mark's salary that wasn't going up his nose was going to pay for the girl's apartment downtown.

The next day, their domestic problems were the sports headline in all of the Chicago papers. Their past wasn't chronicled, nor was it neatly laid out for all to peruse, but the tone of the article indicated there had been incidents of prior abuse. I felt extreme guilt when I read the article. I felt that I had stood by and done nothing. I just helped Ricki hide her problems. Well, at least it was in the open, now. No more secrets. The dominos had started to fall and Ricki's fate was sealed.

In June, I returned from a short trip to South Carolina and saw a moving van in Ricki's driveway. I curiously walked over and found Ricki directing the movers.

"Ricki, are you *moving*? You didn't tell me. When did you decide to do this?" I asked, confused.

"I'm going home, Sally. Back to Georgia. Back to my family. I have to start over. I can't do it here. Too many people know who I am, who Mark is, and they stare at me every time I leave this house. I have to go where no one will judge me.

She continued, "I've enrolled in a junior college down there and I'm finally gonna get that paralegal training I always talked about. An attorney is gonna let me work for him while I'm in school and mama can help me with the kids. It will be hard, I know. And the money will be tight, but I need to know that my children are safe. I need to know that we can sleep without fear. You were right, Sally. I should have done this years ago, when it first started. But it's done, now."

"When do you leave?" I asked, not believing that one of my closest friends, someone I worried about daily, would be out of my life.

"Tonight," she said, "I promised Mark that all of our things would be gone by 6:00 p.m. I'm sorry that I don't have time to talk or say goodbye the proper way."

"It's all right. It's better this way. I don't think I *can* say goodbye to you. Please call me when you get settled and let me know you are okay. I know you'll be happy, Ricki. You're a good person. You're doing the right thing. Keep your head up," I told her, giving her one last hug.

Within the next season, Mark was cut. At the time, I didn't know if it had anything to do with all of the negative publicity surrounding his personal life or if his on-the-field performance really had fallen off-track. Later, I found out he had been released for failing NFL drug tests. Cocaine had gotten the best of him, robbing him of his talent and his life. He had been a star, the starting wide receiver of an NFL team, and he threw it all away seemingly without a thought or care. No other NFL team re-signed him. Eventually, he too moved back to Georgia.

Ricki's dream of becoming a paralegal was fulfilled in the year following her move to Georgia. She sent me a copy of her certification, and I was so proud for her. She was finally creating a healthy environment for herself and her children. In June of 1995, a small, unassuming legal notice in the *Macon Herald* marked the end of her marriage to Mark. Their divorce was only a formality of their year-long separation. Eventually, Ricki married again. Her new husband is an attorney, not someone with a flashy image and a million dollars in his pocket, but someone with a heart, who loves her and her children.

Mark was arrested in 1995 for selling cocaine and currently resides in the Fulton County Jail in Macon, Georgia. Some see him as a tragic hero, a product of his environment on a fateful, inevitable course. And even though I despised him for what he did to Ricki and their children, I just see him as a man, a mortal who lost his way, his sense of right and wrong confused, in a world that allowed him to spin out of control.

The Ass of Alcatraz

For my part, I travel not to go anywhere,
but to go. I travel for travel's sake.
The great affair is to move.
— Robert Louis Stevenson, *Travels with a Donkey*

One of the public's most prevalent misconceptions about NFL wives is that we travel "in style" to all of the away games. Many have envisioned us as part of the jet set, sipping martinis and eating Beluga caviar in spacious first-class seats beside our husbands, the weekend warriors, on their way to battle. It disappoints them when they discover that we usually attend only the home games and have little interest in following our husbands all the way across the country for a four-hour Sunday game. But there are several good reasons that wives usually don't accompany their husbands to their out-of-town job.

First of all, it's really expensive to travel to the away games. We aren't allowed to fly with the team, so we have to buy our own tickets and fly commercial. By the time parking, airfare, taxis, hotel accommodations and a game ticket are paid for, the 24-hour weekend excursion is going to cost more than a big-screen television. And personally, I'd rather watch all of the away games on that big screen. At home. With my feet up.

Secondly, our husbands are there to work, not to entertain us or tour the city. They have curfews and assigned roommates. Since three is a crowd, and Chris would be fined up to $2,000 if I were caught in his room, we save our vacation time for the off-sea son.

Finally, our husbands are usually only gone twenty-four to thirty-six hours. Chris and I love each other, but neither of us is going to wither away and die from being apart for one day. In the time he is gone, I can do three loads of laundry, vacuum the house, go to the grocery store and potty train Cole.

Sometimes though, wives forgo all of the above for a special away game, like one close to our hometown or one that involves playoff possibilities. Husbands generally hate the close-to-home-town games because they have to buy an extra 46 tickets so everybody they've ever known can come see them play.

When informed that dozens of extra tickets must be ordered, husbands usually respond, "Are you crazy? Let me remind you once again that the tickets aren't free and the team will take that money out of my paycheck this week. At thirty-five bucks a pop, I'll be lucky to get a paycheck this week! I may end up *owing* the team money! Who did you invite?"

The standard reply: "Well, several people called me this week to see if you could get them tickets, and I just couldn't tell them 'no.' Your old high school coach called, and the neighbor who used to babysit you called, and your grandmother wants to bring some of her friends from the nursing home. But they have their own shuttle, so we don't have to worry about transportation. And, let's see, oh yeah, that guy that you played soccer with in the third grade....." The list never stops.

In 1994, the Bears played the Forty-Niners in the first berth of NFC playoffs. The game was in San Francisco, and I convinced Stacy Mangum, a Bears' wife who was one of my best friends, that we shouldn't miss the game. We both knew the Forty-Niners would probably humiliate us on the field, but San Fran is a great city to visit, Stacy had never been west of the Mississippi Delta, and I could eat fresh sushi in the stands at halftime. We antici-pated our three-day excursion with excitement.

Our flight left at 5:30 a.m. from O'Hare. It was one of those two-for-one "cheapy" airfares with no in-flight food, but we didn't care because we planned to snooze. I carefully arranged my black satin eye patch upon take-off and said "good night" to Stacy. I immediately fell asleep. Around Utah, which was two or three hours into the flight, I was awakened by Richard Simmons' twin.

He squeaked into my ear, "Open your peepers, dahling. Opie, Opie, Opie! Wakey, wakey, eggs and bakey!"

I thought, "Who the *hell* has Stacy made friends with on this plane...?" Stacy is the friendliest person I have ever known, and I used to tease her about talking to strangers. As I slowly pulled off my blindfold and my eyes feasted upon the miniature Richard, who was doing a warm-up routine in the aisle, I realized that Stacy must have been talking to him since the plane's back wheels left the runway at O'Hare. The five foot two munchkin was wearing a black lycra backless unitard and was consuming the entire aisleway with his runner's stretch. As it had been ten below zero when we departed O'Hare, I hoped that this fool had a jacket *somewhere* on the plane.

Stacy introduced me to Siegfried and told me that he had invited the two of us to his show: *Pinocchio's Banana.* I immediately clued into the type of show it was, but obviously Stacy hadn't. She was asking him if he had to rehearse a lot and if he knew any movie stars.

He continued to stretch in our aisle until we hit California airspace. By the time we reached the airport he was limber enough to run back to Chicago. He waved goodbye and threw kisses to us from the curb as we caught a cab.

I looked at Stacy and said, "Okay, tell me from the beginning how in the world you met that fruitcake."

"What do you mean 'fruitcake?' " Stacy asked.

"Stacy, you do know what kind of show he was talking about, don't you? I'm sure he's a female impersonator."

Stacy looked at me wide-eyed: "No way!"

"Yeah, Stacy. That was what he was talking about. Why else would he have been talking about his Vera Wang dress? It cer-tainly didn't belong to his *wife*! My God girl, you are too naive! I can't believe you didn't realize what he was talking about — you watch Oprah every day!"

Stacy just sat there in the cab, saying over and over, "I can't believe it!"

Stacy's innocence always made me laugh. It was one of the reasons I loved her so much.

Upon reaching the hotel, we decided to eat lunch at Fisherman's Wharf, explore Ghiradelli Square and then top off our day with a tour of Alcatraz. But we were shocked to learn from the concierge that a cab ride was fifty bucks each way. As we were trying to determine if a guided tour would be cheaper, we saw one of our WGN reporter-friends in the lobby. He was desperately looking for someone to interview for the six o'clock news, so we traded a free ride to the Wharf for an interview about the upcoming playoff game.

On our way to the Wharf, we passed two transvestites at a stoplight. Stacy looked at them and said, "Girl, look at how those women are dressed. They look *awful*! Their shoes and purses don't match." We all laughed so hard, Stacy included when we told her they were *men*.

The interview only took a few minutes, and afterwards, we ate crabs on the street, fed the pigeons and watched the seals at Pier 59. It was such a beautiful sunny day, a balmy 68 degrees, and Stacy and I were excited about the Alcatraz tour. We had both changed clothes in the hotel so we would be comfortable for all of our touring. I wore thin tights, a "baby doll" style dress, boots and my oh-so-fashionable leather Chanel backpack. (That stupid backpack was overpriced and uncomfortable, but I just had to buy it. It was the one fashion accessory of the season that I thought I couldn't live without.)

I warned Stacy on the boat ride to the island prison that if we weren't first in line for the story headphones, it could take us all afternoon to tour the grounds. Since we really wanted to see the rest of the city after the Alcatraz tour, I stressed to her the importance of beating everybody else off of the boat. But I specifically didn't tell her about the one-half mile uphill "hike" from the boat to the top of the island, where we would get our headphones, because I knew that she wouldn't want to go. And I didn't want to have to carry her on my back. Stacy *hated* exercise of any shape or form. Even though she was the skinniest person I had ever known who ate Velveeta Cheese and drank whole milk, I always teased her because she was out of breath five minutes into our aerobics classes or when we walked around our neighborhood in Chicago.

When the boat docked, we were the first two down the gang-plank and I told Stacy that we could *not* stop for her to rest on the way to the top, that we had to keep up a good pace to get the headphones first. I prodded her to move faster. About halfway up, she started lagging a few paces behind, and I said, "Stacy, you are going to get trampled by those five hundred tourists behind you if you don't get your butt in gear." She picked up her pace and we pulled away from the pack of primarily Asian camera-carriers.

About three-fourths of the way up the winding hill, I began to feel a "breeze." I attributed it to the height of the island and the fact that we were on the San Francisco Bay. When I turned to make this comment about the breeze, I found Stacy leaning on the railing alongside the trail, unable to speak.

"Stacy, my God, girl, you are so out of shape! This should teach you a lesson. You really should take up the Stairmaster when we get home," I scolded her.

She couldn't respond and I nervously looked back at the tourists who were approaching us like Hirohito's army.

"Stacy what is wrong with you?" I asked when she still hadn't said anything. I then realized that she couldn't breathe because she was *laughing* so hard, not because she was winded from the exercise.

"Stacy, what in the hell are you laughing at? These Japanese are going to run all over us. They are already taking *pictures* of you," I chided her even further.

"Your *ass*! Your *ass*!" was all Stacy managed to say.

"What do you mean, *my 'ass'?* "

"Your ass is *out*! I can see it! Clearly! Your dress is bunched up under that backpack!" She was now crying from laughter.

I almost died! I had been in such a hurry to leave the hotel that I hadn't put on any underwear under my see-through tights. Oh dear God! That would certainly explain the breeze I had been feeling for the last ten minutes. And it was because of that stupid, damn backpack that I just had to buy! My ass was out and everybody had seen it! As I looked down at the Japanese tourists, all I could hear were shutters snapping. I know that I am in some of their vacation albums as the "Alcatraz Flasher."

I began to laugh with Stacy and the two of us had to sit down on the side of the path. We laughed until our mascara was all over our faces.

We were the absolute last people in line for the stereo headphones.

When we reached the cell of the famed "Birdman of Alcatraz," Stacy stopped her headphones, motioned for me to stop mine, and said, "To hell with the Birdman, I've seen this joint with the 'Ass of Alcatraz!'"

Stacy Mangum enjoying the day she saw Alcatraz

Double Your Pleasure, Double Your Trouble

King Soloman loved many strange women.
— 1 Kings 11:1

A recurring nightmare of NFL wives is that they will be the last to know; the last to know that their loving husband has been loving a significant percentage of the female populous of the city in which they live. And even worse than the discovery of infidelity is the realization that the infidel is seated beside you in the wives' room. For years, I have heard rumors of wives and mistresses discovering and confronting each other while watching their significant other play. And although these were some of the more interesting rumors, only once did I come across a potential "cat fight." But in actuality, it was really more of a "discussion" between two girlfriends of the same player who accidentally bumped into each other one cold day in the wives' room.

It was the winter of Chris' second year, and the game had been pretty boring. I can't remember if we were winning or losing, but most of wives had decided that the game wasn't worth our freezing out in the cold. As we made our way into the wives' room and shed layers of scarves, hats and gloves, we all took seats wherever we could because the room was really crowded. We were crammed in there, shoulder to shoulder, like thirty sides of pork.

It was common knowledge that one of the players was not only serious with two different women who didn't know about each other, but that he also gave his phone number to every nail technician, hairstylist and "model" north of Soldier Field. The running joke between all of us wives involved which weekly conquest would occupy his home game seats on Sunday. Even Laura Coleman, my hairstylist in downtown Chicago, and I began every monthly appointment discussing "Romeo," our own nickname for this guy. She would say, "Romeo must have broken up with Girlfriend #1 because he gave So-and-So, our new nail tech, his phone number."

"No, they're still together. He's probably just bored. Tell So-and-so not to get too excited. I doubt that he is looking to permanently expand his already-established *menage à trois*," I would respond.

Of the two girlfriends in 1992, though, one lived in Chicago and one lived out-of-state. The wives were accustomed to seeing "Chicago" at all of the home games but had only seen "Out-of-State" at away locations. "Chicago" was squeezed into a group of people across from me when "Out-of-State" unexpectedly walked in the door. A collective, audible gasp was heard in the room.

Since these girls were unaware that they were both "serious" with the same guy, they were the most comfortable people in the room. Everybody else was afraid to speak. And everybody quit watching the game.

Out-of-state approached the group, smiled and sat down about three feet from Chicago. I had never seen so many people excuse themselves to the bathroom or back out into the bitter cold — myself included. None of us wanted to be there when these two became engaged in conversation and realized (astonishingly!) they were there to see the same player. Freezing my ass off in fifteen-below weather was preferable to witnessing Out-of-State and Chicago's discovery that the biggest thing they had in common was Romeo's penis!

I don't know what happened between them after we all left, but eventually they did find out about each other. And it was an all-out war for Romeo's affections. After years of dueling over him, Chicago married Romeo.

From this experience, I learned that, oftentimes, it was best to ignore things. The way other people lived was none of my business, and sometimes the best thing to do is nothing. Ignorance *can* be bliss!

"Work Hard, Play Hard" ... However, sometimes the consequences of "playing" might be more more than bargained for.

Hello, State Farm? There's Been a Little Accident...

Heaven has no rage like love to hatred turned,
Nor hell a fury like a woman scorned.
                                        — William Congreve

In October of 1993, a Bears' girlfriend was washing a pile of her rookie-boyfriend's dirty clothes at their townhouse. Upon checking his pockets before throwing his pants into the washing machine, she found a suspicious local telephone number, the feminine name underneath enscribed with curly-ques and a fatly-dotted "i." Fury immediately filled her every cell. And instead of waiting four or five hours until her boyfriend returned from work to question him about the scrap of paper, she flew out of the house like a hellcat in her Victoria's Secret pajamas, jumped into his Range Rover and speedily drove toward Halas Hall.

The players were already divided into their morning meetings of offense, defense and special teams. Usually dry and uneventful, this particular morning's special teams' meeting was interrupted by a hysterical, high-pitched call from outside. Players ran to the window as a fellow special-teamer was summoned from below by a wild-eyed, wild-haired woman in shorty pajamas who was standing in the player parking lot. The girlfriend screamed that if her boyfriend didn't come outside immediately, she would come inside and drag him out by a very private body part. After hastily getting permission from his bewildered coach, the player ran out of the building to try to calm his girlfriend and determine the cause of her apparent insanity.

As the other players intently watched and listened from the window, the Sunday game-plan temporarily on hold, the girlfriend showed her boyfriend the crumpled, tear-stained phone number and asked about the temptress. Without giving him a chance to respond, she told her boyfriend that she loved him and couldn't believe he would cheat on her, lie to her, and sacrifice their four-year relationship for a one-night stand. The player responded that he had no intention of calling the seductress, that he had just taken the number so as not to hurt the other girl's feelings. He explained to his girlfriend that he was so sorry for making her doubt his affection and loyalty.

Still angry, not satisfied with his excuse, and unaware of the growing audience behind the facade of Halas Hall, she said, "*Sorry*? You want to see sorry? I'll *show* you sorry, asshole."

She mounted her weapon, the Range Rover, and found her mark – his brand-spanking-new one hundred thousand dollar Mercedes-Benz two rows over in the same parking lot. With him shaking his head and screaming, "No, no, no, noooooooooo," increasingly louder, she rammed it from behind with the sixty-five thousand dollar "Tank-Rover."

She then opened the door, looked at the dumbfounded player and said, "Now, *that* is sorry. *That* is what I think about you and all of your new money, fame and womanizing. Bastard!" She then backed up and rammed the Mercedes again, damages now in the fifty thousand dollar range, the former spacious leg room of the back seat now only commodious to midgets.

The player, upon the second crash, was jarred from his state of shock, the witnessing of one hundred and sixty-five thousand dollars worth of cars being destroyed too much for his eyes, and he physically pulled his girlfriend from the Rover.

"Stop it!" he screamed, "Stop it, you crazy bitch! What the *hell* do you think you are doing? Give me those goddamned keys or I will kill you right here in this parking lot!"

Getting out of the Rover, she said, "You can take these keys, you bastard, and shove them straight up your ass! You can shove this whole NFL *thing* up your ass, sideways for that matter! I'm out of here! I'm going home. Don't you ever call me again. *Ever!*"

With all of the players inside mesmerized by the bizarre scene unfolding before their eyes, the girlfriend stuck her chin out indignantly, carefully brushed off her dotted swiss pajamas and walked down the quiet neighborhood street, into the wealthy bedroom community of Lake Forest. She had no purse, identification or money.

The player sank to his million-dollar knees in the parking lot and cried like a baby. Not only were his prized cars destroyed, but his long-time girlfriend had left him over some stupid, trifling phone number that had been shoved, unsolicited and unwanted, into his pocket by a bimbo he had no intention of calling.

Inside Halas Hall, the fear of God was put into those who had strayed, fear that it could have been *their* wives wrecking *their* trophies publicly. For months after, celibacy and loyalty reigned, the girlfriend's actions causing a ripple-effect similar to the influence the movie *Fatal Attraction* had on wife-cheaters. This story, discussed quietly among players, has become a legend in the league.

The player's coach eventually retrieved him from the pavement of the parking lot and helped him dial the numbers of his insurance agency. Within hours, two tow trucks had removed the morning's carnage, and every living, breathing soul in Halas Hall was aware of *Les Jeux Sont Fais* of the early morning.

The girlfriend had known that her boyfriend's "Achilles Heel" was the pride of his ride. Nothing else would have brought him as much pain as trashing his wheels, his pride and joy, and she had moved in for the kill. Her vengeance cost him two paychecks.

Truth *is* stranger than fiction and the couple got back together. They married, had children and I know for a fact that he will never, ever entertain the thought of having an affair or accepting a phone number from a young nymphet again.

A few momentos from our time in Chicago—
We have a lot of good memories from our years in "The Windy City."

Stress

I was never afraid of failure;
For I would sooner fail than not be among the
greatest.
— John Keats, *Letter to James Hessey*

Stress is the "Ghost of Christmas Future" that shakes a player awake in the middle of the night, forces him to think about the next game or the next year, and tells him that he *can* perform better than he did in the last game. Stress over being the best and winning football games is like a whining child who wants to be picked up. Players can either embrace it and use it to feed their desire on game day, or they can try to ignore it and let it eat away at their self-confidence. But eventually, like the child, it must be dealt with. Most players alleviate stress by working hard in the off-season, coming into July training camp in tip-top shape and feeling good about their own abilities.

In the world of the NFL, stress begins the day of the rookie draft. The player worries *if* he is going to be drafted, what *kind* of team will draft him, what kind of *record* the team has, what *type* of offense, defense or special teams the organization runs and what is *expected* of him. Players also worry about moving, leaving their families, whether they should take their girlfriends, where they are going to live and whether they will make new friends easily. These are worries even *before* training camp starts.

Unfortunately, the average NFL career only lasts about three years. Players train their whole lives for *these* short years instead of preparing for the *other* thirty employable years after the pigskin years end. Businessmen go to college to get their degrees and those pieces of paper enable them to *earn* a living for the rest of their lives. Players must earn a living in a few years that will *last* them the rest of their lives. And so they must play with pain, injury and do whatever it takes to make it back to the game from year to year.

When people read that a player has signed a contract, they think the player has a job for the duraction of that contract, regardless of his performance. Not true. There are no guaranteed jobs in football which means that *every* year players must make the team. Their contract only means that *if* they make the team, the owner will pay them a certain salary.

Therefore, each season, in every game the player must be the best at his position. Teams don't care about how good a player was the year before or that he has been a starter at his position for ten years. A player is only as good as his last game. And loyalty, because of the nature of the NFL beast, exists rarely. I fault no one for this; it is tacitly understood the day a player signs his first contract that he will eventually be replaced. He knows it and the team knows it. Consequently, it is hard for a player to be loyal to a team if another team is willing to double or triple his salary, just as it is hard for management to be loyal to older veterans by keeping them on the roster and rewarding them for years of sacrifice when a younger, cheaper version is available. All of the above is a blue-ribbon recipe for the sometimes intoler-able stress in players' lives.

I couldn't chronicle stress without introducing its bastard brother, failure. Failure is the most rotten thing about the NFL, because even if you succeed for years and "beat" the NFL law of averages, you still eventually fail somehow and are cut, traded or are forced to retire. The job of being a professional athlete has failure built into it from the start. And in the seven years of Chris' career, I have only witnessed one person who closed the door on this game on his own terms. Unfortunately, most players must leave the game when the game leaves them.

◆ ◆ ◆ ◆ ◆

Two years ago when Chris signed as the new punter for the Colts, they also signed a new kicker, Mike Cofer. Mike had enjoyed a healthy NFL career with the San Francisco Forty-Niners, even winning the Super Bowl. Mike sat out the '94 football season to race cars, another talent of his, but was ready for a comeback in 1995.

He and Chris got along well during training camp. Kickers usually become friends because they spend so much practice time together. The beefy lineman continually tease the kickers during camp, telling them that they aren't really working because they don't participate in the bone-crunching contact drills that every other player must endure twice daily. It is all said in jest, but it really makes the kickers a more resolute two-man team.

Just as Chris and Mike had a lot in common, so did Mike's wife, Lisa, and I. In the summer of 1995, we were both pregnant and new wives to the team. It is always hard for a football wife to leave her friends behind and enter a new wives' room when she doesn't know if the wives will be friendly or if they were good friends with the player her husband has just replaced. There wasn't a wives' room in Indianapolis, which made it even harder for us to meet other wives, so Lisa and I stuck together, neither one of us feeling like ourselves because of our pregnancies. We laughingly established a routine of eating crackers in the stands before the pre-season games to quell our queasy stomachs. She quickly became my first friend in Indianapolis.

On the Sunday that the Colts played the Bills in New York during the '95 pre-season, Lisa was in the process of moving to Indianapolis. She got the game on her car radio near Louisville, but the broadcast kept fading in and out of range, so she called me every thirty minutes for updates. In the last quarter, Mike kicked the winning field goal, and we were both ecstatic. Thankfully, Chris and Mike's season had started well.

Lisa and I had been nervous about the pre-season. Anytime a player is new to a team, he must establish himself as a vital component and try to become a "teammate." The media is always quick to criticize a new acquisition, especially if he replaces a popular player or has a rocky start. Mike and Chris had to perform well to be well received. But so far, so good.

Everything was going well until the second game of the season. Then, Mike missed a couple of field goals. And *any* missed field goals are always noticed.

Lisa told me she was scared the Colts would cut Mike if he missed again. I tried to reassure her that they wouldn't, but I was worried too. I have seen people cut for reasons having nothing to do with even performance, and even though Mike had contributed to the team's victories, I could understand Lisa's apprehension. If Mike could just do well the next few games, he wouldn't be in the hot seat.

But that next Sunday, Mike missed another field goal. After the game, he seemed dejected, and I knew he knew what was now on the line. I have always wondered if I could say anything to a friend, or even Chris, after a bad game that would actually help. I usually don't say anything, because this isn't Little League and the players aren't twelve years old. They know, as we do, that their jobs are always at stake.

Our knowledge of this, coupled with never being able to control *any* aspect of the game, is extremely frustrating. As wives, we can only *watch*. We can only watch when our husbands and friends lose, get pulled from starting positions, get screamed at on the sidelines, and get carried off on injury carts. I knew that Lisa must be frustrated at this, thinking there was no way she could throw Mike a rescue line from the stands. It was as hard for her to watch as it was for him to miss.

Mike managed a smile after the game, but I knew he felt terrible. I felt so sorry for him. They had just bought the Indy house and were going to be parents for the first time. The pressure on him must have been enormous.

Lisa and I sat together that next Sunday at the game. In all of the years Chris had played, I had never been that nervous. If I hadn't been pregnant, I would have been drunk. My calm veneer belied my churning stomach. Lisa was so nice and she was my only friend in Indy. I couldn't imagine coming to a game without her being there.

As the national anthem was sung, I said a prayer. "God, please let Mike have a good game. Please God. They are good people. Don't let him be humiliated. Don't let his career end today."

When our offense got inside the red zone and couldn't score, the field goal unit was sent out. Lisa and I swallowed hard. People seated around us knew that she was the kicker's wife, and everybody began staring at her, as if she somehow controlled Mike's fate.

"Stupid people," I wanted to yell, "she can't do a damn thing, so turn around and stop staring!" But I didn't. I was too scared to say anything.

As everybody else in the stands drank beer and enjoyed the party atmosphere of the RCA Dome, time stopped for Lisa and me. I think we held on to each other. I know I closed my eyes. I would know by the sound of the crowd if Mike made the field goal. Their lives were being determined by the kick of a stupid ball. His whole NFL career had come down to this.

When the fans started booing, I knew that he had missed. Lisa and I looked at each other and we both started to get upset. I didn't want to cry because I didn't want to upset her further. I wanted to hug her, and tell her that everything was fine, but I knew that my words would ring hollow. I don't think I said anything. I just sat there.

People were staring. Fans may have paid good money for their tickets, but having a ring-side view of a player's wife's misery wasn't included in that price. I know they didn't realize they were doing anything wrong, but maintaining control with hundreds of eyes on you in a difficult situation is so hard. To act as if nothing matters and to hold your head high takes more courage than fans will ever appreciate, and Lisa was so brave. I had never been more proud of a fellow wife.

We both knew that Mike would never wear a football uniform again. His dream had ended. His career was over and the spot-light of fame was looking for the next star before Mike could unstrap his helmet. Those moments in the stadium after his miss were some of the hardest, saddest moments I've ever experienced during a game. Reality had struck close to home.

I didn't really pay attention to the remainder of the game. I only watched the fans and knew they would go home, go to bed, get up on Monday morning and go to work without realizing they had just witnessed the end of someone's NFL career.

Chris and I didn't talk much on the way home after the game. We both understood what was to come, and neither one of us liked it. I have always taken my friends' losses so hard. And I know I have never told them how much their courage and stamina in playing a game that only takes and never gives has been an inspiration to me. Football is an incredible game of grace and talent, and their skills, heart and passion never cease to move me.

It is hard for players to see friends lose their jobs so publically, and on Monday, Mike lost his job. Chris was upset and called to tell me that Mike's cut headlined the sports section. I felt a profound sorrow for Mike and Lisa, but because of the nature of this business, I also grudgingly understood the Colts' decision. Careers are determined by a player's performance, not by a player's character.

Although this story involves the end of Mike's career, I hope that fans will remember him for his winning field goals and the contributions he made to the NFL. He didn't fail. He fought. Unfortunately, the NFL beat him just like it will eventually beat everybody. *No* player will ever be bigger than this game.

Stress. It is what athletes cope with every day and it is hard on a relationship. Being the wife of an NFL player is learning be a sponge, absorbing the stress that a husband can't. "Accept, learn and move on" should be tattooed on every wife's heart the day her husband signs his first NFL contract.

Does That Make Them Christmas Tree Balls ?

Of thee I sing, baby,
You have got that certain thing, baby,
Shining star and inspiration
Worthy of a mighty nation,
Of thee I sing!
— Ira Gershwin

"Let me see that jacket. Girl, that is *fine*. Where did you get it?" I asked Stacy as she walked into my apartment in December of 1992.

"Diana Ditka. She let me borrow it for Coach Ditka's Christmas party tonight!"

"Why are you borrowing something from her when you already have a closet full of clothes?" I questioned her.

"Well, the defensive wives had a luncheon today and Mrs. Ditka was there. And, guess what? Mrs. Ditka asked *me* to sing at the Christmas party tonight! So she's letting me borrow this pony skin jacket to wear!" Stacy beamed.

"No way! You're going to sing? Yeeeaaahhh! Good for you! Hey, you didn't get the security code for their house did you? Because if you did, I'm raidin' that woman's closet the next away game. She has *the* most awesome clothes!" I teased Stacy.

"No, listen to me. I don't know what to sing. You have to help me," Stacy said, in a quandary.

"Hell, Stacy, I don't know what to tell you to sing. It's Christmas, sing a Christmas carol. You're the one who performed all those years in college and in pageants. Sing something from a performance."

"No, I don't know. I can't remember the words to all of those songs. I only know one or two by heart. What should I do?" Stacy worriedly asked.

"Well, Stacy, it is 4:00 p.m., the party is at 8:00 p.m. and we have to leave here in just three hours. I suggest you sing one of the songs you know."

"Okay, okay. I've got it. I'm gonna' sing 'Wind Beneath My Wings' by Lee Greenwood. I know it word for word so I won't be as nervous." She was resolute in her decision.

"That is a great song. Good choice. Did you know he is really short? Anyway, do you think Mrs. Ditka will give that jacket to you?"

"Oh my God, Sally, don't be stupid. She's not gonna' give me this jacket. It probably cost fifteen hundred dollars."

"Well, ask her if *we* can have it! We could share it!" I tried to convince Stacy that the jacket could be her fee for the performance.

"I'm *not* gonna' ask her if we can have it! You are crazy!!"

Three hours later, the six of us — Stacy and her husband, John Mangum, Kim and P.T. Willis, and Chris and I — were packed into the Willises' Pathfinder, on our way to Stacy's singing debut at *Da Coach*'s Christmas Party. We were so excited to hear Stacy sing. And we knew that any party given by Coach Ditka was bound to be fun.

Stacy practiced chords in the back seat of the car on the way to Coach Ditka's restaurant, the site of the party.

"You need to sing a little lower, Stacy," Kim said.

"I think you need to sing a little slower," I said.

"Ya'll are worse than my singin' coach," Stacy responded. The song "Wind Beneath My Wings" began playing once again from the tape deck. Stacy sang it over, all the way through.

"Stacy, is that the only song you know all of the words to?" Chris asked, teasing Stacy because she could start any song in the world and sing it beautifully; she just couldn't finish it.

"Shut up, I'm not talking to you," Stacy responded, smiling, "And no it is not the only song I know all of the words to. I also know all of the words to the national anthem."

Stacy sang her song through once more, and Kim hummed along with Stacy's singing. P.T. looked into the rear of the car from the driver's seat and said, "Kim, why are you humming? You aren't going to be on stage with Stacy when she sings."

"No, P.T., *you* are going to sing with Stacy, didn't we tell you?" I chimed in, baiting P.T. who thought he was the next Garth Brooks. We all bantered back and forth during the thirty-minute drive, kidding each other and having fun.

Pulling into the parking lot of Ditka's restaurant, we saw hundreds of cars. "Oh y'all! I thought the party was for just a few people! Mrs. Ditka said it would be a small crowd! Look at *all* of these cars," Stacy said nervously.

"I sure am glad I'm not singing," said Chris, cajoling Stacy, "I don't think I could do it, Stacy."

"You guys leave Stacy alone," Kim said.

I chimed in, "She's going to be just fine, right Stacy?"

"I don't know," Stacy shakily replied.

"Stacy do you remember when Lynda Carter was 'Wonder Woman?'" I knew that she would because Stacy idolized all of the former Miss Americas, Lynda Carter included. She could name all of the queens by their year of reign, like some kids can chronologically list the Presidents of the United States. "Well, do you remember, Stacy, when she would get her powers from those bracelets or that belt thing she wore? Well, that pony jacket is going to give you special powers to sing tonight without fear, okay?" I had no idea what I was talking about, but I thought it would take Stacy's mind off of her performance.

Singing in front of Ditka was like being asked to sing at King Arthur's Court. Stacy had sung for all of Mississippi, in front of thousands, but this performance was different. It was for Da Coach.

"Okay, you're right. As long as I have this jacket on, I won't be nervous." Stacy was now sure of herself.

The only person who had been quiet during the car ride was John. John was always subdued, but tonight he seemed invisible.

"What's wrong?" I asked John.

"Nothin'. I just don't think this is a good idea for Stacy to be singin' at this party. I mean, I don't want Coach Ditka to know who I am, to single me out."

"What do you mean, 'know who you are?' You've been playing for the man for three years. I think he knows who you are!" I responded.

"No. Not like that. You don't understand. I just want to blend in with the other defensive players. I don't want to call any unnecessary attention to myself. Once Stacy sings, he'll know me in a different way."

"Yeah, but it will be in a good way, John! She's not gonna' embarrass you, and besides, you're never going to blend in because you are the only *white* boy on defense!" I teased.

John laughed and we all caught up to Stacy, who was discussing her number with the professional band that had been hired to play for the night.

We all hung out, partaking of the lavish display of food and drink, while Stacy prepared backstage for her big performance. I had never seen John so nervous, and P.T. and Chris kept teasing him, saying things like, "Oh, I sure am glad *my* wife's not singing at his party. What if she screws up? Ditka will be pissed!"

"Shut up ya'll! You shouldn't make him more nervous than he already is. Stacy's gonna' do a good job. Leave John alone," Kim and I told them.

The lights dimmed and a crowd of five or six hundred gathered around the stage that had been arranged four or five feet off the ground where the band would perform for the rest of the night. Stacy came out, pony jacket and all, and stood beside Da Coach.

Coach Ditka took the microphone, welcomed everybody to his Christmas Party and said, "We have a special treat tonight. Stacy Mangum, wife of one of our defensive backs, John Mangum, will sing for us. John, she better be good or you'll hear about it next week!" Ditka teased, laughing, and as I looked over at the now paper-white John, I thought he would faint on the spot where he stood!

The music started and Stacy began singing, "Did you ever know that you're my hero? You're everything I wished I could be; I could climb higher than an eagle; If you were the wind beneath my wings...."

I glanced at John and his face had relaxed. Stacy was ON! She was great! She hit every note perfectly and people began cheering before she hit the last, "...and you were the wind beneath my wings." No one cheered louder than our group. Kim and I had tears in our eyes. We were so proud of *our* Stacy.

After all of the dickering about which song to sing, this one now seemed the most appropriate. It was as if Stacy sang the song to John, telling him that he was her hero. The crowd ate it up and Stacy was the star of the night.

No one was more impressed, however, than Coach Ditka. After her performance, Stacy was beckoned by Da Coach to meet his closest friends. As the rest of us watched, we realized that Stacy had managed to break Coach Ditka's sometimes intimidating exterior with her southern charm. Stacy had his group laughing loudly and after a few minutes, she rejoined us.

"What did he say?"

"What was he talking about?"

"What were they asking you?" We all asked her at once.

"Coach Ditka was very sweet and nice," she said, "I never knew he was so funny because all of us were so scared to talk to him." None of us had ever really tried to engage him in conversation because he was Mike Ditka, most famed and revered of all Chicago Bears, past and present.

He then came over to our group and invited us to his personal table for dinner. John gulped again and after Coach Ditka left, he said, "Oh, no! Now he knows *all* of us!"

"John, relax! Relax! He's not going to bite us," I said, "Besides, I'm gonna' ask Mrs. Ditka where she got that pony coat."

We all sat at his long dinner table lined with Chicago celebrities. As we sat down, John whispered to Stacy, "Stacy, Coach Ditka is not your new best friend. Just sit down and don't talk to him unless he talks to you. The less said the better. I am already going to catch grief for this, I *know* it."

About that same time, Bears linebacker coach and dinner table companion, Dave McGinnis, raised his champagne flute and said, "John, Stacy did ya' proud. She can really sing. To Stacy!" Everybody picked up their flutes and cheered Stacy and her performance. Clink. Clink.

Not to be outdone and ever the congenial host, Coach Ditka rose at the head of his table and said, "John, I have just one thing to say. This toast is to Stacy, who sang *her balls off!*"

At that moment, the fine, expensive champagne shot from my mouth, up my sinuses and out my nostrils. I *snorted* with laughter. The six of us then all looked at each other and didn't know what to say! That had been the funniest toast I had ever heard. John was mortified because he knew *we* would never forget it, and Coach Ditka would now know him as "Stacy's Husband" when he passed him in the hall at the Bears' complex. We all touched glasses and drank to Stacy's balls.

Coming from Coach Ditka, that was the highest compliment Stacy could have ever been given! At that moment I knew I would defend that man to the four corners of the earth if ever necessary. In our stupid, politically correct world, he had spoken his heart in his own words and I admired him for it. Always colorful, never predictable, it was the Coach Ditka we all loved and never forgot.

And after dinner, I would find Diana Ditka and ask her about that jacket...

Grace's Story

Every templation he and valor form'd,
For softness she and sweet attractive grace;
He for God only, she for God in him.
John Milton, *Paradise Lost*

"Ya'll can both kiss my ass," Grace teased as Stacy and I told her the vibrant pink lipstick she wore clashed with her fire-red hair.

"Well, don't say we didn't tell you, girl. When you end up in the back of *Glamour* as a 'Don't,' you'll know we were telling you the truth," I laughed, kidding her.

Grace was funny, smart and as southern as a cold, sweaty RC Cola and a Moon Pie bought at a country, back-road dry goods store. With her long red hair and green eyes, she was beautiful but approachable. She was the kind of girl women liked to call their friend; the kind of girl that lured men to your table but never stole your boyfriend.

Grace was married to Tiger Jeffords, a wide receiver from Nebraska, who was always on the verge of being cut. They had been all over the NFL, four teams in four years, and we kept our fingers crossed in the fall of 1992 that Tiger would stick with the Bears, or rather that the Bears would stick with Tiger. We didn't want to lose Grace. Even though we had only known her five short months, since Tiger had been picked up by Chicago, she fit into our group like a kid glove at a debutante's ball.

Tiger was blond, blue-eyed, and as All-American as a fireworks display on the Fourth of July. A sweet farm boy who didn't see a television until he was fifteen, Tiger didn't touch a beer until his eighteenth birthday, had received colored cereal as a Christmas treat, and had oftentimes plowed the family's "back forty" before the morning school bell rung. Tiger's work ethic was fierce, the hard lessons of farm life his backbone. Always in jeans and boots, he and Grace as a couple were comfortable, like a favorite armchair whose seat is a perfect imprint of its owner's backside.

When I first met Grace in the fall of 1992, I thought her entire life must have been peaches and cream perfect like her complexion. I would have never guessed that Grace was the child of migrant workers or that she had grown up hungry. And I certainly wouldn't have thought she would eventually stare in the face of danger because of her husband's fame.

Grace grew up along the apple trail spanning the Carolinas. Her parents, vagabond pickers, travelled where the work was good and where ripe apples were coming into season. Picking the same trail yearly, the family of three began their menial labor in Hendersonville, North Carolina and worked their way through the thimble-sized towns of Hog's Back, Horse Shoe and Long Creek, on their way to the last farm in Walhalla, South Carolina.

As an infant and toddler, most of Grace's days were spent in a worn, cotton pouch that was tied and slung around her mother's waist or in a basket near her mother's feet. At night, in her parent's ever-changing abode, Grace slept on a "pallet," her bedraggled blanket a make-shift bed on a dirty, wooden floor. Growing up, her world lacked continuity and the normal routines of a child. There were no Brownie Scouts, no ballet lessons, nor any spend-the-night parties. Learning to blend into her new housing and schooling environments quickly, Grace became a multi-colored chameleon. She could become anyone she needed to be in order to fit in. By the time Grace was twelve, the skill of being able to rapidly determine what was wanted from or expected of her was instinctual, as innate as her senses of sight and sound.

Once, when I told Grace one of my fondest childhood memories was the smell of a freshly-cut Christmas pine tree in my family's living room, she just smiled sadly and said, "I don't have memories like that, Sally. I mostly remember going to bed on an empty stomach, and wondering if there would even be a Pop-Tart for me in the morning." She then revealed many of her childhood hardships, from having to endure vicious taunts by fellow school children because of her parent's occupation to only taking baths in cold water, hot water tanks being a luxury reserved for senior pickers.

I never questioned Grace about her parents. She didn't have any pictures of them in her home and they never visited during the holidays. I assumed she kept her distance by choice. I did ask her once, though, how she escaped her impoverished background, and eluded the trap of becoming a day laborer.

She told me when she was seventeen, a beauty pageant was advertised in the town paper where her parents had been picking for the last few weeks. The prize was five hundred dollars and a scholarship to Rock Hill College, a small liberal arts institution in nearby Spartanburg, South Carolina. Since her strict, religious parents felt that pageants were sinful, and wouldn't approve of her entry, she borrowed a dress from a recently-met, but kind high-school classmate and competed without their knowledge. When she won and excitedly told them of the college scholarship, they were furious.

"Are you *proud* of what you have done?" they had demanded. "There is no honor in showing you body to win an education. We may be poor, but you have prostituted yourself to get what you want. This is the last time you will shame us. We want you out of this house by sundown."

Hurt beyond words, she left them, and with nowhere else to turn, she lived with her newly-made friend's family until high school graduation. The new family treated her well and provided her with the stability she had craved throughout her young life. By the time she turned eighteen, her prior life had evaporated into the air like the dust trailing behind her family's beaten, old wagon every time they drove away from an apple farm. At Rock Hill, she established a new life for herself and finally blended into the mass of new peers without shame.

Grace thrived her freshman year, soaking up new experiences like a sponge. "Honey, I used to go to the library at Rock Hill and spend *hours* looking at the elegant ladies in *Vogue* and *Harper's*. *Town and Country* was my favorite, though, and I used to imagine that I had grown up in a chalet overlooking a beautiful blue sea and that my last name was Fitzgerald or Biltmore. I had such a great imagination! I wouldn't have survived my childhood without it. I know this sounds horrible, but I used to pretend I had another set of parents. I fantasized that they would show up one day and take me home with them. I convinced myself that the doctor gave me to the wrong people at the hospital," she laughed, "'cept there was no hospital, girl. I was born in my Mama and Daddy's old car. Can you imagine?"

By the time she flipped the graduation tassel on her cap, Grace was ready to take on the world. There was still so much she wanted to learn, and her undergraduate degree was just the key she needed to open the door to worlds about which she had only read. She was accepted to the Masters program at the Univeristy of Nebraska, not because of her great body, but because of her great brain.

She told me that she would do it all again, from being born into poverty to working in a pork-slingin' barbecue joint in college, if Tiger would still be her destiny. He was her knight in shining armor and all of her past miseries were worth suffering if she could spend the rest of her life with him.

"I call Tiger my 'Saving Grace,' girl, isn't that funny? He is my whole life," she told me with tears in her eyes, her voice becoming quiet.

Over the years, I came to love and respect Grace more than the other wives because she never gave up, never had the luxury of being spoiled by caring parents and understood the value of true friendship. Not ever using her childhood callouses as a crutch or seeming bitter because of what she didn't have as a child, she found pleasure in small things like waking up in a clean bed with sunshine on her face. On August 31, 1992 the Bears decided to keep Tiger, and Grace found a new family in Chicago.

In October of 1992, Grace and I were watching the Bears mutilate the Vikings at Soldier Field. It was cold, flurries falling around our cherry-chapped faces and as we bundled ourselves to keep warm I said to Grace, "I don't know why *I* am out here, it only takes seconds for Chris to punt! I'm going back to the wives' room. I can't feel my fingers! Look at Chris! He's warmer than we are! Those bench heaters are so hot that he could punt naked and not be cold! I'll see you inside." Grace laughed and I started to pack my gear.

Abruptly, she grabbed my arm and whispered, "Don't leave. Oh, no. Oh, no." I was about to ask her what was wrong when a handsome young man approached, his mouth in a perfect "O" and his eyes wide with surprise.

"Gracie?" he asked, squinting with a frown, doubt resonant in his voice, "Is that *you*?" He was tall, blond and resembled Tiger.

Grace was at first mute, her eyes nervously darting as if to find an escape route, but she pulled herself together and said, "Yes, Paul, it's me. How are you? I mean, I mean how have you been?" I could tell that Grace was just being polite and didn't really care about an answer to her question.

"Oh, fine. How have *you* been? I lost contact with you after your parents left South Carolina. Nobody knew where you went. I tried to find you." Lowering his voice, Paul gently said, "Gracie, I'm so sorry for what happened. Can we talk?"

Grace still clutched my arm or I would have already headed for the wives' room. I assumed the stranger was a friend, someone she had known years ago, but her behavior seemed so out of character. "I'm here, uh, to see the game with my friend, Sally. Her husband plays. He's the punter," she said, dodging the question, including me into the circle of conversation.

"Is that right?" he said. "I played a little baseball in high school and college. I'll bet it's interesting being married to a player."

"Why don't you ask Grace? Her husband is number eighty-three," I responded and as soon as the words had left my mouth, I knew I had said something wrong.

"*What? What?*" Paul raised his voice. "You're *married* to one of *those* guys?" shocked, he asked Grace.

Grace cut him off abruptly, saying, "Look, let's go under the stadium, okay? I think it would be best if we did that."

I was completely confused, and I didn't want to leave Grace alone with this man. But, she looked at me and said under her breath, "Sally, I'll be fine. I need to talk to him alone. But if I'm not back in the wives' room in ten minutes, come find me."

"Grace, are you sure? I don't mind standing with you," I nervously said.

"Just go. I'll be there in ten minutes." She quickly left my side and I wondered if I should follow them into the shadows under the stadium, but I decided against it and made my way back to the wives' room.

I was nervously pondering whether to alert security when Grace showed up five minutes later than she had promised. Immediately going to the restroom, she appeared upset.

"Grace?" I asked, following her, "Grace, are you alright?"

"Yes, honey. Just fine. Go on back out there and watch the game. I think Chris was about to punt. We were third and fourteen or something. Don't miss it. I'm just fine."

"Okay, but if you need me, I'll just be in the tunnel. I'll be right back. It won't take long for the punt," I said, hurrying from the restrooms.

By the time I came back in, she was completely composed and looked like she didn't have a care in the world.

"Grace, I know it's not any of my business...," I started.

"Honey, I was engaged to Paul a long time ago when I was just a girl. Close your mouth. You could catch a fly with it open so wide. Anyway, Paul was older than me and we met under strange circumstances. We made mistakes that I have tried very hard to forget and when we separated, it wasn't under the best of terms. There's really nothing more to the story. I haven't seen him since 1980." Her body was in the wives' room, but her mind was miles away in South Carolina.

"Grace, are you *ever* going to tell me something normal about your life, or does every part of it read like a Danielle Steele novel? Engaged! You were *engaged* to that man? And you haven't seen him in twelve years?" I queried.

"Yeah, like I said, I was a child when I met him. I just grew up and forgot him. End of story. When I went to grad school in 1988 at Nebraska and met Tiger, I discovered what true love was. What I had with Paul was not love."

"Oh hell, we have to punt again," I said, breaking our conversation, "You have to come to my house tomorrow and tell me this whole saga without interruption. I want to hear everything!" But somehow, I knew Paul wouldn't be discussed.

"Honey, I didn't know a thing about football when I moved to Nebraska," she began at my house on the Monday after the Sunday game. "I'd never seen a college game because there was no football team at Rock Hill. One of my friends in the masters program at Nebraska made me go to the first game of the '88 season with her, and I loved it! The stadium was a sea of red. Honey, people had on red overalls, red pants, red shoes, red *everything*. By the end of the fourth quarter, I even had a little red Cornhusker painted on my cheek. I was hooked after that first game!

"My friend loved sports and knew everything there was to know 'bout football. She taught me all about offense and defense and play callin'. By the end of the season, I knew as much as she did. We went to every home game that year.

"At one of the first games, I noticed a lot of people wearing the number eighty-three jersey and I asked my friend who "Jeffords" was and she told me all about him. She knew everything about Tiger, down to his prospects of goin' pro. 'Course at the time I didn't know what that was and didn't care. I just had so much fun watchin' him play. Lord, girl he could jump so high. And it seemed like he had glue on his gloves because he could catch anything. The harder the catch, the crazier the fans went. Nebraskans loved Tiger.

"I was at a party one Saturday night with some of my friends, after a big Cornhusker victory. Everybody was partying and I was getting beer from a keg when someone tapped me on the shoulder. I turned around and there was this blond guy, with beautiful blue eyes and the sweetest 'ole smile I'd ever seen. He said, 'Scuse me miss, but do you mind if I drink my beer out of your shoe? You have the prettiest little feet, and I'd be honored if you'd let me have that red shoe of yours.'

"I just laughed and told him he was crazy, that I wasn't giving him my shoe.

"He said, 'Oh, by the end of the night, I'll have your shoe. My name's Tiger and I'm not takin' 'no' for an answer.' He stuck his hand out so proper-like and shook mine.

"I didn't know he was Tiger Jeffords, the football player I had been watching, until much later. We had been in a hall, talking through the whole party, getting to know each other, when one of his friends came by and said, 'Great catch this afternoon, Tiger. We're gonna' be National Champs this year. I can just feel it.' Tiger sort of smiled, shrugging it off, obviously not wanting to talk about football.

"I looked at him and asked, 'Are you Tiger *Jeffords*? The wide receiver?'

"He said, 'Yeah, but don't hold it against me. I didn't tell you because girls act funny around me sometimes when they find out who I am. I wasn't tryin' to fool ya' or anything, I just wanted you to talk to me because you liked *me*, not Tiger Jeffords the football player. I know this sounds crazy, so I'll leave ya' alone. And hey, I was just playin' about your shoe, but I do think you have pretty feet!' he grinned, and started to leave.

" 'No, don't go. You're really nice and I enjoyed talking to you. We have a lot in common, and besides, it's not midnight yet. You said you'd have my shoe by midnight and you don't. Are you gonna' quit that easily?' Then, he just reached over pulled off my shoe and laughed. 'If I'd known you were gonna' *let* me pull it off, I would have done it hours ago!'

"But, true to his word, by midnight, that sweet boy had my shoe and my heart." She and Tiger had been together since that first night. And they had survived some of the hardest times of anyone I knew in the NFL.

◆◆◆

"Tiger, we have to sell my car. We can't make this month's payment on the mobile home if we don't sell the Altima," Grace weepingly told Tiger in November of 1991. Tiger had just been released from the Raiders and the Jeffords were strapped for cash. It was nearly impossible to save any money on Tiger's minimum salary and by the time the Jeffords paid for their rental apartment in Los Angeles, an extra car for Grace and their mobile home in Nebraska, they barely got by.

"Let's just wait and see what happens Gracie, maybe we won't have to sell it. The good Lord will take care of us, I know it," Tiger wanted to believe what he was saying, but his words were based on hope, not reality.

After three seasons with three different teams, Tiger was starting to believe that the good Lord had other plans for him. Maybe it wasn't his destiny to play football after college. Maybe it was time to find a real job and stop living day to day, season to season. Tiger was getting tired of being treated like a piece of meat. In 1989 when he was drafted by New Orleans, he felt like he was on top of the world. He had managed respectable stats as the second stringer and was looking forward to challenging the starter the next season. The pink slip in his locker came as a shock.

He wasn't signed by any other NFL team after his release from the Saints, so he played in the World League. He had a great year, leading his division in receptions, and caught the winning touchdown in the World Bowl. His success had snagged the attention of the Raiders, and they signed him for the '91 season. Tiger almost made it through the whole season on their roster, but they already had two million dollar-plus receivers, and Tiger became expendable when they had to quickly sign a right guard because of injuries.

In November of 1991, Tiger felt like he was back where he started. He barely had enough money to get by, and nobody believed in him except Grace. Grace was his life support, his number one fan, and his coach. She went to the football field with him every day to throw, to help him run drills, and to time him in the forty yard dash. She was the only one who still told him to

[79]

keep trying, that his dream could still be a reality. If it weren't for her, he would have given up after the first cut.

"Okay," Tiger said, going into the kitchen where Grace was cooking yet another box of macaroni and cheese, "One more team, one more time, and that's it. If I don't make another team by April 15 of 1992, you are looking at the next insurance salesman for All-American Life. I can't keep doing this to us. We have no roots and it's my fault. I want you to pray with me, Grace," and Tiger and Grace held hands, bent knees and prayed about their decision.

By the time the Bears called Tiger Jeffords on April 1 of 1992, wanting to sign him as their third string wide receiver for the '92 season, the Jeffords were down to their last thousand dollars. Grace had started keeping neighborhood children in their trailer to keep them afloat. The call from the receiver's coach was a sign from above, coming just two weeks before their deadline.

Grace couldn't go with Tiger to the tryout because they couldn't afford two plane tickets. She had always been there every step of the way with Tiger, cheering him on at every camp and every tryout. But not this time. Tiger wanted her to come with him to Chicago, but they didn't have a choice. He promised to call her for luck minutes before his scheduled tryout at 10:30 a.m.

Tiger didn't call until 11:42 a.m., by which time Grace had chewed her nails down to the quick. The Bears had signed him! That was the only reason she didn't yell at him for not calling her earlier. She could have heard him screaming hundreds of miles away if she had only put her head out the window of the double-wide. Grace had never heard him so excited! As the ink was drying on his new contract, she merrily sang and packed their belongings in cardboard boxes rummaged from the liquor store dumpster.

Tiger's first season with the Bears was of legendary proportions. It became football lore that will be retold for years. He broke almost every record ever set by a Bear's receiver. He caught the most passes, had the most receiving yards and scored more touchdowns than any other player in 1992. Overnight, he became a celebrity sensation. By the end of the season, he shared an advertisement billboard in downtown Chicago with The Man, Michael Jordan, and was named to the much-publicized Madden All-Pro Football Team.

Tiger couldn't miss. What he lacked in size, he made up for in tenacity. There was no ball he couldn't catch. Thrown over the middle laid up for the entire defense to clobber, caught. Thrown off the back foot, caught. Thrown into triple coverage, caught. It seemed like Tiger was single-handedly winning games. Just put Tiger in on third down and the Bears would score. In the stadium, when the score was tight and it was third down, fans would begin to chant, "Jef-fords, Jef-fords, Jef-fords," over and over until Tiger made a spectacular, game-saving play. Finally, a team had given him a chance, and he wanted to prove them right over and over again.

Every company in Chicago wanted Tiger to endorse their products and every luncheon organizer wanted Tiger to speak. Terry-cloth towels like the one Tiger wore on the field were copied, packaged and sold in all of the local sport stores. Grace told me that the money they earned from the first month's sales of "Tiger Towels" would pay for their future children's education. Tiger was selling phones on television, clothing in the newspapers and sandwiches on the radio. He was everywhere! On the players' day off, Tiger earned five thousand dollars for delivering a thirty-minute speech about determination and work ethic. The windy city was mesmerized by this young man's spirit, goodness, wholesomeness and intelligence. In 1992, Tiger Jeffords was plucked from obscurity by the football gods and crowned with the laurel wreath.

The Jeffords' life was forever changed. Grace and Tiger couldn't just jump in the car and go with us to The Olive Garden anymore. Every time we went to dinner, frenzied fans would form autograph lines around our table. It was overwhelming for Grace and Tiger, but they never showed it, never cracked from the scrutiny of the public eye and never acted like they were too good for us anymore. They were the same ol' people and we loved them more for their indifference to their sudden fame. In 1992, Tiger went from earning the league minimum to making a cool million from a re-negotiated contract. He finally had the security that had so long eluded him.

Grace told me that all of the money in the world wouldn't change their lives. "Money only means that we've got a roof over our head, sugar. It might be a nice roof, but it's still just a roof. Money can't make you happy. You've gotta' have happiness first. The money is great, I'm not gonna' say that it isn't, but my most treasured possession is Tiger. I'd love him if he were a trash man." Good old Grace. She knew what was important at the ripe old age of twenty-seven. I knew then that Grace and Tiger would beat the divorce statistics of the NFL.

In September of 1993, Grace revealed some of the best news I had ever heard. She was pregnant! She called from the doctor's office, asking me when she should tell Tiger. I told her to drive over to the Bears complex and tell him immediately. Later she told me that she had gotten him out of meetings, but he was thrilled.

"Honey, he is so excited! He is already sayin' he knows it's a boy! But I hope it's a girl so we can spoil her and take her shopping with us!" Grace was so happy and I couldn't think of two people who would be better parents or love a child more.

Every time I went to Grace's new house she had bought more baby clothes. "Grace, those people at Baby Gap must love you. I'll bet they talk about you in their staff meetings, you've spent so much money. And you don't even know what sex the child is! You should stop buying these clothes because that baby isn't going to weigh ten pounds forever," I teased her, laughing that she had only purchased infant wear.

"You know, Sally, you're right, but I guess because I grew up with absolutely nothing to call my own, I just go crazy buying things for this baby. You don't know how I wanted pretty, clean clothes when I was little. I only had old hand-me-downs and stuff other people would have thrown out. I never had new clothes or fancy buttons or pretty bows in my hair. I want to make everything right for this baby. I want to give it everything I missed. I'm so scared that I won't be a good mother because of my own childhood. I just don't want to fail this baby like my parents failed me," she told me with tears in her eyes.

"Grace, the most important thing is your love, not these clothes or this expensive nursery. And you have more love to give than anybody I know. This child will be the luckiest little thing in the whole world. And he or she will be proud to call you 'Mama.' You'll do fine, Grace," I reassured her.

Five days later, Tiger called me after dinner. Trying to hold back his obvious emotion, he told me that Grace had lost their baby. The doctor had stopped the hemorrhaging and Grace was out of danger, but the baby was gone. The doctor had told Tiger that he didn't think Grace could have any children.

Looking out my window as Tiger told me this, I saw Ricki's kids playing in the street and I started to cry. Here was Grace, so deserving of having a baby and couldn't, and there was Ricki, so easily having children that lived a hell within their home. Life, at that moment, did not seem fair.

The game that next Sunday is one I will never forget. Nationally televised, the Bears were playing the Lions at the sold-out Silverdome. I went to Grace's house to watch it with her and keep her company while Tiger was gone. She was still bed-ridden, trying so hard to act happy but her veneer was as transparent as glass. I played along, though, avoided the subject of the baby and let Grace guide the conversation between us. As the game approached kickoff, we settled in around her television.

A famous ex-football player commentated the game, and after his opening comments on expected team strategy he announced, "I had a chance to talk to Tiger Jeffords, the Bears' star wide receiver, before the game and he told me that although he had some personal problems this week, he felt good about today. I found out from other sources that his wife recently suffered a miscarriage."

Grace emitted a low, guttural sound that quickly became a scream. "Why? Why did he just tell this to all of America? Who the hell does this announcer think he is? Is nothing in our lives personal anymore? Does everybody own a piece of Tiger, now? Do they have a right to know everything that happens in my house? Next, he's going to tell all of America how I had an abortion, a bad, bad abortion, and now I can't have any children!" she was standing, screaming at the television and then looked at me.

I was stunned. I wanted to go home and pretend I hadn't heard her. She went into the bathroom and closed the door. Here I was at the heart of someone else's crisis, and I didn't know what to do.

Grace calmed down, returned to the den and sat down. She covered her feet with a comforter and said, "Sally, I've never told anybody what I'm about to tell you. Not Tiger. Not my doctor, although I know he already knows. Not anybody. But I feel like I have to tell somebody now or I will explode. I can't keep this to myself any longer. You don't have to say anything. I just want you to listen."

I nodded, silently.

"When I was fifteen my parents were picking apples for the summer in Hog's Back, North Carolina. The man who owned the apple farm there had a son, eighteen, who was going away to college in the fall. You met him not long ago. It was Paul, the man from the game. My parents worked for his dad.

"Anyway, when I first met him, he was nice, kind, and acted like he didn't care that my parents were workers. He treated me with respect, and I really liked him. When I was working further out in the orchard away from my parents, he would come by in his truck and take me on picnics. We would sneak away, eat real food and talk about life outside of the apple trails. Turns out, he felt as trapped there as I did. His father wanted him to run the farm after college, but Paul didn't want to. We shared a lot of ourselves with each other, becoming close, and learning each other's real dreams.

"After a couple of months, things really escalated. We became secretly engaged and were going to elope. We had even filed for our marriage license at the local courthouse. I carried it in my pocket everywhere I went, like a security blanket. I was only fifteen, but in my world, being married at fifteen was something to celebrate. He was gonna' take me to college with him as his wife. I know how crazy it sounds now, but then, it seemed so logical. I thought I loved him, and I thought he loved me.

"Then, I got pregnant. When I told him, I thought he would be happy because we were getting married anyway. But he was stunned. It seemed as though taking me to college would be an adventure, but taking me and a baby would be a drag. He told me that I had to get rid of the baby, that it wasn't part of the plan. I was so stupid. I just went along, thinking everything would be alright after the abortion. He took me to a doctor, a quack, and without any anesthesia, at age fifteen, I had an abortion. I lost so much blood that by the time he got me back to my parents, who didn't know anything about my being pregnant or my relationship with him, they had to rush me to the hospital. I almost died. I think that was the reason my parents hated me after that. My daddy told me they could never pick there again, because of the shame I had brought upon my family. It had been one of the best farms for them, and my daddy told me that we would all suffer now because of my mistake.

"We left in the middle of the night. They forbade me to contact Paul or ever see him again, and I was so depressed and confused that I listened to them. They told me he didn't really love me and convinced me that he would never have married me anyway. I will never know if that's true, but I tried to forget about him and I never looked back. It's one of those things I have kept buried for so long that I almost forgot it, until now. I can't have children because of that abortion, Sally. I guess it's what I deserve," she was crying now.

"Grace, I don't know what to say. I'm so sorry. Just so sorry that you had to go through all of that, with nobody to support you. But I think you should leave it in the past. It belongs there. Nothing good is going to come of telling Tiger now. We all make choices that are hard, but don't look back, Grace. Move on. My God, you were just fifteen. Be thankful you're alive, that you escaped that life. Don't let this ruin what you have now, with Tiger. Let it go, Grace. Just let it go." I hugged her and she cried for a long time.

I remember thinking that all of America was watching the game and was focusing on Tiger's sorrow. But who was consider- ing Grace's heartbreak? Nobody knew what she had been through. Nobody knew the secrets she must keep, the demons she must fight every night before she drifted off to sleep. The public only saw the facade, the beautiful face behind Tiger's image. No one would have guessed the pain in Grace's soul. I wondered how many times women across America had said, "Wouldn't it be fun to be Grace Jeffords?" I wondered now how many of them would think it fun if they had to carry her baggage and her scars.

In November of 1993, Grace went for a typical jog around her subdivision. She ran the same neighborhood streets daily and had even competed in the twenty-six mile Chicago Marathon. On her third mile, she noticed a woman in a grey Sunbird who stared at Grace when she passed. On her sixth mile, the same car crossed the center line and whizzed by at a high rate of speed, forcing Grace to jump from the road to avoid being struck. Grace tried to read the car's license plate as she was falling, tearing her medial collateral ligament in the process, but the searing pain in her knee distracted her attention.

A neighbor who witnessed the incident stopped to help and took Grace to the hospital. Grace called Tiger from the emergency room, and he rushed from the Bears' training complex. When Grace described the car and the woman to Tiger, his face fell. He said, "This is my fault, Grace. She could have killed you. I'm so sorry. I could have prevented this."

Neither Grace nor Tiger knew at that moment that this incident would be the crossroads of their marriage. Grace would have to decide between believing in Tiger and believing hard facts. The relationship that had survived financial problems, job firings, job relocations, and new-found fame and fortune was now on the brink, with trust teetering at the precipice.

♦ ♦ ♦ ♦ ♦

Mad, confused and shaking, Grace shouted, "Do you *know* this woman, Tiger? Please don't tell me you are having an affair with her! What the hell is goin' on?"

Tiger responded, "Oh god, no! Grace, I'm not having an affair. *Never*. I would *never* do that to you. I think the woman you just described, though, is the same one who has been putting notes on my car in the Bears' parking lot for a couple of months. I didn't tell you because I didn't take any of them seriously. At first, her messages just said that she was a fan, an admirer, and that she wanted me to call her sometime. But she never signed anything or gave me her number, so I didn't think it was a big deal. *All* of the players get those kind of notes. I didn't think it was odd until she started putting nude pictures of herself under my windshield wipers.

"I kept hoping that she would just leave me alone. I didn't think it would amount to anything, but I should have at least alerted Mr. Groh, the Bears' FBI agent to what was going on. Management is always warning us about wackos, but I didn't think it would happen to me. I'm calling the police, now. Mr. Groh needs to know everything so he can track her quickly. I wish I hadn't thrown all of that stuff away that she left on my car. This is all my fault! I'm *so* sorry, Grace."

When the police arrived, Tiger started at the beginning, with the first note. There had been two months of cards, flowers, cologne on his birthday, and finally the nude pictures. He told the police and Mr. Groh that the notes had neither threatened Grace nor made any reference to knowing the street address or community in which they lived. The police explained that since she had obviously tried to run Grace down with a car, this stalker was a very dangerous individual and police surveillance needed to be posted outside of the Jeffords' home for at least one week. Also, there would be a unit watching Tiger's car in the Bears' parking lot in hopes she would return.

Grace was befuddled. She didn't really think Tiger would cheat on her, but she also found it very hard to believe that a woman would pursue Tiger this doggedly without any encouragement from him. There must be something Tiger was leaving out, to spare her feelings. He must have led this woman on in some way, allowing her to believe he was interested. Grace decided to keep calm, however, until she reached the bottom of this.

She called me late in the afternoon to let me know she was okay if "by chance I had heard an overblown rumor."

"Well, Grace, it wouldn't be overblown if I heard that someone tried to *kill* you would it?" I had been worried to death since Chris called from the complex to tell me about Grace's near-miss. It was so typical of Grace that she didn't want everybody else to be upset.

After we hung up, I re-checked all of our door and window

locks. It spooked me to think that someone would want to physically harm a player's wife because of a sick crush. Grace had
never even met this woman. And from what she had said, this
woman didn't even *know* Tiger, yet wanted to hurt Grace. This
was nuts! I had heard it all, now.

I didn't say anything to Grace, but I started thinking that
maybe Tiger had egged this woman on in some way. Even though
I loved Tiger and wanted to think he was above having an affair, I
couldn't imagine a woman going to this extreme without *some*
promise of returned affection.

The next few days were quiet. Nothing strange happened while
the police were watching the Jeffords' house, nor did the mystery
woman make a love-note run to the Bears parking lot. Maybe it
was just a fluky thing after all, we started to think, or maybe the
woman who had left the notes wasn't the same woman who had
tried to hit Grace. The only link was the similar physical descrip-
tion by Grace and Tiger, but even they began to doubt themselves.
Everybody started to relax a little, thinking we had *all* over-
reacted.

Two weeks after Grace's accident, the Bears played out of
town. Grace adamantly told me she wasn't scared, that there was
no reason for Stacy and me to babysit her while Tiger was gone.

"The police are gonna' cruise around my house all night and I
will have the security alarm rigged so tight that a fly could set it
off. There is no need for the three of us to sit around and give
each other the willy-nillies when nothin' is gonna' happen. I'll be
fine," she assured me.

I thought she was crazy, because if I had been in her shoes I
would have invited everybody I had *ever known* to stay with me
and I would have kept *all* of the lights on until dawn. But Grace
didn't seem to be scared of anything...

Until 3:30 a.m. when she called me scared out of her wits. The
stalker had just called Grace *at home*. She had called their un-
listed number, which had just been changed the week before.
Grace and Tiger had only given the new number to a few people.
Even the head coach didn't have their new number. How in the
world had this crazy woman found it? Grace said the woman
identified herself as the "second Mrs. Jeffords" and threatened

that the swerving car had only been a warning. She then informed Grace that Tiger had professed his love for her, that he was planning to leave Grace.

Grace hung up immediately and called the police, but with no tracers on the Jeffords' phone there was no way to find out from where the woman had called. By the time Grace rang me, she was hysterical and wanted to call Tiger. I told her not to, that it would only upset him and what could he do? He was seven states away and playing a game in less than twelve hours. And the Bears weren't going to let him fly home because of a crank phone call; hell, I knew men who had missed their baby's *birth* because of team obligations. I told Grace to wait and tell Tiger when he got home.

"I'm sick of having to put these stupid games before everything else! I just want to talk to Tiger! I want to hear him say that he doesn't know this woman. I want him to tell me that all of her talk is crazy gobbledegook and that everything will be okay. But you're right, the game comes first. I'll tell him when he calls me from the plane."

I understood Grace's frustration. She was making yet another sacrifice for football that would forever go unnoticed. If fans only knew this side of professional sports, this part of being a wife, then they might not think we were so fortunate.

Eight hours later on that same Sunday, just one hour before kickoff, Grace got another phone call. The woman told Grace to look in her mailbox, that she had left Tiger a gift. Grace, trembling, called the police again and the dispatcher called the cruiser that was supposed to be watching Grace's house. The cruising surveillance team had momentarily left, distracted by the noise of a sounding burglar alarm two blocks away, but was back in front of the house within five minutes and had reported no suspicious activity of any kind. However, with the threatening nature of the two calls and the recent events, the surveillance team beckoned the police bomb squad to check the mailbox.

While Tiger was making his first catch against the Bucs, his house was being surrounded by police personnel. Large, foam protectants were being placed around his mailbox and two policemen in astronaut-like suits were approaching the metal box with extreme caution. Grace watched from a camera inside of a police van parked two blocks down the street. Her immediate neighbors had been evacuated before the bomb squad proceeded, and Grace thought about the neighbors now. Those same neighbors who had been so happy, so *honored* to have Tiger Jeffords living next door were probably ready to plant their own bomb in the Jeffords' mailbox since this stalker had caused so much distressful commotion within the neighborhood. A once peaceful subdivision where parents let children ride bicycles freely down the streets and sidewalks, the common areas were deserted, as parents feared that another attempt on Grace's life would endanger those of their children.

There was a loud pop when the mailbox door was opened! Grace was watching from the mini-van's camera, and the noise ricocheted through her body. She thought it was a bomb until she saw streamers falling to the ground. The stalker had rigged the mailbox with a party favor that resembled a small champagne bottle, popping open to release dozens of small streamers. This woman's idea of a joke was not funny. The sound had scared everyone. Grace still thought the mailbox might explode before her eyes, but instead, the bomb expert signalled the "all clear" and removed a large, paper-bag wrapped object.

After the second check of the Jefford's property uncovered no suspicious objects, Grace was allowed to return to her house. Her kitchen resembled a commando station, so many machines and personnel were active within the room. Someone had even used her coffee maker to supply the "troops" with brew. The scene was surreal. Grace hadn't even thought of the game or Tiger's performance. And she wasn't going to get to now — on the kitchen table was a black notebook with a large color picture of Tiger on the front.

"This is the 'gift,' Mrs. Jeffords," a burly detective told Grace. "It seems to be a scrapbook of sorts, like something my grandmother made for me when I played football in high school. I can't find anything strange in it, just newspaper clippings and Bears programs throughout Tiger's career. We would like for you to look through it though, and see if anything strikes you as unusual. Maybe you'll see the significance in something we didn't.

We've already checked it for prints and found nothing, so you can touch it."

"Do I have to? I mean if you didn't find anything, I'm sure I won't either. I don't want to touch it. I'd rather not, if it's okay," said Grace, still shaken.

"I understand how you must feel Mrs. Jeffords. But, we really need your help. Detective Margoulis can flip through the pages for you. If you want, though, you can wait until Mr. Jeffords returns home tonight, because he'll have to look through it, too."

"Okay, if someone else flips through it, I'll look and see if anything looks strange."

As the detective opened the cover and began leafing through the many pages, Grace noticed how neatly the clippings were arranged and how precisely the articles had been snipped out of the paper. It was obvious that this album had taken hundreds of hours to prepare, a labor of misguided love.

Grace kept thinking to herself that this woman was really _in love_ with Tiger. The more she tumbled the idea around in her mind, the more sick she felt.

Tiger came home to madness and after spending hours with the police, answering questions and looking at evidence, he was cornered by Grace, away from everyone.

"Tiger, I want to ask you something and I want to know the truth, okay? Please, please don't lie to me now. It would only do more harm than good. Did you ever have an affair with this woman? Because I am finding it harder and harder to believe that she would do all of this without any reason. If you did something Tiger, tell me now. I need to know."

Tiger began crying and held his head in his hands. "Grace, I'm so sorry. I would never, ever hurt you and I swear to you on my life that I don't know this woman. We've never been face to face. I promise. You have to believe me. Hell, the police act like _they_ don't believe me. I feel like I'm going crazy, being punished for something I didn't do. When I told you years ago that being a football player's wife meant sometimes tolerating obnoxious fans, I didn't mean this. Nobody should have to go through this. This is just madness and I don't know why it is happening to us. You've been so good to stick by me through all the bad days, when I was cut and didn't have a job. Grace, please don't start doubting me now, please. We've been through too much. I love you with all of my heart. Please believe me."

A crisis like this either breaks a marriage or makes it stronger. As Grace had looked through the scrapbook earlier in the day, she knew most wives would begin to doubt their husbands. Most wives would believe an affair must have occurred to evoke a response that strong. No woman would chase a man this tenaciously, risking incarceration, if he hadn't led her to the action. But Grace loved Tiger and trusted him. She believed everything he had just told her and she decided that she wasn't going to start doubting him now.

"I believe you, Tiger."

The police were now monitoring Grace and Tiger's every move. The officer assigned to Tiger shadowed him at the Bears' complex. He stood watch outside the meeting room doors. He waited outside the locker room. He stood on the sidelines of the practice field. He did everything but catch the ball for Tiger. Tiger's teammates teased him about his "shadow" relentlessly, but were actually glad the police were protecting Tiger so closely.

Grace, against the advice of everybody, decided to attend the Bears' home game on Sunday. All of us felt that it was just too risky for her to be in such a large crowd of people. Especially since the stalker had just struck seven days previously. But Grace was determined.

"This isn't gonna' get the best of me. I'm not scared of that woman. What's she gonna' try at a game, anyway? She can't hurt me there," Grace informed us, and we all knew that it would be futile to argue with her once her mind was made.

That Sunday, Grace's "secret service" looked like they were just friends of hers in for a visit and a game. After two quarters without incident, they felt like the stalker wasn't in the stadium. No strange occurrences had been reported and no one except other wives had approached Grace.

Grace wouldn't even watch the game from the wives' room. Since she stubbornly refused to listen to reason, we sat in section 115, row 14, seats 6 and 7, which were Grace's normal home seats. The secret service boys were in front and back. My mind wandered until the third quarter.

It was third down, six to go, and I knew the quarterback would throw to Tiger. Everybody in the stadium knew it too, including the other team. It was a bad throw over the middle, with Tiger having to extend himself, arms over head, which left his ribs exposed on both sides. Of course he made the sacrifice for the team and caught the ball, but he didn't get up. Even after all of the defenders started walking away, Tiger hadn't moved. It looked like he had been knocked unconscious and our medical staff ran onto the field.

Grace never panicked in these situations because Tiger got banged up frequently. She had just recently told me that she wasn't buying new sheets until the season was over because all the "strawberries" on his hips bled like crazy and stuck to the sheets after a Sunday night game. As I looked at Grace, I thought to myself that absolutely nothing rattled her cage. She was being stalked, her husband was the injured time-out and she still wasn't shaken. I would have been on my third Valium and fourth beer, but Grace was as calm as the lake beyond the stadium.

The medical staff took Tiger into the locker room, beyond our sight, and Grace wanted to walk through the tunnel to check on him. She left with the boys, and I suddenly felt alone. Just to think the crazy woman could be watching Grace as she snaked her way to the player tunnel gave me the creeps.

One of the boys came back to tell me they were going to the hospital, that the doctor thought Tiger had two cracked ribs and had possibly punctured a lung. I had been so concerned about Grace, I hadn't even stopped to think about Tiger. Grace was riding with the detectives to North Shore Hospital, and I told them to tell Grace that Chris and I would come by after the game.

The rest of the game was dismal. We lost and I knew that Chris wouldn't be looking forward to a hospital visit afterward. The *only* highlight of the day was that the stalker had remained quiet.

When we arrived at North Shore Hospital there were five police cars outside with their lights on. I didn't think much of it, because the downtown hospital emergency rooms treated so many victims of violent crime that police were often called to investigate. But when the Channel 2 news crew pulled up beside us, I started to wonder about all of the activity.

Recognizing one of the reporters, I asked him if something was up. He told me that the Jeffords' stalker had been caught, that the police were escorting her out of the hospital momentarily and he was there to get the story.

I was stupefied. "How? What happened?" was all I could ask.

"I don't really know. My station just told us to get a quick shot and sound bite of her being escorted into the police car," he quickly told me.

I was arguing with one of the security guards from the hospital to let us onto Tiger's floor when Grace heard my voice. She told them we were friends and took us back to a waiting area adjacent to Tiger's room. She quickly told us that Tiger's lung wasn't punctured, but that he had two broken ribs. Unfortunately, the doctor predicted he would be out for the next two games. She then proceeded to tell us how the stalker had been caught.

Grace had arrived at the hospital with the detectives about fifteen minutes later than the ambulance carrying Tiger. She went directly to the emergency room desk. Upon explaining to the admissions nurse that she was Tiger Jeffords' wife and that she wanted to go back to his cubicle, the nurse looked at her strangely.

"Well, that's odd because his *other* wife is back there, too. It never ceases to amaze me what you little groupies will do to see those players. You should be ashamed! Now go on and get out of here before I call security. His *real* wife doesn't need to be worrying about women hanging around in the emergency room trying to get a glimpse of her husband," the nurse said, rolling her eyes.

Grace didn't bother with a response and barely heard the end of the nurse's lecture. She ran to the detectives who had just settled themselves in with two year old copies of *Field and Stream* and

People and hurriedly relayed what the nurse had told her. They rapidly explained the situation to the hospital's security guard and physician on call and were quickly escorted to Tiger's bedside.

When they rounded the curtain of Tiger's cubicle, they found the stalker holding his hand and singing softly to him. Tiger, having been heavily medicated before the ambulance carried him from Soldier Field, was asleep. The detectives swiftly surrounded the stalker, who caused no scene, and removed her from the emergency room.

Grace had only glimpsed the woman and said that she had a crazy, distant stare in her eyes. She readily confessed to the police that she had stalked both Grace and Tiger, and the detectives took her to the police station. And out of their lives forever, hoped Grace.

"Boy, am I gonna' have a story to tell Tiger when he wakes up," she laughed, in spite of all the turmoil. "The last thing Tiger probably remembers is going up for that ball. He's gonna' think *I'm* the one who got hit too hard when I tell him what happened. The police said that with her confession, she would probably have to serve time for this. I hope she does. This has been so horrible."

Eventually, the woman stood trial and Grace and Tiger both were called to testify. The crazed fan, who worked for the phone company, had access to the Jeffords' phone number and home address through her work. During the trial, she told the court she became fixated on Tiger because "he was handsome." She admitted that he had never responded to her notes and invitations, but she kept pursuing him in hopes of kindling a relationship. She felt that if Grace were "out of the way" Tiger would have returned her affections. Found guilty, she was sentenced to six years, and Grace and Tiger tried to forget the whole ordeal. After the trial, none of us ever discussed the stalker again, not even in jest.

♦♦♦♦♦

In January of 1997, Chris and I gathered around a small television set in an Atlanta airport trying to catch glimpses of Tiger in the Super Bowl. He was the starting wide receiver for the Green Bay Packers, having left the Bears through free agency. He had just finished one of the best seasons of his nine-year career and was going to the Pro Bowl for the third year in a row. He had started his career on the "bubble," lucky to make the final roster and now was an NFL poster boy. Drug-free, alcohol-free, and faithful to his wife, Tiger was a college-degreed, well-spoken team leader. And he was still the same ol' sweet Tiger he'd always been.

The camera panned the players' family section in New Orleans and landed on Grace and their two daughters, Macy and Maddy. The girls, twins, had been born to Grace and Tiger in 1995, after Grace endured several surgeries performed by the leading fertility specialist in Chicago. I had never seen such spoiling as Tiger gave those two little girls, both the mirror image of Grace. And as the camera showed Tiger smiling up in the stands at Grace after catching his second touchdown pass of the evening, with the Packers on their way to winning the Super Bowl, I couldn't have thought of two people more deserving of success and happiness.

Linguini and Cigars Don't Always Mix

Unquiet meals make ill digestions.
— William Shakespeare, *The Comedy of Errors*

Most of the stories in this book are from the perspective of
NFL wives. The following anecdote, however, is not. But it
is one of my absolute, all-time favorites, and I couldn't
write a book without including it. So, even though this is a
"quarterback sneak" on my part, I hope you like it

◆◆◆◆◆

On the first day of Bears' rookie camp in 1992, the veteran
players nicknamed the beefy, Italian rookie lineman from the
Bronx "Joey Buttafucco." The epithet remains five years later
even though "Joey" is a starting offensive lineman in the NFL and
could easily manhandle the guys who lovingly refer to him as
such. He was always one of the most popular players on the team
because of his great sense of humor and his ability to laugh at
himself, and I spent many an after-game night at Planet Hollywood doubled over from one of his stories.

When Joey was a junior in high school, he had a crush on a
classmate named "Carla." Carla was from the same Italian background as Joey, and he saw her cute petiteness as the perfect
complement to his bulky physique, like a garlic-baked bread is to
lasagna. He finally summoned the courage to ask her on a date
and she said "yes." But, before he could take her out of her

house, he had to meet her entire family. So she invited him to dinner, which I understand if you are from an Italian family in New Jersey, is similar to a car inspection. Instead of pumping your tires to capacity with air, however, your stomach is pumped full of food. And everybody in the family looks under your hood to make sure you're worthy of being driven.

Joey arrived on time with flowers for Carla's mom and some of his family's homemade, home-jarred marinara sauce for Carla's grandmother. He was ushered into the heart of the family's home, the kitchen, and the aroma of the sauces and pastries only made him grow more ravenous for the wonderful smelling food. Joey had only snacked for the last twenty-four hours because he wanted to have a robust appetite. He explained to me that the more he was able to eat, the more virile and worthy he would appear in the eyes of the elder Italians.

While Joey was waiting for supper to begin, he dedicated himself to charming Carla's family. He was very attracted to her, even more so after meeting her nice relatives, and he decided to ask her to be his escort at next month's homecoming game. He planned to invite her after dinner if all went well.

After drinking several rounds of homemade lemonade while waiting for the dinner bread to bake, Joey needed to use the restroom. When Carla showed him where to go, he thought it odd that the bathroom was located beside the dining room, but he quickly finished his business and returned to the kitchen in time to help carry out the heaping, steaming platters of food.

Lasagna, ravioli, linguini and Italian sausage were eaten in abundant amounts by all. Joey stuffed his two hundred and fifty pound frame until the last strand of linguini remained. The table was cleared and everyone enjoyed eating their Tiramisu and telling youthful stories about Joey's new "girlfriend."

Within ten minutes, as Joey managed to take the last bite of desert, his stomach told him that he shouldn't have eaten so much food. He eyed the restroom, but painfully realized its close proximity to the dining room where everyone was still seated. He would just have to wait until he got home. But, *my God*, could these people talk! And talk and talk! When he realized he couldn't make it home, he started to sweat. Joey *knew* that if he used this ever-so-close bathroom, these nice people would *hear* him. And he wouldn't be able to blame this on the dog like he did at home. He couldn't, at seventeen years of age, imagine a greater source of embarrassment. He could already hear the remarks from his high school buddies at school the next Monday. But it didn't matter anymore because *he had to go. And soon.*

He excused himself, went into the small bathroom and immediately opened a window. He turned on the water and searched the cabinets for deodorizing spray. He thankfully found it and began spraying before he unbuttoned his pants. Upon the close of the last "chord" of the Italian sonata playing in his stomach, he tried "shooing out" as much air as he could through the window. He still thought the room smelled like something had died, though, so he used the only weapon he had: the spray. He used a quarter of the can spraying the ceiling, walls and door, and he finished the can off on the commode itself. Joey then buried the can in the back of the cabinet, hoping no one would ever realize he had emptied it. He then washed his hands and returned to the dining room.

He waited for some kind of comment about his lengthy absence when he rejoined the others at the table, but no one acknowledged that he had been gone long enough to knit a small sweater. Joey decided that they probably had noticed, but were polite enough not to verbally observe it. He was *safe*, home free.....*until* Uncle Leo rose from the table, grabbed the newspaper and went into the bathroom.

"That man is going to be asphyixiated by all that 'English Rose,' " Joey thought. He had sprayed enough to neutralize the entire neighborhood block. Seconds passed, then minutes. Joey relaxed. "Thank God, he hasn't suffocated," was Joey's last tranquil thought.

Just as Joey turned to ask Carla to homecoming, KABOOOM!!! The explosion happened so fast, no one had time to react. Suddenly, the door to the bathroom blew off its hinges and Leo was flying through the air, into the floor of the dining room, screaming and grasping his ass. His whitey-tidies were still in place around his ankles, but the commode was in a thousand pieces, scattered throughout the dining room and bathroom. A big, white chunk of the porcelain god was firmly planted under Leo's ass.

Someone frantically dialed 911 to report the explosion and to request an ambulance for Leo. Miraculously, his had been the only injury suffered. Leo couldn't speak except to scream, which prevented him from explaining what had transpired moments before the explosion. Joey knew exactly what happened when he saw the remnants of Leo's cigar melded to his charred hand.

Leo had entered the bathroom, pulled down his pants, sat on the commode and, unfortunately, decided to combine his two favorite activities. When Leo lit the Cuban cigar, the deodorizer had ignited like a flamethrower between his legs, blowing him off of the toilet and into the dining room.

The seventeen year old Joey was speechless. "*My God, I almost killed Uncle Leo*," he thought to himself. The man had to be removed from the scene by stretcher. Quietly, Joey asked if there was anything he could do and exited quickly.

He never asked Carla out on that second date, and his third cousin had to escort him to the homecoming game. Leo recovered, but it is speculated that he still wonders which mafioso laced his cigars with explosives. Joey, now a three hundred pound much-feared maniac on the field, still prays every night before sleep that Leo will never discover the truth!

Did You Say You Knew Dionne Warwick?

Why don't you come up sometime and see me?
Come on up, I'll tell your fortune.

— Mae West

The regular season of the NFL officially begins around September first, with each team having pared its roster to fifty-three players. Fans see the team running through half-clad screaming cheerleaders, taking the field for the new season's first game without realizing the many changes to the team's physiognomy that have occurred since the last season. Many cuts and signings happen in the early off-season, but there is a also a spurt of movement prior to and during July's training camp. And although training camp cuts strike throughout the four to six week bivouac, the final August 30th boot is the unkindest cut of all.

It is bad news if a player suffers a cut this late, just before the regular season begins, because it is difficult to catch on quickly with another team. The other teams have usually filled bare spots in their rosters by then, and a player oftentimes finds himself unemployed for the entire season. The good news is that if you make this last cut, you'll probably be on the team's payroll until January.

Most NFL teams only have one punter and one kicker on their regular rosters. With so many injuries during the season, a team cannot afford the luxury of back-up kickers and punters when they have a greater need for back-up linemen, wide receivers and quarterbacks. Many teams will, however, take two kickers and two punters to training camp, and will release one of the tandem at the end of camp. During Chris' second year in the league, he and another punter participated in the Bears' training camp. The previous year, Chris had been injured during the pre-season and wasn't activated to play until the last four games of the regular season. So the Bears had been forced to keep their punter from the previous year, Maury Buford, since Chris couldn't play in the first twelve games. But it had been a fluky thing to have two punters on the roster, and Chris and I knew that at the end of training camp in 1992, either he or Maury would be out of a job.

I was nervous about the final cut. I felt like Chris would make the team, but with the volatility of the NFL, players and their families never completely relax. The final cut was going to be hard on Chris either way. If he made the team, that meant the Bears had cut Maury, and he and Maury had gotten to be good friends. Maury wasn't obnoxious about competition, and Chris really respected Maury's cordiality and ability. If Chris didn't make the team, we would be packing and looking for a new home. Since both of them had made it through all of the regular camp cuts, it was coming down to the wire. The last cut was on August 30, 1992.

I love to run, and prior to having Cole it was my first activity of the morning, even if I didn't get up until the crack o' noon. On that August day, when our lives were still undecided, I awoke uncharacteristically early at 5:30 a.m. Fear of the unknown had left me sleepless and wondering whether the day would end with me clambering through Kroger's trash trying to find sturdy moving boxes or unpacking the rest of my boxed sweaters and coats.

Chris had already left for work when I awoke, and since there was no one except my dogs to converse with and no way to expend my nervous energy except to run, I pulled on my tights, grabbed my keys and headed for Bally's, an exercise club in close-by Northbrook. It was still so dark outside that I had to use my

fog lights to drive. The club, however, was brightly lit and crawl-
ing with meat-seekers at 6:00 a.m. I *hate* the moron who approaches sans sweat and throws his Mercedes-Benz keychain
down beside a piece of exercise equipment like a fish lure seeking
a bite. I hoped that none of the desperados approached me this
morning, because I was so high-strung over the afternoon cuts,
that I just might have expressed my true feelings loudly.

As I stretched, I listened to the drive-in morning show of Eddie
and Jo Bo, two of my favorite Chi-town disk jockeys. Funnier
than hell, they always crossed the line of good taste and were
never politically correct, but that was their appeal. I usually
listened to them when I warmed up, switching over to a homemade Van Halen/AC DC/Stone Temple Pilots cassette tape for my
actual run. The loud, head-banging music blocked out the sound
of my own desperate gulps for air and kept me running, as I
envisioned fat falling behind me on the track.

But just as I was reaching to switch my cassette player from
radio to tape, I heard Jo Bo say, "And this morning, we have a
special treat. 'Mary Threadgoode', famed psychic, will tell us who
will be cut from the Bears today at Halas Hall, so stay tuned. Will
it be Maury Buford or Chris Gardocki? We'll ask her right after
this." Advertisement music began and I started to breathe again.

"Oh my God," I thought, "I have to call Kim." With my headphones on so I could hear Eddie and Jo Bo come back from
break, I ran to the women's locker room and called Kim Willis,
one of my best friends whose husband was the Bears' back-up
QB. It was only 6:00 a.m. but I didn't care.

Kim's machine picked up, "Hello. Kim and P.T. aren't in right
now, but if you leave a message after the beep, we'll get back to
you." Beep.

"Hey, Kim. It's me. I know you're there. Pick up. It is *so*
important. Pick up. Get out of bed. I need..."

"Hello, Sally. Do you know what time it is? If you don't I will
tell you. It's 5:55 a.m! What are you doing up at this time?" Kim
groggily asked me.

"I'm so sorry to wake you up, but you *won't* believe this. Listen
to me. Go tune your radio to Eddie and Jo Bo. A psychic is

coming on in a couple of minutes to tell whether the Bears are gonna' cut Chris or Maury. You have to listen with me. I'm all alone with the pervs at Bally's and I don't want to hear this by myself," I frantically explained to her.

"I now know for sure that you *are* crazy. I've thought it for a long time, but if you are telling me that you are in Bally's, listening to a stupid psychic on the radio, and you actually *believe* what this woman is about to say, I *know* you have gone over the edge!" Then I heard a deep sigh. "Hold on, let me get my radio so I can listen to this new-age babble with you!"

Eddie and Jo Bo came back from commercial break, and with me standing in the Bally's locker room surrounded by naked women, with one ear on the phone and one ear on my headset, they introduced Mary Threadgoode as one of the most accurate psychics in the Midwest. My mind was racing. Did I really want to hear this? I felt like I would throw up on the fat lady in the lovely plastic shower cap next to me, who kept staring as if I were being too loud or too excited for that time of the morning.

Kim was still hanging on and listening as Mary began her Bear predictions. She discussed three or four other players before she "got in tune with" the punter position.

Channelling her psychic energy, Mary said, "I am picking youth over experience at this position. The Bears will go with the young man who has a funny-sounding last name. I am feeling that the younger fellow can play more than one position. And in the long run, this will be better for the team."

My heart started beating again. "Yeah, yeah! Whoooo!" I yelled in the phone to Kim.

Kim was laughing at me. "You are so goofy! I'm glad Ms. Mary, or whatever her name is, predicted that, but she doesn't work at Halas Hall, Sally. She works 'out there,' " Kim teased.

After I calmed down, I said, "Yeah, I know. But she did say something that is true. Chris *can* kick off and be the back-up kicker. I wonder how she knew that?" I pondered, impressed with Mary's abilities.

"Duh," Kim said, "she probably *read it* in the Bears' media guide from last year! No magic crystals were needed for that tidbit of knowledge. I'm going back to bed and pretend you *didn't* call me at 5:55 a.m. to make me listen to a *psychic* with you over the phone!" Kim laughed heartily.

I thanked Kim for listening when I needed her and hung up the phone in the locker room. Phew, I didn't know if I believed good ol' Mary, but it sure beat hearing that Chris would be cut.

I finished my run, now energized, and went home. I was vacuuming when Chris called.

"Well, they cut Maury this morning," he informed me, not in the mood you would expect from someone who just found out he made an NFL roster. Understanding his feelings, I didn't tell him that I had already heard from a psychic that Maury would be cut. Chris was in no mood for such silliness. "It sucked," Chris said, "Maury is just such a nice guy. It's hard for me to be happy when he doesn't have a job because of me."

Chris was experiencing for the first time the Catch-22 that all NFL players face when they make a team at the expense of someone else's career. The Yin is the happiness a player feels when he makes the team. The Yang is the regret that he has replaced someone else and, in this case, a friend.

But I wanted Chris to enjoy this day for his own accomplishment and focus on the positive, so I went to Baskin-Robbins and had them decorate his favorite chocolate ice-cream cake with the words, "Welcome to the NFL." I knew it was a *little* tacky (!), but he needed something funny to lighten his mood. We talked about many things that night, including the high standard Maury had set with his kindness in the face of competition and how Chris should be proud of himself for making the team.

To this day, I still get nervous during final cuts. A player and his family often don't anticipate that the lightning bolt is going to strike them. Even when all is going well, it is sometimes hard for players and their families to sit back and enjoy their good fortune and the scenery from the field or the wives' room. Always knowing the end is somewhere near, the NFL experience never becomes routine.

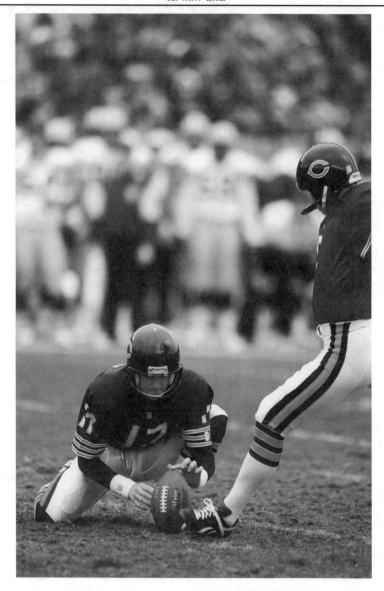

The Bears-Packers game is a huge deal, ask anybody from Chicago or Green Bay — Chris holds for Kevin Butler during one of their exciting match-ups

Can You Use Your Psychic Abilities To Locate A Lost Pet?

Strange, when you come to think of it, that of all
the countless folk who have lived before our time
on this planet, not one is known in history or in
legend as having died of laughter.

— Sir Max Beerbohm

In 1993 and 1994, I was a Monday-morning regular on a
Chicago radio show hosted by media personality Brant Miller.
We discussed Bears' games, players' personal lives and made
up spoofy songs to highlight important games. The show had
a funny, quirky flair and our audience always wondered what
we were going to do next.

During the '93 season, Brant had Mary Threadgoode as a guest
on his show. Our plan was for me to call in, out of the studio, and
ask her to predict the outcome of the upcoming weekend's Bears-
Packers game. Brant thought it would add to the building excitement of the much-discussed game, and I was looking forward to
telling Mary that she had almost given me a heart attack two
years ago, on Eddie and Jo Bo's show when she had predicted the
Bears' final cuts.

While I held the studio line, I listened to callers' questions for
Mary. The people calling in had significant queries about their
love lives, their job horizons and finding misplaced, dearly-loved
objects. I was amazed at Mary's responses, the callers intoning
that she was correct in many of her answers.

And if I live to be 150, I will never forget the final caller's request. The lady said, "Mary, I've lost my pussy. It is grey and furry and I can't find it anywhere. I'm so upset because I just don't think my pussy can be replaced."

I *died*. I didn't know if the woman was a serious caller and was actually referring to a lost cat, but I knew that Brant, who had my same warped sense of humor, would be fighting to keep his laughter from being broadcast over the airwaves. And there is nothing harder than trying not to laugh on the air when you get tickled. No matter what you do or say, all you can think about is laughing. (Especially if you share booth space with funny people like I have. In Indianapolis, I appear regularly with Dave Wilson and Jeff Pigeon and the morning crew on WIBC-AM. They are some of the funniest and most talented people I have ever met, and if I get really tickled, I have to leave the studio or flip my mike off!)

I loved to play jokes on Brant, so when he got to me, immediately after the lady with the cat problem, I couldn't resist. And I knew Brant would be sitting on the edge of his seat in the studio, with his finger on the three-second delay button, just *knowing* I was going to say something that could get us in trouble. Screw the Packer game, I thought.

"Hi, Mary. I'm Sally Gardocki. My husband is the Bears' punter and I had originally called to ask you a question about the game, but I am so worried about that woman who just called in. The item she lost *is* irreplaceable, and I'm sure she was *very* attached to it. I want you to call her back, get her address and tell her that after Bears' practice, I can send a few of the players over to help her locate her lost pussy. They wouldn't mind *at all* and I'm sure it would be a great help to her."

I could hear air escaping Brant's nose, but the only thing he said was, 'Let's go right to break."

He flipped to my line and we completely lost it for five minutes! I laughed so hard that I cried and he kept saying, "Ohmigod. We're gonna' be fined!" But we just laughed. It was one of the funniest moments in my interesting radio "career." I can't even remember if I went back on after the break and asked her about the game. I know that I shouldn't have said what I did, but the opportunity was there and I took it.

There are so many moments in football and in Chris' career that are serious and extremely important. And as wives, we must maintain solemn demeanors, especially when we are losing. But I love to laugh and need to find humor in everyday events to keep my sanity. I think that a good sense of humor lessens the heavy burdens of stress and competition that a football career can bring. So as long as Chris has a job in the NFL, I'll keep my good sense of humor.

Stacy and I innocently enjoying a Bears game — before being swooped down upon by les fans diabolique

Les Fans Diabolique

From fanaticism to barbarism is only one step.
—Dennis Diderot

very stadium has them. Every player loathes them. Every beer vendor worships them. Every NFL wife is scared of them. I am referring to the obnoxious fan. I do not mean the wonderful people I have met in the stands who under-stand the money they spent on a ticket will *not* guarantee a victory or stellar performance by their favorite player. I am also not talking about the fabulous people who are kind to me whether we win or lose, the people who share personal aspects of their lives with me or the individuals who buy me whiskey sours pre-game to calm my nerves! No, I am talking about les fans diabolique, who tend to fall into three categories: Boo Birds, Drunks and Groupies.

The first group swoop down on their prey, à la Hitchcock's *The Birds*. "Boo Birds" appear beside you, coming from nowhere, to annoy and pester at the slightest provocation. They don't know when to sit down, when to shut up or when a normally docile group is about to turn violent and beat them silly in the stands.

You can smell the second group before you see them. These are the Drunks — individuals who make it their business to be drunk before, during and after the game. They are famous for staring, groping and scaring young NFL wives. Usually inebriated to the level of anesthesia, they are numb to a swift kick aimed at the knee or groin, and security frequently has to be called in to control them.

The last group, who epitomize the saying, "Why buy the cow when you can get the milk for free?" are the saddest. "Groupies" (also known as "BWNF" or bimbos with no future) disgust the wives and contribute to the high divorce rate among professional football players.

Having experienced close encounters with all three groups, les fans diabolique remind me of a freckle I have above my lip. I wish it weren't there, but after seeing it for so many years, I don't really notice it anymore when I look in the mirror.

Big, Fat Boo Bird

One of the unspoken wives' rules is "Never argue with fans." It is easy to state this rule, but very hard to abide by it. I am feisty and nothing irritates me more than an ignoramus with a numerical roster who doesn't understand a damn thing about football. I managed to hold my temper through my son Cole's eight-month bout of colic, but keeping my mouth shut in the presence of boo birds is even more challenging than Cole's screaming ten hours a day. Through the years, I have mellowed in my response to them, but I still don't hesitate to have security escort the truly unruly fans from the stadium. It matters not to me that their season tickets will be revoked.

During Chris' first season, though, unaware of the wives' ejection power, I used my mouth as a BB gun against the feathered breast of three big, fat boo birds in Soldier Field. The incident transpired in late September when you could still eat a hot dog in the stands without it freezing to your lower lip. Since rookie tickets were the worst in the stadium, I sat with the beer-drinking crotch-pickers whose favorite pastime was to see which one of them could get the attention of a player. As if the players really listen to these idiots! Anyway, after two quarters of enduring their obnoxious screams, and after realizing the dampness I felt on my back wasn't from a humid lakefront evening, but from their slobber, I mentally put on my durable, Chuck Norris boxing gloves.

I collected my thoughts and composure, left my seat and walked to the trio of compatriots two aisles above me. I briskly informed them of three things:

One, I was the wife of a player.

Two, if they were going to scream my husband's name, they had better pronounce it correctly: it was G-A-R-D-O-C-K-I, not G-A-R-D-I-C-K-I, and that they wouldn't know a real dick if it hit them in the nose.

Three, if they thought they could do a better job than the players, they should get off of their hot-dog-stuffing, beer-guzzling, pretzel-eating fat asses, go down to the locker room, and ask for a uniform.

The men were mortified, a whole section of fans clapped, and I returned to my seat. Ten minutes later, after cooling down from my "victory," I realized I shouldn't have voiced my opinion because people would judge Chris by my mouth — which is not only unfair to Chris, but also goes against everything my mother taught me about lady-like behavior.

So, I don't argue anymore. I just get one of my security buddies to grab the offender by the scruff of the neck and haul him out of the stadium. But as the boo bird passes me on his way out, I enjoy looking into his eyes. My eyes say to him, "Yeah. That's right. Nobody is laughin' now, are they? Nobody except me!"

Oh, Say Can You See *What???!!!*

It was a rare, beautifully clear and warm day at Soldier Field in October of 1993, and at halftime Stacy and I were discussing the importance of buying Donna Karan-brand knee socks over others because Donna's stayed right above your knee and didn't loosen or slide down your calf. We were both wearing stylish kilts with the half-thigh-high-half-knee-sock fashion trend of the season and thought they were the coolest thing since sliced bread. Chris told us that we looked like Catholic school drop-outs, but we didn't care.

Stacy and I spotted *him* at the same time. He was about fifty feet away, with his back to us, singing loudly and off-key. He looked about forty-five years old and wore only combat boots, camouflage green shorts that were so cut-off they were briefer than a Chippendale's costume, and a wide-brimmed, ear-flapped jungle combat hat that was tied beneath his chin. Drunk beyond belief, the man was causing large groups of people to disperse in fear of what he might do.

I looked at Stacy and said, "I will bet you anything that within five minutes that luscious hunk o' man over there will be over *here*, on us."

"You're crazy! That man isn't going to come over here. Besides, he'd have to scale these metal bars around our section and crawl over one row of seats to get to us. Your 'weirdo magnet' isn't that strong," Stacy laughed.

The weirdo magnet to which Stacy referred was a running joke among my closest friends. While some women have "dork magnets," "rich-men magnets," or "married-men magnets," my magnet only attracts predators with weird, sexual problems, those drunk, high or stoned, or any combination of the above. Joe Combat was definitely drunk, and from his dress, well... I knew we'd eventually see.

I won the bet. Within three minutes of our spotting Joe, he had scaled the metal hand-rails around our seating section, had crawled over the first row of wives and was practically standing on top of me. "Rot-gut" is the term I would use to describe his aroma. He was *stinking* drunk and smudged with dirt.

"Hello, purdyy layydies," he slurred.

"Hello," I weakly responded and glanced at Stacy, who was holding her laughter between her pursed lips. "Stacy," I said between my teeth, "go get the Andy Frain security guards."

"Andy who? Who is he? What are you talking about?" Stacy asked, confused.

Still keeping eye contact with the weaving drunk, I discretely whispered again to Stacy, "The security people, Stacy. Get up and go get them. Now!!"

Stacy had no idea of what I was directing her to do, and as she looked questioningly at me, Joe began to speak again.

"Ladies, I fought in Vietnam for *you*. For you, so that you could sit out here in the sunshine and breathe free air. Do you appreciate my sacrifices?" he demanded.

"Yes sir, I certainly do. I respect what you have done," I replied, now getting a little scared, afraid he might have a flashback, afraid that he was *actually* Lt. Calley, the infamous Vietnam vet tried for the horrendous massacre at My Lai.

"Do you mind if I sing the 'Star Spangled Banner' to you, if I pretend that you are the flag?" he asked.

"No sir, if you feel the urge, you just go right ahead. Stacy, my friend here, is a better actress than I, though, and she would probably make a much better flag. She's skinnier. Why don't you sing to her?" I said, trying to divert his attention and somehow alert the security guards to our situation.

Joe leaned in to me and began singing loudly, "Oh, say can you see...", he was so close I could feel his hot breath against my cheek. Out of the corner of my eye, I could see the yellow-jacketed security guards mounting the railing, climbing over the first row, and approaching Joe from behind. "What so proudly..," was the last thing we heard before the guards grabbed Joe, practically knocking him into my lap.

They took him away, but I could still feel his presence. His smell was on me. Stacy and I were in shock. He screamed obscenities at us as they carried him away, kicking. Although Stacy and I later laughed about Joe's shenanigans, it was very scary to think we could have been in a potentially dangerous situation.

I now watch all activity in the vicinity of my stadium seat. If anybody looks remotely suspicious or acts like they are going to pull a stupid stunt, I call the security guards, who have become some of my best friends. And every time I hear the "Star Spangled Banner," I think of Joe Combat and Stacy's flag impersonation!

I Hope You Like Your Crotch!

While working with an NFL committee a few years ago, I learned that seven of ten NFL marriages end in divorce and the average life expectancy of an NFL player is forty-nine years. To me, that meant if a player's wife hadn't killed him by the age of forty-nine, the law of NFL averages would take care of him.

All joking aside though, I've seen too many relationships fail. Most of them collapsed because one party started taking more than they were giving. As anyone who has ever had an intimate relationship knows, being a happy couple requires a lot of work, every day, to keep the relationship fresh. Many factors, such as fame, fortune and time apart, can contribute to the demise of an NFL marriage, but one of the worst relationship killers is the ever-present "groupies."

The first time I ever saw groupies was in the lobby of the Hyatt Hotel in New Orleans in November of 1991. It was my first away-game trip, and I had come with fifteen other Bears' wives. As I walked into the lobby with Carla Woolford, wife of then-Bears' cornerback Donnell Woolford, I was astounded. Wall to wall, as far as I could see, were women of all shapes and sizes: big hair, short hair, tall legs, fat legs, fake boobs, saggy butts, street attractive, dog ugly. All were dressed in varying degrees of lingerie or exercise wear. Literally, lingerie decorated with satin and lace or bike pants like the kind I wore when I jogged.

I turned to Carla and said, "My God! Is the Hyatt hosting a lycra convention this weekend? The cotton industry must be going down the tubes since this stretchy stuff was invented. Who *are* these people?"

Carla said, "Honey, you sure do have a lot to learn if you don't know who these women are. They are groupies. They are here to meet our husbands," she responded.

"What are you talking about?" I asked.

"These women are worse than hookers. Instead of making the players pay for sex and getting out of their lives, they hang around and sue them for paternity, or worse, yell 'rape.' Some of the stupid ones think they can find a husband down here in the lobby. They don't realize they become disposable after the guys have had their way with them," Carla informed me.

"You don't mean that players actually *sleep* with these cheesy-looking women, do you? Carla, some of these women are down-right UGLY! I don't believe this," I said in disbelief.

"Okay, let's just sit here and watch for a minute, then. You'll believe after you see. Let's get in a corner where the players can't see us," she suggested.

As we sat there and watched, I *couldn't* believe it. Players, married and single, would stop to talk to these women. I was absolutely floored. Some of these guys were married to women much more beautiful, classy and refined than these groupies, yet were handing out their room numbers like campaign workers distributing flyers outside a polling booth on election day!

"Why, Carla? Why do they do this? I just don't understand!" I asked.

"Oh, honey, nobody understands it. Some of the wives just chose to accept it, to have a blind eye."

"Not me," I almost yelled, "If Chris were doing this, I'd be wearing his nuts as earrings as a warning to my next husband. I wouldn't stand for this."

She just laughed and I told her I was serious. I couldn't believe a self-respecting woman would *tolerate* that kind of treatment from a man, or would be down in the lobby half-naked trying to *find* a man. It was my first encounter with the groupies and I learned a lot about their modus operandi.

After seven years of observation, I have two thoughts regarding the groupies. First, I trust Chris and believe he places high importance on our marriage and wouldn't succumb to their trashiness. Second, my policy is to ignore the groupies hanging around outside the locker rooms and in hotel lobbies. To acknowledge and notice them is to give them confidence in what they do.

Through the years, their audacity has never ceased to amaze me. Usually glaring and hateful toward the wives, the groupies cling to themselves. Some, however, are very stupid, and on several occasions, will approach our husbands when we are standing at their sides. The few times this has happened to me, the groupie approached Chris, looked smugly at me, handed *me* her camera and asked me to take her picture with him! Bimbo! I smiled sweetly, played along with the game, but instead of focusing on two faces, I took a picture of the girl's crotch. I figured if she were relying upon her "hidden talents" to get her through life, she needed to memorialize them (it) in a photo.

I've always wanted to be in the car when those girls pick up their pictures from the photo mart and realize I knew what they were trying to do! I would love to hear what they have to say! Some of them probably don't even get the joke, but I still think it is fitting.

We wives have built-in bimbo detectors and never mind photographing true fans with our husbands. Don't worry if you've approached a wife and asked her to take your picture. If you have a picture of two smiling faces, the wife thought that you were nice and well-intentioned. If, however, you have a picture of your crotch...

Perks and Stars

The best things in life are free.
— Buddy De Sylva, *Good News*

The celebrity is a person who is known
for his well-knowness.
— Daniel Boorstin

The fringe benefits of playing in the NFL are numerous. But two of the best perquisites have to be the "freebies" we receive (such as dinners, clothing and movie passes) and the opportunity to meet famous celebrities. Some of my favorite memories involve both perks...

How's That Heidi Fleiss, Anyway?

Planet Hollywood, the fun, chichi restaurant owned by famous movie stars, was *the* hangout after Bears' home games in 1993 and 1994. Mark Weissburg, the general manager in Chicago, and his staff always took care of the Bears, their families and friends. Not only were food and drinks gratis, but Planet Hollywood did special things for us, like give us gift bags full of their merchandise, reserve their largest "VIP" rooms so we wouldn't be cramped, and introduce our whole group to visiting stars like Bruce Willis. And since others appeared there regularly to promote their movies, we often got invited to mingle with them at premiere parties.

On one such occasion, an assistant manager asked me if Chris and I would like to meet Charlie Sheen. Mr. Sheen was appearing at the Planet Hollywood in Chicago to promote a newly-released action movie in which he was starring, and they were planning a big luncheon shindig. I knew that Chris couldn't meet him because he would be at practice, but the event sounded like such fun. I knew that Stacy would go if I prodded her, so I told the manager to expect the two of us. Since Chris and John teased us endlessly about *playing* all day while they *worked* all day, we slyly headed downtown without telling them.

As Stacy and I drove the thirty miles to the restaurant, we made a list of things *not* to say. The main subject to avoid was Heidi Fleiss, the supposed Hollywood madame to whom Mr. Sheen had allegedly paid over $40,000 for the services of prostitutes. The topic of his "hobby" had caused a media frenzy and was getting more press than the release of his new movie.

"Don't mention prostitutes or Heidi Fleiss," I said mantra-like, over and over to myself in the car. No prostitutes. No Heidi Fleiss.

We valet parked, were escorted in to a private booth and enjoyed lunch. Mr. Sheen arrived later, to a media blitzkrieg, with hundreds of camera flashes and microphones being shoved in his direction. After a short while, Stacy and I were escorted into his private room and were introduced. My absolute first thought was, "Why did *you* pay women for sex?" He was *so* cute and I couldn't imagine why he would be involved with *prostitutes*. I was thinking this to myself when I realized he had asked me a question. Oh, God! I didn't know what he had said. All I could think about was Heidi Fliess! I could just see her in that gray Armani wrap-dress being arraigned in court! Charlie Sheen was still looking at me, waiting for an answer. Shit! I then said something, probably completely unrelated to his question, but he responded positively. Thank you, sweet Jesus. I thought I had blown it!

We talked to him for a few minutes and he was very nice, polite and even seemed to be a Bears' fan. He surprised and impressed us by asking specific questions about our husbands. He had genuine manners! We asked for a picture with him, even though his "people" weren't encouraging it. When we explained to him that pretty women always got their pictures made with our husbands, but that we never got our pictures made with anybody that would make *them* jealous, he laughed and kindly obliged, which delighted us.

As we were finishing our conversation with him, a dishwater blonde, named Ann or Amy or something, who was there to interview Mr. Sheen for her television station, began complaining loudly. She was apparently mad that *we* were talking to Mr. Sheen when *she* was supposed to be interviewing him. "Who *are* those girls? What are *they* doing here? Doesn't he know *I* have a schedule? I don't care if they are Bears' wives. They're probably bimbos anyway."

We could hear her behind us. Stacy and I had done nothing to her. I turned and stared *hard* at her until she had gotten the point. She huffed off. We were having fun. She couldn't have pried our impressed butts out of there with an electrified pitchfork. *Especially* after what she had said! We lingered a few more minutes.

After a while, Mr. Sheen's entourage decided to move to another location and we were asked if we would like to follow. I think that our reply shocked him more than being caught with his pants down at Heidi's. We thanked him, but told him "no," that it was about 3:30 p.m. and we needed to go home to cook dinner for our husbands! If we went anywhere else, we would get caught in the afternoon traffic and would be late getting dinner on the table. He looked at us, baffled, as if he were thinking, "This is so lame, they can't be making it up." Stacy and I didn't realize we led such pathetically boring lives until that point!

We left Planet Hollywood and got our film developed at a one-hour photo booth while we shopped in the grocery store. We grabbed some food, picked up our pictures, which were splendid, and went to our separate homes to prepare dinner. When Chris returned from practice, he asked me what I had done that day and I nonchalantly told him that Stacy and I had been to lunch with Charlie Sheen. He chortled.

"Oh, yeah, Pamela Anderson from *Baywatch* came by the complex and we all had lunch with her! I think her boobs are *real*. Then David Hasselhoff sang us some of his German chart-busters before we went back out to practice!" He joked further, "I'll bet you and Stacy didn't do a thing except fix dinner ten minutes before we got home. Ya'll have probably been layin' on the couch watchin' *Oprah* re-runs all day."

I then produced the t-shirts Planet Hollywood had given us that Mr. Sheen had signed. Chris was still unfazed. He accused me of going to a lot of trouble for a hoax. When I produced our pictures from Planet Hollywood, he said, "What are those? Ya'll really *did* meet Charlie Sheen? And you had lunch with him? Charlie Sheen, the *actor*?"

"Yes. Stacy and I actually get a lot more done between 7:30 a.m. and 5:00 p.m. than ya'll think. And next week we're supposed to meet Mel Gibson for lunch, but don't worry, supper will be on the table by 5:30 sharp."

Stacy and I always managed to have fun and meet interesting people. I'm sure that Charlie Sheen doesn't remember us, but we will always remember him and the day that we engaged in conversation with a supposed Hollywood "bad boy" who was actually a polite lamb.

I Wonder if Donny Wore Undies Beneath His Amazing Technicolor Dreamcoat.....

When I was eleven years old, my grandmother took me to see the Osmond Brothers perform at Memorial Auditorium in Greenville, South Carolina. I wore my first pair of big-girl, suede clogged-heels, some elephant-legged flower-child pants and a t-shirt that read, "I ♥ Donny Osmond." My grandmother wore cotton balls in her ears.

When Stacy suggested that she and I attend an evening performance of *Joseph and the Amazing Technicolor Dreamcoat*, a play in downtown Chicago starring Donny Osmond, my thoughts went back in time to Memorial Auditorium — my cool-woman clogs and fat little Jimmy Osmond pounding the keyboards while sexy-hunk, big brother Donny belted out the tunes of my childhood. My infatuation with Donny Osmond ended about the time the heels of my clogs wore down. Stacy's still existed in December of 1993.

Stacy told me that, as a child, she would sit for hours in her room, imagining herself the next Marie Osmond, trilling with the Brothers O on her hand-held tape recorder. Donny's clear voice beckoned Stacy's imagination to a bright stage and adoring fans, leaving Pearl, Mississippi in the dust. Stacy's voice eventually did earn her the first runner-up title in the Miss Mississippi pageant and secured her membership in a popular college vocal ensemble. And throughout her years as a songbird, Donny Osmond still remained her idol and her hero.

Spending an evening with Donny Osmond dressed as a lost cast member from *Godspell* was the *absolute* last thing I wanted to do on a Thursday night. Thursdays were my night to watch "Seinfeld" and "Wings" and I had no intention of paying forty-five dollars to hear Donny's choral poem of goodness, even if he was half-naked. Stacy bribed me by paying for my ticket and telling me she would drive. That sealed the deal. In three years of going to Sunday Bears games, Stacy had *never* driven. I was the Carol Brady of our group, taking everyone to the games in my station wagon à la Montero. The younger wives were all scared, with good reason, of the fast bumper-car-drivers who maneuvered the downtown traffic like Grand Prix racers.

Just a few months prior to Stacy's invitation, I had taken Stacy and Stephanie Matthews, another Bear wife, downtown to shop at the Water Tower on Michigan Avenue. They were scared to drive themselves, so I was determined to not only take them but to make them feel comfortable navigating the environs of Chicago proper and give them the confidence to do it alone in the near future.

"After this trip, you girls should not have any fears of doing this alone. Once you see how easy it is, you'll be doing it all the time. There is just one interstate, which you follow to the Ohio Street exit, and then you make a left on Michigan Avenue. Simple! I can't believe ya'll have been scared to drive down here by yourselves!" During the ride I kept reassuring them of how easy it was to find a parking space and of how friendly the downtowners were.

It began drizzling and I decided to park our new Montero in the underground garage of the Water Tower. I usually used the self-park between Michigan and Superior Avenues, but parking underground would keep us dry and we'd only have to catch an elevator to be in the middle of the shopping orgy. As I steered the Montero underneath the hanging, overhead bar going down into the garage, I heard the distinct sound of metal striking metal.

I stopped the car's descent and quizzically looked at Stacy and Stephanie, saying, "Did y'all hear that? Was that my car?"

Stacy and Stephanie in unison replied, "Yeah. It sounded like something hit the luggage rack."

"*@#!," I muttered under my breath as I exited the car in the now-pouring rain. As I inspected the top of the car, I found the luggage rack *wedged under*, not just touching, the overhanging garage bar which read, "Clearance: $7^1/2$ Feet." Great! Now that I knew my car was at least $7^1/2$ feet high, how would I extract it from its perch? As I was pondering this, and trying to convince Stacy and Stephanie there wasn't a problem, I noticed the traffic trying to park in the underground garage was backing up behind us and was, in fact, snaking out onto busy Michigan Avenue from our bumper-to-bumper sidestreet entrance.

Dismally realizing I would have to back up to extricate us from this mess, I approached the driver's side window of the car immediately behind me. The driver, a scowling man with Coke-bottle glasses, grudgingly rolled down his window.

I said, smiling, "Hi. I need to back up because my car is too tall. Ha, Ha! Silly me. It's a new car and I didn't know it wouldn't fit. You know how we women are about cars...only thing I know is how to put gas in it! I'm really sorry to have to ask you to back up. I'll go tell the cars behind you."

Before he rolled his window back up he snarled, "Stupid bitch! It's raining. I'm late. What were you *thinking?* Or *were* you thinking?"

I stopped dead in my tracks and wheeled on him, "Look, if you want to get out and throw down right here, we can. My hair is already frizzed for the day, my Donna Karan jacket is ruined, and I'll bet you don't weigh one hundred and twenty pounds soakin' wet. I could kick your little ass like it hasn't been kicked since you were a snivelling twit in grade school. I'm trying to be nice, but what will it be?" He rolled up his window and stared ahead. That was his answer. Good decision on his part, I thought.

I was now soaked to the bone, but I had to explain my predicament to the other ten cars behind him. They were, thankfully, much more polite and made a path for me to retreat.

I climbed back into my car, unaware that Stacy and Stephanie had heard the dialogue between Pee Wee Herman and me, and said, "See, it's no problem coming down here to shop, girls. Just a little glitch in the plan. We're back on track, now."

They both looked at me and said, "No way will we *ever* come down here by ourselves! You almost had to fight that man to get him to move his car! This just isn't fun."

I had done more harm than good by bringing them down here and challenging that little weasel to a fight. Later, in the food court of the mall, we saw the man *again*. He snarled at me from a hundred yards distance, and I flipped him off. He disappeared quickly.

Anyway, when Stacy volunteered to drive to *Joseph*, it was a shock. So I *had* to go, leaving Chris to videotape Jerry, Elaine, George and Kramer.

I must admit that the play was entertaining. The story line was engaging and the actors were talented. When Donny Osmond was on stage, Stacy's face brightened like that of a child on Christmas Morn'. It was clear that she still adored him.

After the curtain fell, Stacy looked at me and said, "Let's go find the stage exit and get Donny's autograph. I want to see him up close!"

Without missing a beat, I responded, "Stacy, what are you thinking?! We are in *downtown Chicago*! It is after *midnight* and you want to walk around the *outside* of this building, in alleyways in the dark, to find the stage door? *Hello, hello!* We would be mugged! We are not in Pearl, Mississippi, Stacy. We can't just traipse around outside looking for the stage entrance."

"Puuuuuhhhllleeeeeeaaaasssssee, it would mean so much for me to see him," Stacy begged. I relented, as always.

"Alright, but I can't *believe* we are doing this and I am agreeing to it. If I get mugged because of Donny Osmond, I will never forgive you!" I teased her, laughing.

Within twenty minutes of searching, we found the stage door. We stood along with twenty-five or thirty pre-pubescent 12 year olds. "Stacy, would you look at us? What is wrong with this picture?!! Look at who wants his autograph and look at us! *We* have boobs! I can't believe we are doing this." I was laughing so hard I could barely talk.

After we had lingered beyond the time a normal person would have waited and become completely convinced Donny must have worn a muscled body suit that had to be peeled off layer by layer under that damn Dreamcoat, he finally appeared at the stage door. Stacy and I, at my insistence, were dead last in line for his John Hancock. It was *way past* the bedtimes of those little girls who so desperately wanted to meet him.

He sat inside a Chrysler Lebaron and signed the play programs for his adoring fans. After a thirty or forty minute wait, Stacy kneeled at his altar and began weaving a richly-colored story of her past years of reverence. It began, "When I was a little girl in Pearl, Mississippi, I listened to you on forty-fives in my room..."

The Coach

Wars may be fought with weapons, but they are
won by men. It is the spirit of the men who
follow and of the man who leads that gains
the victory.
— George S. Patton

The head coach sat behind his desk and examined the filmed
play unfolding on his dark office wall. It was well past
10:00 p.m. and the training complex was empty, save for
the underpaid trainers who were washing dirty uniforms in
the basement. The coach rubbed his eyes and rehashed the
video of the day's team practice once again. He just couldn't
make a decision about the receivers. All four were good, but he
could only keep three. And he had to post the final roster for the
upcoming season at 10:00 a.m. Tomorrow, he must release five
more players to meet the requirements of the NFL's Collective
Bargaining Agreement, and he was stuck on the receivers.

As he ran his fingers through his hair, trying to clear his mind,
his thoughts wandered to his wife, probably asleep in their bed by
now, and his children, now grown with children of their own. He
wondered why he had chosen this profession years ago because
he knew he had missed chunks of time in his loved one's lives.
And he regretted that. But as he glanced back at the figures
moving on his wall, catching balls across his marked-up black-
board and plaques of personal accolades, he remembered why he

had chosen this job. He loved this game. He loved these players. And he loved being in the center of it all. He realized that he hadn't chosen this profession. It had chosen him.

Fans always ask players to compare the different head coaches for whom they have played. And since every coach is so different, it is difficult to make a fair comparison. Each coach has his own way of running the show. Some coaches delegate authority and let their assistants call the plays, whereas other coaches *invent* the play and control every aspect of it. I have seen coaches who rant and rave, but still retain the respect of their players. And I have seen coaches who will never successfully motivate men.

I believe the best coaches are men who feel they have nothing to prove. They are confident in their actions and instincts and aren't afraid to listen to their players. It has been my experience that the older, more accomplished coaches relate better to their team.

Younger coaches have more difficulty handling the pressure to win and are quicker to shuffle and re-shuffle their starting lineups because of some media moron's mouth. It seems more difficult for young egos to accept that their failure resulted from the play *they* called or the fact that *they* moved a guard to a tackle position. Instead, they find subtle or even overt ways to project the losses onto the players, away from themselves. It is easier for them to point the finger at a player, assistant coach, or even a referee who had a sub-par game. And in some ways, I don't blame them for this. Younger coaches aren't given unlimited years to prove themselves and some of them wear the hats of general manager, head of scouts, player personnel director *and* head coach.

Older coaches, on the other hand, have fireplace mantles for shoulders. The older coach has survived years of media speculation, doubt and criticism. He has learned that to point a finger at someone else leaves three pointing back at himself. Older coaches are the Obi-Wan-Kenobis of the NFL. The Masters of the Universe. They are survivors and the best teachers of men-boys. Seasoned lessons from a trustworthy coach are as invaluable as Lynn Swann was to Terry Bradshaw.

Fans also ask players, "What makes a coach a great coach?" All of the great coaches I have ever heard of or known have had two common traits: respect for their players and honesty. If a coach respects his players and is *always* honest with them, the team will enjoy success. If the players are happy, the coach is happy and vice versa. And if everybody is happy, the team will win. Or will die trying.

Mutual respect between the players and the coach is a locker room "must." Mutual respect means listening with open ears and sometimes accepting another's opinion for the good of the team. When it is 4th and 18 on their 35 yard line with twelve seconds left in the game and the players must perform better than they ever have to win, it is mutual respect that gains the conversion and ensuing touchdown. Faith in each other and belief that each play counts brings that winning season. Mutual respect is what motivates a player to give his all even though he thinks a better play could have been called, and what prompts a coach to call a fake play even though he doesn't *really* believe the kicker can throw more than twenty yards. Lack of mutual respect is a 6-10 season, a bad attitude in the locker room, allowing your punter to quasi-dance in the endzone after punts, and a coach being seduced by the media temptress to release cuts to the press before telling his own players.

Honesty is the counterpart to mutual respect. If a player can't believe the words of his coach, a promise of the world is just blowin' smoke. A player has to feel a little job security to play his best game. And if a coach tells a player that he is "the man" or that he has the starting job, the coach better mean it and not try to cut or trade the player the next day. Dissension disseminates through the locker room like a potent stench when a coach lies.

◆◆◆◆◆

I think the value of honesty is best exemplified in the following story. The events transpired many years ago, and the player who relayed it to me has long-since retired, but the significance of the account endures.

It was cuts week and "Jason" was a rookie on the "bubble" of getting cut. The night before the third pre-season game, Jason prayed for the opportunity to show Coach Ditka that he was worthy of making the roster. His prayer was answered during the game when it become 3rd and 3 and Jason was called off the bench as the "goto" tight end for the next play.

Before Jason ran onto the field, Coach Ditka drilled his eyes into Jason's and snorted, "Don't drop the f----in' ball, son."

"Yes sir!" was Jason's only reply as he ran onto the field, snapping his chinstrap on the fly.

The huddle was all business and ever tense as the play was called. Jim McMahon, the brash, demanding quarterback, planned to loft a slant pass to Jason. Jason would then burst for three yards and run to the sidelines, converting the first down.

The play's success was a necessity because the Bears needed at least three points to win the game and wanted to avoid a fourth-down punt with only 3:54 remaining. Jason got set, the ball was snapped and as he ran his route perfectly, turning on the precise spot where his hands were aching to grip the spiraling ball, out of the corner of his eye, for a lightning flash of time, Jason sensed a defensive back barrelling for him. He blinked, the pigskin hit him on the numbers and it fell to the unforgiving dirt. Jason looked up to see the punter replacing his baseball cap with a helmet and he knew that contrary to Coach Ditka's admonition, he most certainly had f----ed up. Hell, he even wished he was on the special teams unit so he wouldn't yet have to confront the disappointed Ditka, but face him Jason must.

Jason put his head down, so the white Reebok logo on his shoes was the only thing he concentrated on as he crossed the sidelines. He stood near the 10 yard-line, away from everybody. Although the team later rallied to win on a defensive interception, Jason felt like a failure and just knew that he would be cleaning out his locker the next day.

After the game, in the locker room, other teammates told Jason to "shake it off"; that *The Drop* wasn't a fatal mistake. But *The Coach* hadn't even glared at him since *The Play*. Jason showered slowly, taking it all in — the clanging of the metal locker doors, the dingy white tile in the shower stall, the smell of sweat, dirt and blood still fresh in the air — because he didn't think he'd be back here again. Dressing methodically, Jason realized he was the last player to give his wet, clinging uniform to the trainers.

He didn't even want to think about facing the waiting press with their invasive questions: "How could you have dropped it?" "Wasn't it perfectly thrown?"

As Jason turned to leave, he noticed Ditka noticing him. Ditka's nose was still flared, but his voice had quietened. "We could have lost because of your mistake, son. You can't play in the NFL if you're worried about your ass gettin' hit rather than catchin' the ball."

Jason thought that was it. He thought that Ditka wasn't even going to wait out the week to cut him.

But instead, Ditka said, "You're a rookie. You're going to make mistakes. Tonight was one of them. And you're not ever going to forget it. But you had a great camp and played well in the other pre-season games. I'm going to keep you. Trust me. Just relax next week and do what you're capable of." With that and without hearing the responsive excuse Jason had been formulating in his mind, Coach Ditka turned and left the locker room.

Three years later at his first Pro Bowl, as Jason was holding his heart during the Star Spangled Banner, he remembered his first year, how far he had come, and what he had learned from Coach Ditka. He realized that being able to trust and believe in his coach's words allowed him to achieve his potential. When Coach Ditka had said, "Trust me," Jason relaxed and was inspired to prove his coach right in making the decision to keep him on the roster. It was a big step in his rite of passage to manhood.

Honesty and respect... they are the most powerful tools a coach can utilize.

We are very fortunate that our families have been able to share Chris' success — in the photo above. I'm with my mom and dad at one of Chris' games. They always enjoy watching him play.

Sloane's Story

The awful thing is that beauty is mysterious as
well as terrible. God and devil are fighting
there, and the battlefield is the heart of man.
— Fedor Dostoevski, *The Brothers Karamazov*

The black Mercedes convertible squealed to a stop alongside the parked, red BMW. Bannon Scott, the frenzied driver, vaulted over the car door, bypassing the handle, and began running toward the immense two-story Tudor mansion.

Hair askew, sweaty-palmed, he started screaming as soon as he got inside and reached the bottom landing of the spiraling, suspended staircase.

"Sloane! Sloane! I know you're up there! Get down here *now*. You can't hide this from me anymore. Oh no, sugar pants, I know *everything*. DO YOU HEAR ME? I KNOW EVERYTHING!!!" Bannon's voice echoed in the marble entrance hall, shaking even the petals of the carefully arranged day lilies upon the mahogany sideboard.

Upstairs, Sloane was coiffing her hair in the mirror. Her fingers stopped, poised above her bangs, when she heard Bannon's tone. "Bannon doesn't know what he's talking about," she thought to herself, "If he did, he would have just marched up these stairs without any warning and wrung my neck!" Sloane realized she had finally grown tired of the game she had played for so long. She may as well tell him the truth now. She wanted to look good for this. Her judgement day. Ha! Well, at least she still had one surprise for him. Bannon may have found out what she had been secretively doing, but she would bet her right silicone boob that he didn't know who she was doing it with. Moron! She loathed his perfect blond hair and perfect white teeth. And all of the groupies who screamed and waited for him after every game. And all of his smiling-faced endorsements. And all of his smooth-sounding radio commercials. As she carefully applied her blood-red Viva Glam lipstick, she smiled to herself. Her little revelation would fix him. She couldn't wait to reveal the whole truth, eye to eye.

"Bannon, honey, quit that yelling! I'm coming down," sugar-voiced, she started downstairs.

On every team throughout the League there is one couple who is *the couple*. The are the most famous, rich, beautiful and seemingly perfect ones of their crowd. But there is always more to their story than what meets the eye. And the stories, the rumors and the innuendo that tend to surround these couples are usually well-contained. But there is always someone, somewhere, who knows the whole truth.

In the fall of 1993, the Bears signed one of the hottest quarterbacks in the league. It was big news, and the fans were rabid for information on Bannon Scott and his beautiful wife, Sloane. *The couple* was coming to Chicago, and we wives, like the fans, wanted to know all about them. Specifically, we wanted to know about Sloane. And Grace, having known her briefly in Los Angeles when Tiger played for the Raiders, had the scoop that the press never would...

Rebecca Sloane Stevens was born with the blue blood of Boston coursing through her veins. Growing up as a Beacon Hill brat, she had always enjoyed the best money could buy. Her spoiling commenced in infancy with a European nanny because her mother, a nervous, high-strung woman, needed her sleep and couldn't be bothered with a crying infant when metropolitan Boston was relying upon her to organize charity balls for thousands of patrons. The pampering continued throughout her teenage years; she always wore the best clothes, attended the finest schools and associated with the scions of other long-standing Boston dynasties. At her family summer house in Cape Cod, Sloane lifeguarded and honed her sailing skills from hobby-level to those of a well-versed yachtswoman during her three-month breaks.

Sailing became Sloane's real passion and one that she pursued endlessly during long summer vacations. When Sloane graduated from high school in 1979, her father presented her with a forty-five foot schooner so she could toddle around the Cape, in style, with her girlfriends. The salt water and cool sea breezes were the strongest pulls in keeping her east-coast bound for college — that and her daddy's money.

By the time she entered Boston College in the fall of 1979, Sloane was gorgeous, well-bred and one of the most sought-after dates north of Manhattan. During her college days, she sharpened her skills at her other much-practiced hobby, which was tormenting the hearts of men. Understanding her beauty's allure, she used her thick-lashed blue eyes and long, straight blond hair to lure men into her tantalizing web. Sloane Stevens enjoyed addicting men to the drug of her body and then witnessing the ensuing withdrawals they suffered when she cut them off. Their hearts and emotions were her playthings. Having never met a man she really cared about, she was ruthless. Her games escalated from seeing if she could get a man to buy her a drink to seeing if she could get a man to propose. Sloane's "sport-dating" led her to hone yet another of her talents, acting.

Upon graduation, Sloane decided to try acting as a profession. She had modeled as a teen and college student and had performed in summer stock at the Cape. She would never win an Oscar, but her killer body and face just might earn her some "fun money," as she was able to rely upon her daddy's cash to pay for her necessities. She felt that pursuing a career in acting would certainly be more fun than finding a job in the real world. When she revealed this new-found desire to her father, he pulled his well-connected strings and within three months of graduation, Sloane was the most sought-after "extra" in Hollywood.

Famous producers were all too eager to return favors to Sloane's eminent father, helping to create an overnight sensation in her popularity. It had been difficult to leave her beloved Boston and stomping grounds at the Cape, but California was a new and exciting experience for Sloane. The addictive rush of sailing was soon replaced by the thrill of being selected, from a sea of competition, to appear in a new television series about life along the shores of Malibu.

In 1984 at the cast party for "Malibu Sunsets," the new drama in which Sloane had a recurring part as the villainous mogul's mistress, the strangest event of her twenty-three year life occurred. Engaged in a rather boring, but necessary conversation with a shaggy-haired assistant director, Sloane suddenly felt an urge to look across the room. Staring directly at her and mouthing the words to the background music of Ozzie Osborne's "Crazy Train" without self-consciousness, was the most beautiful man she had ever seen. She suddenly felt weak-kneed. Men *never* had this affect on Sloane. Usually the opposite occurred. Her eyes were glued to the six foot four physique with sweeping blond hair and hazel eyes. The young buck reminded her of Robert Redford, circa 1970, as the alluring bandit in *Butch Cassidy and the Sundance Kid*. She didn't know who he was, but she was going to find out, now.

Sloane's eyes never left those of the gorgeous stranger as she slunk across the room in her best B-actress seductive prowl. The stranger kept his steady gaze, an invitation to share more than cheap gossip and expensive champagne at this oh-so-typical Hollywood party.

When Sloane was within arm's length, she purred, "I *know* I didn't give *you* mouth-to-mouth this season, but maybe we can create our own resuscitation scene later on."

Bannon choked on the gin and tonic he had been trying to sophisticatedly sip as he was enjoying the scenery and false bravado of these actors and actresses. But that line strangled him. He was amazed at the audacity of women these days.

"Don't think we've met, Miss...." he ventured, the native Alabamian always polite.

"Stevens. Sloane Stevens. And I *know* I haven't met you. Are you the new actor MGM is touting this year? I'll bet you are. I've heard all about you. Half of the women on this set want to have your children!"

Bannon laughed, "Uh, I hate to disappoint you, but no ma'am, I'm not an actor. Just a 'friend of.' That's the only reason I am here. Hell, the most I've ever acted is pretending like a tackle didn't hurt. Name's Bannon Scott. I play football for the Raiders."

Sloane was transfixed. A football player. This was an exotic animal to her, a species she had never tried to tame. Intrigue and the sparkling eyes of Mr. Bannon Scott kept her fascinated.

"So, Mr. Scott, what do you think of this fancy party? Or do you frequent these on a regular basis?" Sloane asked, wanting to know if she had any competition from other starlets on the rise.

"No. This is my first one and I have a feeling it will be my last. I'm more comfortable with a cold one and a big screen TV, if you know what I mean. All of this pretense is for the birds. I wouldn't have chosen to play in this city as a matter of fact, but the choosing is done by the teams. Players don't really have a choice where they start their careers or end them, for that matter. So, here I am. Like a whale too close to the shore," Bannon confessed, surprising himself in doing so. He normally didn't reveal much of himself to anybody, much less a stranger. But Sloane was so beautiful, so intoxicating. He was comfortable talking to her. And he was picturing her naked in his mind.

The next Sunday was a series of "firsts" for Sloane. The afternoon of her first professional football game began with her first experience of not being center stage and ended with her realizing that she was falling in love for the first time. After only one week of being wined and dined by Bannon Scott, Sloane was a goner. She was so mad at the silly feeling of lightheadedness she experienced every time Bannon looked her way. The mushy, sweet feeling in her stomach was virgin territory for Sloane Stevens. She had fallen hard and fast, and for the first time in Sloane's life, she loved another human being. But she would never let Bannon know it because of the power he would then hold over her. This was the most exciting game she had ever played because *she* was risking burn by the heat of the flame this time.

Sloane was impressed by the mystique Bannon held for so many women. After the game, hoping for a peek at Bannon, his female fans were lined up deeper than the fashion slaves in front of Filene's for its annual sale. All of those waiting for Bannon to appear from the locker room screamed his name, waved scraps of paper and jerseys and hats, and prayed they would get an autograph or picture. As Bannon exited the much-guarded locker room, he ignored the throngs of fans and went straight to Sloane to escort her to his convertible Jag. The onlooking women were rabid with jealousy. They wanted Bannon, and if they couldn't have him, they didn't want to see him with another woman. Sloane was just glad they were behind a high fence. The fevered adoration of Bannon only made him more attractive to Sloane. The object of her desire was the object of everyone else's.

Bannon was one of the most eligible bachelors in Los Angeles. A first-round pick from Florida State University in 1984, he was the Raiders' quarterback of the future. An instant millionaire after the draft, Bannon had gone on to prove his worth, earning the starting position by the end of his rookie season. He was magic on the field, and one of the most handsome, desired and popular professional football players since Joe Namath.

Bannon and Sloane had more in common than they realized. Everything had always come easily to them. They never had to work too hard to get what they wanted. And the gift of beauty had been bestowed upon both of them from birth. It seemed they were meant for each other.

They became one of the most photographed couples of 1985. Always together, Bannon and Sloane perfectly complemented each other. The tabloids had chronicled their every move since that first cast party. The public seemingly couldn't get enough of them, their picture-perfect images. Perfect, snap. Perfect, click. The cameras loved them.

It wasn't that Bannon didn't love Sloane. He did love her. He knew he did. This was the perfect woman for whom he had always searched: his dream girl and his trophy. He wanted to marry her and had even begged her to run away in the middle of the night with him to Vegas to make it legal. But she wouldn't.

"Not yet," she said, "I'm still not sure of how I feel. And I really want to pursue my career as an actress. I don't know if I would have as much appeal if I were married. Maybe next year, Bannon. I just need a little time." He thought that if he married her, if he was a taken man, his dark, deep secret would disappear.

His problem had existed since the sixth grade, when his friends bet him that Joni Buchanan wouldn't go to the Friday night dance with him. He had been a quiet youth, never really having time for girls or their silliness, because of his hectic after-school sports schedule. But his friends were starting to tease him, saying that he didn't like girls. He had to show them. He was scared to ask Joni because she was the most beautiful girl in school and if she said "no" to him in front of his friends, he would never hear the end of it. But he had prove to his friends that he not only liked girls, but that he could get the most sought-after girl in the sixth grade. He was so nervous before he asked Joni to be his "date," but when she agreed to meet him at the dance, he was elated.

He had floated on Cloud Nine until he got to the school gymnasium that Friday night and found *Joni there with another boy!* She had only agreed to be his date to play a cruel joke on him! He ran from the dance, only allowing himself to cry when he was a block away from the school, but he could still hear the taunts and laughter of his peers in his mind. The next Monday, his male friends sided with him, previously unaware of the "joke" Joni had staged, and assured him that girls were worthless. At the age of 12, Bannon had decided all girls were evil and mean, and that he would make them all pay. And for the next six years, every young girl who tried to love him had her heart broken.

By the time Bannon entered college, his retribual game had become his standard treatment of women. He was a popular god on campus and could have any girl he wanted. And he did. His caddish behavior unfortunately befell some of the most sincere and beautiful co-eds. And even though it was no longer his agenda that women suffer because of the long-past slight by Joni, he had just become indifferent to others' feelings. He didn't know any other way. He knew that he needed to change, but he couldn't find "the one" who was worthy of his love; the one girl who was deserving of his complete honesty and who could heal the scars of an embarrassed sixth-grade boy. Until he found her, he knew he would continue jumping from woman to woman.

The thrill of the chase became Bannon's excitement, his addiction to women stronger than any drug. "Could I get her in bed?" was the ever-present question when he approached a woman. It wasn't the act itself. It was just the challenge, the game. He knew the sex would be a let-down. He always left them after the conquest, because the thrill was gone until the next head-turner appeared. But then he met Sloane. She was different. He had started to believe she was "the one."

Bannon's nickname among his teammates was "Cass," short for Casanova. They benignly whispered behind his back that Bannon's addiction to women stemmed from his healthy ego. But they were wrong. It was the insecurity of a twelve year old that caused Bannon to prove, over and over, that he was attractive to women. Bannon's self-doubt was fueled by his fear of obligation. The "C" word for Bannon was "commitment." He wanted to keep them all at a distance and never let them inside his head or heart. He wanted them to *want* him, not *love* him. What most of his best friends saw as womanizing was really a deep-seated fear of falling in *real* love and being hurt and shamed once again.

Sloane was different because Bannon felt things for her that he had never felt for another woman. Women had even tried to blackmail him into loving them with false pregnancies and attempted suicides. But nobody ever succeeded. And now, when he found someone he wanted for life, he couldn't convince her to marry him. He was exasperated and knew that if she didn't commit to him soon, the cycle would start over, the addiction would still be there, calling to him.

Brad's Platinum Club was located in the heart of Venice Beach. Inside the glitzy canopied building, the dreams of beautiful young women died hard and fast. The girls' long-dreamed-of "auditions" before famous directors and producers transpired on the small dance stage rather than a studio stage lot. Brad's became one of Bannon's favorite haunts when he first moved to town. Starting as a once-a-week male bonding session between Bannon and the offensive linemen, the performances at Brad's quickly became one of Bannon's after-practice routines. Bannon came alone, a baseball cap pulled tight around his ears, needing to be incognito in his obsession. The strippers were some of the most challenging sells Bannon had ever tried to make, which made them all the more attractive. He had managed to stay away from Brad's during the first months of his relationship with Sloane, but her efforts to make him want her by backing away were driving him back to his old ways.

On October 16, 1985, Bannon kissed Sloane on his way out to meet "the boys" for their weekly dinner and poker game. Sloane bitched about the secrecy of these excursions, and Bannon knew that if she ever discovered that the poker game was held at Brad's, she would throw him out of their apartment. Keeping this one secret from her was the last remnant of the former Bannon. It was the last bastion of the crumbling fort that had protected his heart for so long.

He had never cheated on Sloane, but this game she was playing with his emotions was starting to make him crazy. What if she was only teasing him like Joni Buchanan had? What if she wasn't really "the one?" What if the allure of other women was still present? He was so confused. He wanted to do the right thing, but he didn't want to be the laughingstock again. It wouldn't just be his sixth-grade class at Gettys Middle School. He knew that it was dangerous for him to go out without Sloane when he felt this way, but as he pushed on toward the club, he was determined to get the answers he was seeking.

The boys were waiting for their paladin, Bannon, and as he sauntered in the door, they cheered. They respected Bannon because he was one of the best quarterbacks in the NFL, which helped many of them make the Pro Bowl yearly and earn their million-plus salaries. But they loved him because Bannon was a babe magnet. The boys enjoyed watching the women flock to Bannon and jockey for position within his "harem." In the past, a few of the linemen had reaped the benefit of Bannon's cast-off spoils. He was their bait, and he only attracted the most exotic and beautiful fish in the pond.

Only the highest paid strippers danced at the Raiders' table.

No beginners, chubettes or pre-surgery bodies. Only the centerfold women, those who embodied men's fantasies. Tonight, Brad was showcasing a new girl, unsullied as yet by this business. The boys were roused by the prospect of virgin skin. Especially Bannon because of his perplexed state. Maybe this was the "test" he needed.

Desiree began an exotic water dance. With whips, leather, bath suds and hot water, she created a stage fantasy that ensnared the attention of all club patrons, especially Bannon. Giving her two hundred dollar tips per gyration, Bannon had spent over one thousand dollars by the end of Desiree's performance. Because of his generosity, she targeted him for the rest of the night, dancing every number at his table.

After the bar closed, and the boys had gone home, Bannon found himself in the employee parking lot, waiting for Desiree. When she finally left the club she was surprised to find Bannon sitting on the hood of her car.

"Hi," he began, "I know I'm really not supposed to do this, to talk to you after the club closes, but I thought that maybe you would like to get a drink somewhere."

"Well, I'm not supposed to. Brad has a really strict policy about this. You know, I'm new here, so I don't think I better. Thanks, but I think I'll just go home. Besides, I'm really tired," she replied.

"Oh, well, I understand. Are you sure it's not because you have a boyfriend?" Bannon queried.

"Oh gosh, no, Mr. Scott. I don't date much. I really just don't want to get in trouble. Thanks though," she said as she slid behind the wheel of her vehicle.

Nothing incited and intrigued the former Bannon more than initial rejection. It made the thrill and pursuit that much more of a challenge. Instead of feeling like a junkie on a high after spending time on the wagon, Bannon now hated the sudden rush of adrenaline. But he decided to give in, to let his emotions definitively answer the questions in his mind. He needed to discover the *real* Bannon, for better or worse, to see if he were destined to be a family man or a gigolo.

Desiree provided Bannon with fantasy fuel for the next few

weeks. Sloane didn't suspect anything and Bannon went to Brad's four times a week, allowing his passion to become a runaway train. And after three weeks, Bannon slept with Desiree. Only then did he realize which man was the real Bannon. He had never felt such guilt after a conquest, and the thought of losing Sloane killed him. No woman would ever be as important to him as Sloane and now he had the answer he had sought. He really loved Sloane. From this point on, he was going to be a one-woman man and he would wait for Sloane, no matter how long it took, to decide the same thing about him.

He dumped Desiree without fanfare. At first, she was hurt because she had really liked him and had thought the feeling was mutual. But then, her anger took control when she saw his picture with Sloane in the paper just one week later. When she read in the article they had been a happy twosome for over a year, she was incensed. She felt like Bannon had just *used* her and had never intended for her to be his girlfriend. Did he think that he could just treat her like insignificant trash to be thrown away at his whim? She would show Bannon. He had been unaware of her fetish when they had slept together, but he would see it now. Oh yes, she would give Bannon a *real* show, one that he could watch over and over and over.

Desiree had no trouble finding Sloane. Since she and Bannon were one of the most tracked Los Angeles couples, it was simple to locate the studio lot where "Malibu Sunsets" was filmed Monday through Thursday. Desiree easily convinced the security guard at the lot gate that she was an extra, just working for the day on the series. Desiree looked the part, a slim California beauty, and her excuse for not having a pass seemed plausible. She easily entered the studio set.

Finding Sloane's dressing room was more difficult, but when Desiree saw "Ms. Stevens" on the door of the eighth trailer on the lot, she knew she had found her mark. Sloane was alone, rehearsing her few lines. She smiled at the knock on her trailer door. "Probably someone lost on their way to hair and make-up," Sloane had thought to herself.

"Hi there! You missed it by two doors. The wonder-working

trailer is that green one," she kindly told Desiree.

Desiree was surprised by Sloane's friendliness, and even had a moment's hesitation of pursuing her plan, but there was no turning back now. "Uhm, I think I have something that you might want to see. Here," Desiree mumbled as she thrust the video tape into Sloane's hands and quickly turned to leave.

"What? Wait a minute! Who are you? Don't leave! Wait!" but Sloane, only in her robe, wasn't going to chase the girl across the lot, so she let her go and stared at the tape in her hands. Her curiosity piqued, she fumbled around the trailer and put the tape in her VCR.

When she saw Bannon, naked, doing tricks that would have earned him a permit with the local stuntman's union, and the date of just three weeks ago flashing in the upper right corner, Sloane felt like a stake had pierced her heart. Here was the only man she had ever loved disrespecting her in the worst way she could imagine. Hell, she didn't even have to imagine it! The image was right here on her television screen. So *this* was the real Bannon. The *real* Mr. Scott. After one year of dating him exclusively and giving him her soul, this is how he returned her love. Dog! Cheat! Bastard!

Being honest with someone and loving them with abandon had just brought her the worst pain of her life. But she shed no tears nor broke any precious objects in her trailer. Instead, she resolved to make Bannon pay dearly for his mistake. And she decided to make him pay for the rest of his life.

The same day that Sloane's eyes were shockingly opened, Bannon came home from practice to a house fragrant with the mingling smells of fresh flowers and home-cooked lasagna. Sloane had outlined the plan on her way to the grocery store from the studio lot. In her kitchen, she perfected the scheme in between the kneading of dough and the chopping of tomatoes. And as she carefully planned it step by step, she became more resolute in her method of attack.

Next week was their one year anniversary and as Bannon stood in their kitchen looking at his beautiful, sweet Sloane, he thought to himself that he should really treat her to a new car or something grand. She had been so good to him and her love had turned his life around. He still felt guilty about the fling with Desiree but was glad that he had discovered his true love for Sloane. He had even started seeing a therapist after his slip with Desiree because he wanted to be the perfect husband for Sloane.

"Bannon," Sloane said, breaking his reverie, "I've really been thinking about what I'm going to say and I want you to know that I've never been more serious about anything. You are my world, my universe and this past year has been the happiest of my life. I can't believe I'm going to do this, but it's what I feel in my heart and I just have to say it." She stood up, breathed deeply and handed Bannon an envelope. "Open it," she instructed him.

"But Sloane, honey, our anniversary isn't until next week. I haven't gotten your gift, yet. I can't open this until I have something to give you," he protested.

"No, this is a pre-anniversary gift, Bannon. Please open it! I think you'll be surprised!" she pleaded. Relenting, Bannon opened the gift and squinted his eyes in confusion as he looked at it.

"Plane tickets. What are these? What is this?" he asked.

"Bannon Scott," Sloane cleared her throat, "Will you marry me? Say 'yes' and we're on the next plane to Las Vegas. Say 'no' and I'll walk out of here tonight and never bother you again."

Bannon was stunned! Marriage! "Sloane, are you serious? Don't tease me about this. I want nothing more in the world than to marry you. I've come to realize what you mean to me, and I would wait for you forever if you feel like you need more time. I thought you wanted a big ceremony later on. What changed your mind?"

"Why wait any longer when I know what I want? You didn't answer my question. Will you marry me?" Sloane waited for his response.

"You know that I will. I can't believe this! Okay. I have to call my parents. I have to call some teammates. This is the best day of my life! You are going to be Mrs. Bannon Scott by tomorrow morning. I just can't believe it!" he said again.

Sloane smiled broader than ever, sweetly, letting Bannon pick her up and kiss her. "You fool," she was thinking, "You stupid, stupid fool. I can't wait until you know the truth. Then you'll know how you hurt me. One day *you* will feel the pain that you made me feel," And as she packed her bags for Vegas, she thought this would be the best game she ever played.

Every tabloid in America ran the story. Every Raider discussed it. Every woman on the set of "Malibu Sunsets" was jealous. Mr. and Mrs. Bannon Scott were the newest beautiful, young, rich, and in-love couple to steal all the headlines. Readers immediately wanted to be in their shoes, live their lifestyle, and share their happiness.

Bannon had never been happier in his life. His therapy was going well and his love for Sloane was strong. The vows he took were for life. Come hell or high water. He loved Sloane even more than football and the glory of throwing winning touchdowns. He had turned his life around for her unconditional love.

Sloane had to share a private smile with herself as she looked at the cover of *People*. There she and Bannon were, smiling, perfect in their wedded bliss, the Ken and Barbie of 1985. The perfect couple. The only thing that kept Sloane smiling was the prospect of telling Bannon, at just the right time, that she hated him. That she had tricked him into marrying her out of revenge for breaking her heart. That their union was a joke. That she didn't love him when she asked him to marry her and that she never would. When he saw the video tape that she kept in a lockbox at First Trust Bank in Bel Air, his blood would run cold. When, oh when, would she tell him the truth? Before he left to go to summer camp? Before a big playoff game? Or before his first start in the Super Bowl? The ball was in her court now, she thought to herself. She was the real player with the cannon arm, not Bannon Scott.

◆◆◆◆◆

The one-stop-light town of Platteville, Wisconsin in August of 1993 was a zoo. Platteveille, the summer home and training camp of the Chicago Bears, was thick with zealous Bear fans. The enthusiasts ranged from families on summer vacation to hero-worshippers who sported logo tattoos and haircuts in the likeness of their favorite player's number. Fans clutching sweaty, ever-changing paper rosters rubbed shoulders with the elite of the Chicago media. The biggest trade in the last five years had been made, Bannon Scott of the Raiders for a tandem of Bear linebackers, and the hot, new quarterback was spending his first training camp as a Bear in the lap of Wisconsin cornfield luxury. The last trade of this historic proportion was Jimmy Johnson's exchange of Herschel Walker for a whole team. Bannon was the highest-rated QB in the NFL and the Bear fans and media were acting as if we had already been presented with the Lombardi Super Bowl Trophy for the '94 season.

Kim Willis and I had driven two hours to Platteville for "family weekend," the only weekend during the six-week training camp when wives and families of players and staff were encouraged to visit their husbands. Family weekend was a much anticipated, traditional event, usually occurring the second or third week of camp. The highlight of the three-day visit was a Saturday scrimmage game, after which the players had no curfew until Sunday at 6:00 p.m. Players typically spent Saturday night and Sunday morning with their families at a nearby resort, enjoying a well-deserved break, knowing they wouldn't be coming home for four more weeks. Since couples and families don't see each other for such a long stretch of time, they usually spend every minute together during this weekend, beginning with dinner after the Friday practice.

Pietro's Pizza was the most popular Platteville restaurant, and Chris and I kicked off the routine of family weekend by going there with two other couples. The small parlor with the same decor from year to year was hopping with customers, all of them Bears, hot and sweaty after the 3:30 p.m. workout. We were talking animatedly between tables when Bannon and Sloane Scott sauntered into the restaurant.

As a couple, they were stunning — absolutely breathtaking. I had never seen a more beautiful woman than Sloane Scott. Tall, slim, not an ounce of fat on her body and with the face of an angel, she was more spectacular in real life than on the magazine covers she frequently graced. She possessed the hypnotic beauty to which most women would never measure up — which was partially due to obviously purchased body parts. Bannon was equally as handsome, but in a more natural, approachable way. He could easily have been in movies, so charismatic and genial he appeared. These two "stars" looked so out-of-place in the middle of Wisconsin cheese-land. It was akin to imagining Tom Cruise hangin' out at a Saturday night tractor-pull. Everyone in Pietro's stared as they made their way into the modest establishment.

They approached our table and Chris introduced me to the Scotts. Bannon seemed to be the sort of person he looked, friendly and polite, but Sloane, hardly acknowledging us wives, openly voiced her disgust with these less-than-four-star surroundings.

Upon asking her if they were staying at Beaver Creek, the beautiful, quaint cabin community in which we all annually lodged for family weekend, she replied, "If you mean that dump twenty-five minutes between hell and no place, yes. I was scared to put my clothes on the bed, it smelled so musty." Then, turning her repulsion on Bannon, she said, "Please don't tell me we are going to have to eat *pizza*, Bannon. This is just awful! Look at this place! I'm going to the car. *I'm* not eating in here!" and with that she whirled out of the restaurant like a dervish.

Bannon let her walk out the door without a backward glance, like it was a scene experienced countless times beforehand. He seemed unaffected, however, joining us and sharing our picked-over pizza. It didn't take long to realize why he was so popular with both men and women. He was funny and knew when to back-slap the guys, yet understood the import of a well-placed compliment toward a wife.

After about forty-five minutes of sitting with us, I asked him if he shouldn't check on Sloane, who I assumed was waiting in the car outside Pietro's.

"Oh, I'm sure she's gone by now. I'll just catch a ride back to the dorms with Chris. Sloane is probably polishing off her first bottle of Dom or Crystal in the bar at Beaver Creek," he informed us.

"Oh," was my only response, but I was thinking, "Wow! She isn't going to see him for the next four weeks and she doesn't want to spend all of her time with him?" I thought it odd that she would just leave him with us. And that she didn't bother to come back inside to tell him where she was going. But later I learned that her unexplained disappearances were a recurrent theme in their relationship.

The first phone call in October of 1993 surprised me. Although Bannon and Sloane had a townhome two streets away from us in Lake Bluff, and I frequently saw and spoke to Bannon when I jogged by, I didn't know him that well. I certainly didn't know Sloane any better than I did that first day in Pietro's. She had continued to be contemptuous during our few, short encounters, and that was fine with me. I just cut a wide path around her, not wanting to become entangled in her web of animosity.

"Sally? Hi. It's Bannon Scott. I hope I didn't catch you at a bad time?" he started. "Oh, no Bannon. Whatcha' need?" I responded, thinking he would next ask to speak with Chris.

"Well, I feel sort of stupid calling you, but I don't know what else to do. I know that Sloane has called you before about where to shop and stuff, so I thought maybe you could help me. I'm actually embarrassed to ask you this, and if you don't pass any of this information on, I would appreciate it, if you know what I mean."

Wondering what in the world was going on, I nevertheless responded, "Sure, Bannon. I completely understand."

"Well, it seems as though I've come home to an empty house, and thought you might know where Sloane is. She usually leaves me a note, but I've looked all over and I can't find one anywhere. There aren't any messages from her on the machine and I just thought she may have mentioned something to you about going downtown to shop or get her hair cut," his voice sounded embar- rassed, not desperate.

I immediately felt for him. I couldn't imagine calling one of Chris' friends to track him down because he didn't respect me enough to let me know where he was. "Oh, Bannon, I'm really sorry, but I don't have a clue where she might be. I know that Laura at Elizabeth Arden trims her hair occasionally. Maybe she went down there and got caught in the downtown traffic on the Kennedy. You know, if you leave from downtown after 3:30 p.m., you're going to get stuck," I said, trying to fill the gaps.

"Yeah, okay, well maybe you're right. I'll call down there. Thanks. I really appreciate it. Sorry to have bothered you over something so silly," he stated.

"No problem, Bannon. I don't think it's silly. I hope you find her. If you need anything else, just call," I said, and hung up.

After the phone call, I asked Chris if he had seen Sloane around.

"Now why would I see her? She's not my friend," Chris responded.

I briefly explained that Bannon didn't know where she was.

"She's probably downtown spending all of his money," Chris replied.

"Yeah, that's what I told him," I said, smiling.

"God, those people have the weirdest relationship I have ever heard of. Did you know that she goes back to California a lot without *telling* Bannon?" He continued, "Can you imagine? I just stay out of the conversation when Bannon talks about her. It's almost like he wants one of us to say, 'Yeah. My wife does the same thing,' except nobody's wife does. And I don't want to know about Bannon Scott's problems off the field. It's just not any of my business, you know?"

I knew then that the Scotts' lifestyle had been bandied around the locker room. And I knew that there was probably a lot more to the story than I had heard if Chris had already formed an opinion about Sloane.

Two days after Bannon's phone call, I was jogging with Peepers and Rhett. As I rounded the curb catty-cornered to the Scotts' house, I saw Bannon opening his mailbox. As I raised my hand to wave, he walked quickly to the middle of the road. I didn't want to stop, but he obviously wanted to talk so I pulled off my headphones. Out of breath, I said, "Hi, Bannon. What's up?"

He looked at the ground and said, "I still don't know where Sloane is. You haven't heard from her, have you?"

I thought she would have been back by now. Chris hadn't said a word about her still being gone. "You're kidding! Oh, Bannon, no, I'm really sorry! I haven't heard from her. Where do you think she could be? Have you called the police?" I asked, concerned.

"Well, I contacted Mr. Groh, the FBI agent who does part-time work for the Bears, and he's trying to locate her. I have called everybody we've ever known, from Illinois to California, and nobody has seen her," he told me, shaking his head. I could tell he was upset. He continued, "I'm just fixing dinner, trying not to think about it. Mr. Groh is supposed to be here in an hour to tell me what he's found out, if anything. I don't know what to do. She has never been gone this long. I mean, Sloane is strong-willed, I guess you might say, and she just picks up and goes sometimes, but this time just feels different."

I could tell he was a mess, really worried. "Well, Bannon, if there is *anything* Chris and I can do, just let us know, okay? Please?" I didn't know what else to say. It sounded like Sloane had just gone crazy and run away.

As I turned to leave, he asked, "Why do you think she would do this? I've never been able to understand why women do some of the things they do." Then, "I'm sorry for interrupting your jog. But I don't really have anyone here that I can talk to."

I turned my earphones off and tethered Peepers and Rhett. I knew they weren't going to get their run tonight.

Bannon began with the night of the cast party and how boldly different Sloane was from the other women with whom he'd previously been involved. He told me their story from the beginning, of how he realized she was the only person he really ever loved, to the present, with his confusion over her recent behavior like disappearing for days at a time. The Scott's world was one of glamour, of having to "dress up" for dinner in their own home to avoid gossip between neighborhood butlers, of yachting from romantic-sounding ports like Bimini and Catalina in the off-season, and of having Diane Sawyer call their house for an inter-view. Their high-society world was as foreign to me as Ricki's abusive one. I even told Bannon that maybe I wasn't the person he needed to be talking to, that mine was a much simpler exist-ence than his. "Bannon, I'm ashamed to admit it, but Chris and I eat dinner on our den *floor* every night in front of the *television* like two heathens," I laughingly told him.

Grinning, he said, "I need a dose of reality, Sally. I've forgotten what it's like to heat up Stouffer's and eat out of the plastic container. I need a real friend."

It was my guess that I was Bannon's only friend who shopped at the Gurnee outlet mall, ate fast food and went to movies before 5:00 p.m. to get the discount.

Sloane breezed in four days after she "disappeared." Detective Groh hadn't been able to reveal anything to Bannon about her apparent evaporation into thin air. She finally told Bannon that she had been on the Dutch side of Martinique, visiting an "old family friend" at his parent's palatial estate which overlooked the Caribbean Sea. Sloane was tan, which made her stand out like a sore thumb in October in Chicago, and appeared rested. Maybe she was telling him the truth. I didn't know, but it wasn't any of my business.

Bannon called me from the Hilton that Saturday night before the game, when all of the players spend pre-game night under a curfewed "quarantine," to thank me for listening to his troubles. I assured him that it wasn't a bother. Later that night when I told Chris about the phone call, he said that he felt sorry for Bannon.

"Why? What do you mean?" I asked.

"Well, you know, I don't think he really *talks* to any of the guys on the team. I mean he's friends with everybody and he goes to dinner and plays poker and golfs with us occasionally, but it's like nobody really *knows* him. He's a good guy, but we definitely only see what he wants us to see. He's really guarded, even though he occasionally mentions his difficulties with Sloane. You may be one of the few people who knows the *real* Bannon Scott."

After we hung up, I thought about Chris' comments. It never ceased to amaze me that the players perceived as having it all were usually the ones who led the most empty lives, surrounded by many but friends with few. The thought was not comforting.

Over the span of the next year, Bannon revealed things to me that I would never have imagined. He explained everything about his addiction to women and even told me about his treatment every off-day Tuesday with a local therapist. He shared his mistake with Desiree and how he still shuddered to think of what he had done behind Sloane's back. Even though they weren't married at the time, he still struggled with whether he should tell her the truth.

His obsession was becoming less of an issue for him because of his dedication to therapy, and as long as he avoided strip clubs and pornography, he could keep his demons at bay. No one on the team knew about his problem, and after one year of convenient excuses to avoid the frequenting of local skin parlors with the team, the players quit inviting him to the after-dinner activities. Instead, he just did the weekly dinner gig and poker match with his "o" line, then politely excused himself.

I think Bannon needed to tell someone other than his therapist the truth about his life. I believe he told me everything because he could sense that I cared; because he needed simple, uncensored friendship. The rest of the world saw Bannon as the image of NFL success. I saw Bannon as a grown little boy, still the ever-changing chameleon in a world that refused to accept him for the less-than-perfect, absolutely normal man that he was.

In early December of 1994, Carter Martin carefully examined his facial pores in the expensive vanity mirror mounted in the bathroom suite of his eighteen-room mansion. Carter was outwardly attractive in a flashy way, sexy with his longish hair and scintillating smile, but he was only a beautiful shell. Many times over he had earned the nickname "Use and Abuse," a moniker given to him by his teammates. Carter never met a woman he didn't like. And women never walked away liking him.

Playing the position of center for nine years, he had earned a lot of money, but not a lot of publicity. Being almost invisible bothered Carter. He was tired of having to *tell* women who he was. He wanted to be more recognizable, but that would be difficult since the usual camera shots of Carter were of his butt. He thought he had a nice butt, but what he needed was "face time," a look-see inside his helmet. Every woman in Chicago would know him then.

As he lounged around his house on the Bears' Tuesday off in his Versace silk robe, he wondered why the Bears' public relations office only highlighted that idiot, she-man Bannon Scott. Bannon could have as much action as he wanted in Chicago, but he didn't even try to get it. Pretty-boy Bannon. Carter smiled, wickedly, and thought to himself, "Bannon Scott may get all of the camera time, but he doesn't have jack on me. Nosiree, not jack."

Two months prior to Carter's ruminations about Bannon, Sloane was sitting alone in KaPow!!, the hottest new dance bar to hit downtown Chicago. It had quickly become the hangout of local celebs with its separate VIP bar. The club had an overall feel of "cheese and sleaze" with its too loud music and obnoxiously narcissistic patrons. Sloane loved it.

She was on her second glass of champagne in the VIP room adjacent to the bar, and as she watched people shuffle to and fro, her mind wandered over the last year. Her relationship with Bannon was worse than ever. Having denied any feeling toward him for so long, she didn't even feel married to him anymore. She needed something to make her life exciting again. She had recently convinced Bannon to buy her a sprawling Tudor mansion in Lake Forest, but even that didn't make her happy. And the flings she had carried on with other men, like her "family friend" in Martinique, weren't exciting anymore because Bannon would never find out about them.

She began thinking to herself as she started her third glass of Crystal that they didn't even have anything in common anymore. He had become such a stick in the mud. He didn't drink, didn't smoke, and didn't laugh. Maybe tonight she would just go home and tell him the truth. Maybe she should stop waiting for the "perfect time" to shatter his world. If she did it now she could go back to California and maybe land a part before the new season's filming started. She was thinking all of this when, out of nowhere, a handsome man in a tacky suit appeared in the mist, surrounded by the fog coming off of the dry ice KaPow!! used for ambiance.

"Sloane Scott? Bannon's wife? Is that you?" Carter asked, unsure if he should approach, not wanting to see or be nice to

Bannon. He had to tolerate pansy-boy every day at practice and this was Carter's off-time, his time to roam.

Sloane eyed him. "Yes. Who the hell are you? Didn't you know that Leisure Suits went out of style in the late seventies? Where did you find that get-up? Is it vintage or Merry-Go-Round from the mall?" she asked viciously, shattering Carter's perfect image of himself.

But he was attracted to her at the same time he was repelled, "Uh, no, this is Gucci. I guess it's Retro. Maybe too Retro, on second thought," Carter had to smile in spite of himself. Sloane was a spitfire. She had too much bite in her for Bannon. Carter couldn't imagine the attraction.

"Are you alone or is Bannon going to jump out from behind the bar?" Carter queried.

"No. Are you kidding? Bannon, drink anything other than a Perrier? Or have fun? No. He's probably tucked safely into his king-size four-poster bed by now. What are you doing here? Don't you have practice tomorrow?" Sloane asked, nicer now, recognizing Carter.

"Yeah, I have practice, but I always come here on Tuesday nights. Ladies night and all. It's usually pretty fun. Never know who you'll meet. Even Sloane Scott," he said, flashing that smile and raising his beer in a toast to her champagne flute.

"To possibilities," Sloane said, smiling, her mouth a flash of white teeth and red lips.

Returning the toast, Carter said, "I like that. To possibilities."

Sloane was already turning a thought over in her mind, a wicked, iniquitous vision that would kill Bannon. And the night was still young.

The next morning Sloane stumbled out of the four-poster bed with the hangover from hell. Smiling to herself as she headed to the bathroom in the Lake Forest mansion, she caught her image in the mirror. "Not bad for a football player," she thought to herself in spite of her pounding head, "not bad at all."

In the mirror behind her, Carter Martin returned her mischievous smile.

♦ ♦ ♦

The affair between Carter and Sloane was built around their mutual hatred of Bannon. Carter was jealous of Bannon's fame and Sloane blamed Bannon for making her marry him (at least that's how she saw it). Instead of whispering sweet nothings to each other, Sloane and Carter's foreplay consisted of bashing Bannon. The more they uttered his name, the more they felt the desire to betray him. He was an invisible party to their affair, the loathing of him their strongest attraction. They both knew this affair would spear Bannon in the heart. And that was the only reason their affair was kept alive.

After a while, Carter only tolerated Sloane because a betrayal with a teammate's wife was the worst form of treachery. Secretly, though, he wondered how Bannon had put up with her for nine long years. He thought Sloane was evil, a harpie who insulted his every choice in fashion, food and fun. By the end of the '94 season, Carter found himself looking forward to the time Sloane wouldn't be around his house, telling him where he should place his "cheap art deco" furniture, laughing haughtily that he had mistaken the "crap" he proudly hung on his walls for art, and instructing him on the importance of conversation. He wanted to yell in her face that he didn't give a damn about conversation; that she was only there as *his* toy, *his* sexual Nautilus machine, and that he could care less about the dictates of her world. Sex and self-pleasure were his world, and she had merely been an overnight stop on a cross-country trip. She was nothing special, not even the best he'd ever had, and he couldn't wait to be the one to break it to her. Now *that* was going to give him pleasure. She thought she knew the rules of this game, but Carter was determined to teach her a lesson. He wanted to kill two birds with one stone.

Similarly, Sloane found Carter acutely unattractive, but knew that their tryst was the best payback for Bannon's long-past mistake with Desiree. She couldn't tolerate much more of Carter's tackiness, though. She had decided to dump him on her way out of town, maybe from her car phone en route to the airport. She had decided to continue this dalliance for a few more months, then head back to LA, finally leaving Bannon. Her affair with

Carter would be the perfect icing on the cake. In Carter she had found her holy grail of betrayal. Bannon would die of embarrassment and shrink with humiliation that she had bedded a teammate. Oh, there was such irony in the fact that Sloane and Bannon had touched the same ass. That thought allowed her to tolerate Carter the Yahoo just a little longer.

Bannon, in a glum mood, moped around his study and stared at the wall of game balls hard-earned. Sloane was gone, who knew where to, and Bannon felt alone. As he looked at his many awards, he pondered his true success in the NFL. Sure, he had made millions and would never have financial problems, but he played this game to *win*. And even though he was one of the top-rated quarterbacks in the League, this was the eleventh year of his career, the middle of January, and the season was over for his team. The Super Bowl elusive yet again, in the four corners of his private sanctum, Bannon allowed himself to question his own ability and his present goals. Maybe he should be thinking of retirement, of passing the jock to a younger version of himself. These doubts and insecurities were floating in his mind when he heard his private line ring. After pausing for a second, debating on whether to let the machine pick it up, he instead reached for the receiver, deciding that a conversation with anybody was more preferable than this piteous self-wallowing.

"Hello?" Bannon's cheery voice betrayed his real mood.

"Hey, Bannon. It's your neighbor and favorite ass, Carter. I was just packing up some stuff to go on a short vacation from this hellish outpost of the North Pole, and I thought that if anybody was as depressed as I am about our failures this year, it would be you. So, I thought you might want to come over and have a beer and shoot some pool before you go back to LA. I've got some cold ones over here with your name on 'em. Whaddaya say?" Carter was praying that Bannon would take the bait.

"Sure, Carter. You're right. I'm just sitting over here pouting. I might as well come over to your house and make you just as miserable! Just kiddin'. I'll leave my troubles at your doorstep and we'll just shoot pool and try to forget that we've come in last place in the NFC Central again. Maybe your company is just what I need. I'll be there in five," Bannon said and as he hung up, he thought that this diversion would be good for him. He didn't know it would change his marital status.

Carter's mansion was three streets over from Bannon and Sloane's in the same manicured neighborhood. Built by expensive contractors, their houses were similar in size and had the same accents of Corian countertops, Baldwin Brass fixtures, and Sub-Zero appliances. Carter's gameroom was the envy of half the team. His carved Olderhausen pool table was a one-of-a-kind and his surround-sound stereo system provided greater clarity than the speakers of nearby Riverbend Cinemas.

Bannon rang the door bell and heard the roar of a bear. He laughed to himself about Carter's flashy style. When Carter didn't answer, Bannon pushed the partially opened door and heard Carter yell to him, "Hey, man I gotta' take this call. Come on in. I'll meet you in the gameroom in just a minute. Sorry."

Bannon stepped inside the marble entry, which opened grandly to the second story, and thought it odd that a single man would have such a collection of furniture. Bannon almost chuckled out loud thinking that if he weren't married, he'd probably just have a bed, a refrigerator and the most kick-ass audio-visual system in Chicago. He made his way back to the gameroom and was waiting for Carter when he decided to flip on the television, to watch, in spite of himself, the teams who had made the playoffs. He was looking for the remote to Carter's big screen when he saw it.

Nonchalantly, a little skewed on its side, there was a plastic video tape jacket with the word "SLOANE" written in thick black letters.

Bannon's id took over his entire body and he moved trance-like to the VCR with the tape clutched in his hand. His mind was not even weighing what he might do if Carter came into the room and caught him. He was focused solely on determining if this Sloane was his Sloane. He placed the tape in the video and watched. As his wife came into focus, nude on Carter's bed, Bannon said "What..." out loud, not completing his thought. When Carter entered the screen, laughing and discussing parts of Sloane's

anatomy, Bannon stifled the urge to vomit. When Carter and
Sloane began having sex, Bannon did vomit. All over Carter's
hand-hooked Bokahhra silk rug.

As Bannon turned to leave the room, he encountered Carter at
the door.

"So, I see that you found your wife's audition tape for 'Carter's
Little Harem.' She was good, my man. But I don't know how you
tolerate her attitude. Sorry you had to find out this way, Bannon.
I really wasn't trying to hurt you. You know, things just happen,"
Carter was beaming inside, so gratified that he had been the one
to break it to Bannon. To see the look on Bannon's face was
worth one week's paycheck. Hah! Who's holding the cards now,
Big Man? Carter wanted to add insult to injury.

Bannon was just standing there, looking into the dark abyss of
Carter's empty soul. He knew that Carter wasn't sorry and didn't
care. In a flash, before Carter could move, Bannon clocked him in
the jaw.

On his way out the door Bannon yelled, "Ya' know what? You
two deserve each other, Carter. Tell you what, you can have her.
I'll tell her that you told me she's the love of your life. Good luck,
old buddy, you're gonna' need it!!"

As Bannon's black Mercedes yelped to a stop beside Sloane's
BMW, indicating that she had arrived back from wherethehellever,
Bannon contemplated what he was going to say. He was furious,
embarrassed, humiliated, but ten minutes after his discovery he
wasn't really shocked anymore. Sloane's behavior over the past
few years had become intolerable, her unexplained absences
leading Bannon to doubt her fidelity to him and, unbeknownst to
Sloane, he had already placed some of his money in secretive
funds which would escape any kind of divorce settlement. Although he had protected himself financially from Sloane's claws,
he knew that emotionally he would be scarred. He really had
loved her and had tried to make it work. But now he knew that
their union had been a sham.

Sloane locked eyes with his and smiled at him all the way
down the steps. This was it, she was telling herself, this was her

moment to break Bannon's heart. Just as Sloane began, her speech more rehearsed than an Oscar acceptance, Bannon shut her up.

Bannon, who had poured himself a drink while waiting for her grand entrance, was seated, comfortably now on their Baker sofa, and began with, "Sloane, I'd like to congratulate you on becoming locker room fodder for the rest of this century. You've outdone yourself this time, old girl, but you sure stooped below any level I would have imagined when you picked Carter Martin as your co-conspirator. Did any horns blow or balloons drop from his bed-room ceiling congratulating you as his hundredth lay of *the season*? Or does each of his girlfriends receive a certificate for one hundred dollars from the Versace store on Oak Street? I'm just curious, Sloane. Could you fill me in on the little details? Like how long you've been cheating on me? If there are any other teammates you would like to tell me about? Oh, but before you do, let me give you this. These are the keys to the house in LA, where I expect you to be and stay for how ever long or until you die. You're out of my life, sugar pants. I should have done this years ago, when you became the most frigid bitch south of Ant-arctica."

Sloane was numb. This was supposed to be *her* scene, *her* decision to leave. *Not* Bannon's. He had the upper hand *again*. And he was throwing *her* out! "Well, Bannon. It seems as though you've been doing some investigating. Here is one more little piece to the puzzle. I never loved you! I married you for spite. I knew all about Desiree and your affair with her. Don't think you're better than me!" Sloane said, but the statements lacked the steam she had imagined, and failed to evoke the emotion she had envisioned from Bannon.

"You pathetic whore. You mean to tell me the whole *thing* has been a lie? You *never* loved me? Not even in the beginning? Hell, it was you who wanted to marry me! Oh, this is beautiful, just beautiful. Get out, Sloane. Get out now before they take you out of this house in a body bag. I don't have another word to say to you," Bannon took a deep breath.

Sloane turned, "You're right. It's done. I'm out of here. My bags have been packed for over a year." She left unceremoniously, disappointed that the final scenes weren't directed by her. "That stupid shit Carter," she thought, "he spoiled everything by telling Bannon first." Oh well, what's done is done. At least she could go back to her beloved LA where the beach, the sun and the buff bodies were always visible. She picked up her cell phone as she jumped into her car, and dialed the familiar number. "Ricardo," she purred into the receiver, "it's been such a long time. This is Sloane Stevens. I've missed you....."

◆ ◆ ◆ ◆ ◆

The Bears versus Oilers game in September of 1995 began with a long drive downfield capped off by a thirty-three yard Bears' field goal. Bannon was beginning his twelfth year in the NFL, this time as a back-up, but playing first-string against Houston because of the starter's sprained thumb. He was thinking to himself how much he still loved this game. The camaraderie, the competition, and the hard-work sweat he felt on the back of his neck were familiar comforts.

He never saw the defensive tackle approach his left side. Bannon Scott's last play, his last memory on the field, was dropping back five steps after taking the ball from the rookie center and then feeling excruciating pain explode in his foot. Hours later, at North Shore Hospital, he didn't remember being carted off the field, or being driven by ambulance to the emergency room. In his full uniform sans helmet, he had been immediately wheeled into the operating room. He numbly listened that same night as doctors informed him that he was lucky to still have his toe. They explained that he had to be operated on in his uniform, pads and all, because his toe had practically been ripped off by a defender's cleat that had cut clear through the top of his shoe. A damned toe injury was not on Bannon Scott's list of most dreaded injuries, and it certainly wasn't how he had pictured himself leaving this game!

As he laid there, staring at the plain room with no flowers, cards or visitors as of yet, he pondered his NFL career. How could he have been on top of the world one minute and have the rug whipped from under his feet the next? It was difficult for him to think that the game could go on without his presence. It was so hard for him to realize that there wouldn't be a "next season" or summer training camp for him. He suddenly felt like a grain of sand on a hundred-mile beach.

The next day, with the reality of his career's end staring him in the face, the phone beside his bed rang. "Hello?" he answered.

"Bannon? It's Sloane. Look, I just saw the replay of your injury on television. I just wanted to tell you that I'm sorry, Bannon. I know I'm probably the last person you want to talk to, but I know how much you loved that stupid game and I know how hard this is going to be for you. I just wanted to tell you that if you need me for anything, I'm just a phone call away." Sloane's voice sounded like she was calling from a well, so far away she seemed in space and time. Their divorce had gone smoothly, considering all of their assets. Sloane wanted no money from Bannon. Not one cent. She only wanted her car and the LA house, and that was fine with Bannon. More than fine. Amazingly, his resentment towards Sloane had dissipated. He didn't hate her anymore.

"Thanks, Sloane. Hey, I really do appreciate your call. It was time for me to hang it up, anyway. I guess this was a sign from above. You know I would have never quit this game. I'll give you a call if I come west," he said kindly, but having no intention of calling. Still, it was better to be friends than enemies. After all, they had spent eleven years together. And some of them had been good. Or at least Bannon wanted to remember it that way.

After he hung up with Sloane, his orthopedist came in and told him that he could go home tomorrow. He would be in a cast for a while, but with some therapeutic work, he should he able to walk without a limp or a cane. This news uplifted Bannon's spirits a little. At 8:00 p.m., he couldn't resist. He turned on the television to watch the Monday Night Football match-up between the 49ers and the Cowboys. As he watched Frank, Dan and Al, he smiled and thought to himself, "I could do that. How hard can it be to look good and sound smart?"

◆ ◆ ◆ ◆ ◆

In September of 1996, Chris and I went to The Keystone Grill in Indianapolis to watch a Thursday night game between the Bears and the Vikings. Since a few of our friends were still on the team, we tried to catch their games whenever possible.

After the general TNT introduction, Bannon Scott appeared on the screen. Polished, handsome as ever and sounding like an old pro, he prognosticated the starting game. Chris and I looked at each other, smiled and shook our heads. Bannon was great! He knew just when to deliver stats, mix in a few personal stories, and tell the viewers what to watch for in the next play.

I thought about my last conversation with Bannon, and his excitement over his new career. I was proud of him for landing on his feet after retirement and for turning down Sloane's latest offer.

Chris turned to me and said, 'I hope they aren't broadcasting this game in California, because if Sloane sees this..."

"Don't even finish that thought! And besides that he's done with her," I teased. And as we continued to watch the game and Bannon's commentary, I kept thinking, "Good for you, Bannon. Good for you."

The three musketeers: Kim, Stacy and Sally. We were never as mischevious as Sloane, but we always managed to have a good time.

Agent

Friendship is constant in all other things
Save in the office and affairs of love;
Therefore all hearts in love use their own tongues;
Let every eye negotiate for itself
And trust no agent.
　　　　　— William Shakespeare, *Much Ado About Nothing*

"**O**h my God! Can you believe this? We did it!" I slurred to Chris and Steve Mandell, one of our business partners. We were sitting in a trendy bar in Union Station in Indianapolis, celebrating the new four-year contract that Chris had just signed hours before with the Colts. I had the signing bonus in my purse and kept glancing at it from time to time. I had never before seen a single check for that amount of money. And although the money was important, we were most excited about the fact that Chris would be playing for a team about which he could be energized. We all laughed and slammed yet another shot of Tequila. We had tamed that wild horse, free agency, and had saddled the Colts.

My business partners, Steve Mandell and Eldon Ham, and I had negotiated a contract that Ted Phillips, vice president of the Chicago Bears, had said was impossible. Ted had intimated that the Bears' offer was the best Chris would get and we shouldn't waste our time testing the murky waters of free agency. But we all knew better. The Bears' offer had been *laughable*, an insulting joke, and it was a pure white light of joy for Chris to leave them in the dust.

Three months before, in December of 1994, Chris was nearing the end of his fourth season with the Bears. His contract would expire after the last game that year and he would be an unrestricted free agent, meaning he could leave Chicago and play for any other team who wanted him. The season wasn't going well for the Bears — or for Chris individually. Chris had been successful his first three years in the NFL, posting some record-breaking numbers. But something wasn't right this year, and I was determined to discover the problem. Chris wasn't happy when he got up in the morning and he wasn't happy when he returned from work in the late afternoon. He said the game just wasn't fun anymore, a complaint I had heard from several of our friends after Coach Ditka's departure. And when a player ceases to enjoy playing, one of two things should occur: the player should either quit, or, when he's an unrestricted free agent, find a team for which he can enjoy playing.

"I just don't like this anymore, Sally. I can't do it. I can't make the changes they are asking me to make," Chris told me late one night after an uncharacteristically bad game.

"Well, at least you have a choice, Chris. You'll be a free agent in a month. Don't even *try* to make the changes they're asking. Obviously, they don't know anything about football anyway because we can't win any games that count. I mean the only team we can whip is Tampa Bay! And nobody cares how they did it in *Dallas*. The Cowboys' game plan obviously doesn't work here! Just try to keep your own game intact and it will be better next year when you're playing for a real team. You'll beat the Bears, Chris. You'll have the last laugh. I promise. Just keep your head up." I wished that I could give those morons at Halas Hall a piece of my mind. Criticism is fine when it is from the mouth of knowledge. But when it is spoken by someone who doesn't even have the experience to *make* a judgement, *and* it is spoken condescendingly, I get angry.

I knew that the last game of the season would be Chris' last as a Chicago Bear. I loved the tradition that George Halas had established, and I appreciated the fact that the Bears had given Chris his NFL start. However, there had been too many changes within the organization since his rookie year. We felt like it was time for us to move on. I would rather Chris take a pay *cut* and go to a team he felt good about rather than continue playing in a system he didn't enjoy. With that decision resolved, we just had to determine who would be his agent and help him find a new "home."

♦♦♦♦♦

Most NFL agents are like that scum ring that just won't rub off your tub, no matter how hard you scrub. They are always there, lurking, trying to take advantage of players, making money I feel they don't really earn. Most of them take up to 6% of a player's contract for doing, at most, one hundred hours of work. Outrageous! To illustrate, if a player is under contract to pay his agent 6%, he owes $60,000 to his agent out of every million that he earns, every year of the contract. If the contract is for four years, the player winds up paying the agent $240,000 for one hundred hours' work! That is $2,400 dollars an hour!

Besides charging outrageous fees, agents don't even have to be professionals to hang out their shingle. The only requirement of an NFL agent is that he pay a yearly fee which registers him with the National Football League Players Association. He isn't required to pass a test, be honest, or play fairly. He just has to pay eight hundred bucks a year and he is handed a license to steal from unwitting players. Theoretically, one could become an NFL agent without a college degree or any background in finance or law.

I believe the smarter route for players is to hire an attorney, a professionally trained negotiator, and pay him an hourly fee or negotiate a fee cap. Attorneys are regulated by state bar associations and are held to standards much higher than those of the Joe Public. I'm not saying that a law degree is the absolute litmus test for finding great agents, but at least if an attorney breaks a fiduciary standard, the player is protected two-fold, by the regulations of the bar association and the laws of the state in which the attorney practices.

Determining a player's value and his asking price are not as difficult as people may think. A player is only able to earn what the market will allow and with one phone call to the NFLPA, a diligent agent can ascertain the contract salaries of same-position players across the League. The agent can then compare his client's performance record with those of his peers and determine a "sliding scale" of his client's value. This isn't an absolute formula though, and just as a homeowner doesn't know the exact value of his castle until he sells the property, the agent must seek other offers before he concludes that the offer on the table is the best one. The agent must also factor in considerations like whether the player is a starter or a Pro Bowler, which will increase his value, or must try to downplay an off-season DUI or an unexplainable lack of performance the previous season, which will usually cause a player's salary to decrease or remain average.

The most important job the agent has after ascertaining the player's value, however, is the negotiation of the contract. Negotiation is an art and few agents are Matisse; most are merely finger-painters. Wanting a certain salary and getting a certain salary are two different things. I feel that an agent earns a *reasonable* fee when he negotiates and delivers a contract that reflects the player's wants.

◆◆◆◆◆

After talking to several agents, Chris and I decided to rely upon the people we trusted most: each other and my two business partners. Steve and Eldon had been part of our extended family since Chris and I moved to Chicago in 1991. They were attorneys who had been negotiating contracts of all kinds for years and were two of the most honest and trustworthy people I have ever met. We decided upon a realistic fee and went to work.

There was much groundwork to do before February 17, 1995, the commencement of free agency. Until then, agents weren't allowed to discuss *anything* with any team other than the current team for whom their client played. In early January of 1995, I sat down to discuss Chris' future with Ted Phillips, who negotiated most of the Bears' player contracts.

My meeting with Ted went poorly. He basically told me that the Bears weren't pleased with Chris' '94 season performance and began negotiations by offering Chris a contract that paid *less* than the average salary of NFL punters. It was insulting because just the season before, Chris had broken 20 year old Bears' punting records.

I spent the first ten minutes of the meeting explaining to Ted the importance of receiving a reasonable offer from him. I didn't want my time wasted with a ridiculous proposal, but that was the road he had chosen. And if that was the stance the Bears wanted to take, I was willing to be tough — and go elsewhere.

The Bears' attitude wasn't a revelation to me. I had seen in the past how other players had been treated, and I knew going into the contract negotiation that the Bears' offer would be unreasonable because their pattern was to offer low-balls until the eleventh hour. Their silly tactics were one reason they had lost so many good players they had really needed in order to be competitive on the field.

I also knew the Bears organization would try to use Chris' '94 season record against him, and this made me mad because Chris' '94 performance directly related to a new kicking style that Chris had been *made* to adopt. After four years of successful play in high school, three years of college honors and three progressive years in the NFL, the Bears had decided to change Chris from a two-step punter to a three-step punter. This would be the equivalent of an American being dropped in the middle of England, where they drive on the left side of the road, and being told to adopt a new style of driving after driving on the right side of the road for all of their vehicular life! It could be done, but was not something that could be mastered overnight. It required the deprogramming of habits formed by years of repetitive practice. And even though Chris had tried to forget his style and all that he was comfortable with and adopt something totally foreign, the Bears weren't willing to accept responsibility for any of the performance numbers that were less than par.

After that meeting, I realized what we *didn't* want and knew that *all* of my efforts would be focused outside of Chicago. Our target cities were narrowed even further when Chris limited the search to teams who either played most of their seasons in warm weather or in domed stadiums. If he were going to leave Chicago, the goal was to find a more environmentally friendly stadium. And only four of these teams were looking for punters. They became our first priority.

Free agency is a cross between "turnover the fruitbasket" and "Simon Says." There is a constant shuffle of players between teams until the whistle is blown at the start of the first pre-season game. The punting changes in the '94 off-season tell the story. Chris went to Indianapolis and replaced Rohn Stark, who went to Pittsburgh and replaced Mark Royals. Mark Royals then went to Detroit. Dan Stryzinski signed with Atlanta, leaving Tampa, who then signed Reggie Roby, who had left Washington. Washington then signed Matt Turk. It was my job to stay aware of these changes, to "read" the market before the ink dried on the new contracts, and to make sure in this high-stakes game of "musical chairs," that Chris' butt was firmly seated when the music stopped playing.

Everybody told me I was crazy to be involved in Chris' representation, that wives were not supposed to do this. "Why aren't you hiring a regular agent like everyone else?" they all asked. I didn't worry though. I felt comfortable doing the "grunt" work, the gathering of statistics, contracts of other players and the important phone numbers and contact names we would need on the 17th, because I knew that Steve and Eldon would ultimately do the hardcore negotiation. I felt confident about our triumvirate of representation.

I began assembling a portfolio summarizing Chris' NFL career, which answered questions before a general manager could ask them. I knew, for instance, that player personnel from other teams would be curious about Chris' punting stats in '94 and why they were weren't as impressive as his other three years in the League. I didn't want to just point a finger at the changes he had been forced to make in his style, so I researched, game by game, the punting statistics for the entire season. I discovered that Chris had in fact outkicked his competition in almost every game and that the wind had been an undeniable factor in *every* punter's performance in Soldier Field in 1994.

The average wind shear for the '94 season home games was over 50 miles per hour, even reaching 85 miles per hour the Halloween night that the Bears played the Packers on Monday

Night Football. (This was the same night that the American Eagle plane crashed in the Indiana cornfields about forty-five miles away from Soldier Field, killing all aboard.) I had to call an obscure federal agency in Asheville, North Carolina that monitored wind speed near airports to get this information. Thank God Meigs Field, the old downtown Chicago airstrip, was close to Soldier Field.

The point of all of my research, though, was to show that while other punters only had to play in windy Soldier Field once a season, and played the remainder of their games in more environmentally-controlled stadiums which increased their gross averages, Chris was stuck with Soldier Field for eight games. And my research paid off. It enabled the general managers from the targeted teams to understand that '94 had been a fluky year for Chris; that in fact, he was one of the better punters in the NFL and deserved a salary which reflected this.

◆◆◆◆◆

The morning of February 17th, Chris and I awoke at the Waldorf Astoria in New York City, where we were attending Toy Fair for GamePlan, the game company Steve, Eldon and I owned. I didn't really wake up because I had never really gone to sleep the previous night. I had *never* been so nervous in my entire life. Not when I took the LSAT for admission to law school, not during my first law school exam and not when I sat for the South Carolina Bar. Chris had put his career in my hands and I *couldn't* disappoint him.

Before we left the hotel, I tried to make several phone calls to special teams coaches and vice presidents of player personnel. All busy lines. Everybody else had my same idea. "Fine," I said to myself. I would go to plan B, which was to mail all of the portfolio packets. I gave the hotel concierge a stack weighing twenty pounds, all postage pre-paid, and asked him to be sure they were mailed that day. I could re-try my calls from our showroom cubicle in the Toy Building on Fifth Avenue.

Chris and I hailed a taxi and chatted nervously during the fifteen-minute ride. We shared a laugh about our previous visit to Toy Fair in 1993. It had been Valentine's Day, five o'clock in the afternoon, six below zero, and we couldn't hail a cab to save our lives. I had on a short-skirted suit from Bebe with a pair of high-heeled Chanel pumps, and told Chris that walking was definitely not an option. Ninety percent of my legs would be exposed. I would be *dead* by the time we arrived at our hotel, eighteen blocks uptown. But after one hour of standing in the driving snow trying to hail cabs, we decided to walk. Freezing while walking was preferable to freezing while standing. By the time we walked thirty minutes in the blinding snow from the Toy Building to our hotel, I was delirious. No shopkeepers along the way would let us in their buildings to get warm. I was crying, tears freezing on my lashes. I had told Chris that if I froze to death to tell my parents I loved them and to please take good care of Peepers and Rhett. It took me two solid hours after arriving at the hotel to unthaw and think rationally.

We were laughing about that memory when we arrived at the showroom. We settled in with our lists of phone calls to make, and Bill Tobin, vice president of player personnel for the India-napolis Colts, was the first person I tried to contact. Previously employed by the Chicago Bears, Mr. Tobin had drafted Chris in 1991, and I had always held his opinion in high regard. He had always been honest and forthright with us, and I hoped that he could at least give me some pointers on who to call next if he wasn't looking for a punter. The Colts, as a domed team, were on the top of our list and since Mr. Tobin was already familiar with Chris' abilities, he was my premier priority.

Mr. Tobin was starting his second season with the Colts and had already taken them to a better than .500 record in one year. He was the ultimate chessmaster in the building of powerhouse teams, creating the dynasty teams of the '80s Bears, and we felt good about the Colts' future under his direction.

After a few tries, Mr. Tobin answered his phone and I quickly re-introduced myself to him since I hadn't seen him recently. I explained the nature of my call. I told him that Chris was a free agent, and asked if he would be pursuing any punters for the '95 season. He told me the Colts *were* interested in Chris! I was delighted and we quickly arranged for a scout to fly to our home in

South Carolina and work Chris out the following Thursday. On the Saturday after the workout, Chris and I would fly to Indianapolis to personally sit down with Mr. Tobin and tour the Colts complex.

After my conversation with Mr. Tobin, the Colts became the focus of the free agency scramble. We politely fielded calls from the other interested teams, of which there were eight including the Bears, but I knew in my heart that we were already leaning toward the horseshoes. Each time we had driven through India-napolis on our way from South Carolina to Chicago, we had always said what a nice town it appeared to be. It was so clean, and Chris and I frequently joked that maybe someday we would live there. I always said to Chris as we passed the Hoosier (a.k.a. RCA) Dome, "See, Chris, if you played here, we'd be home now instead of having to drive another two and a half hours!"

We would laugh and Chris would say, "Man, it would be awe-some to punt in that Dome and not have to worry about wind and snow." Our jokes suddenly seemed prophetic.

On Saturday, we were back in South Carolina and set to meet with Hank Kuhlman, the special team's coach, on Thursday. Between Saturday and Thursday, two other teams had called and wanted Chris to work out with them. But we really wanted the focus to stay on the Colts. It just seemed like a great fit for Chris. So, with the other teams on the back burner, Chris and I went on Thursday to the Clemson Holiday Inn to meet Hank and take him to the university's stadium where Chris would run drills, punt, kick off and kick field goals.

We hit it off with Hank immediately. Hank appreciates Miller Lite, country music and good barbeque, the requisites of a good ol' southerner. He cleverly weaves rich, home-grown quotations like, "Is a frog's butt water-tight?" into his conversation. Chris' workout went well, and after sharing an evening of cold beer and superb barbeque in a Clemson hole-in-the-wall where dogs served as free-roaming napkins and peanut hulls littered the floor, we looked forward to seeing Hank in a few days in Indianapolis.

Steve and I were still trying to keep other interested teams at bay until we made our Indianapolis trip. This was difficult, though, because free agency moves so quickly. The first players to sign are usually the ones who make the bigger bucks, and the punter signings had begun. The day before we were to visit Indianapolis, Dan Stryzinski signed with Atlanta, reaping a $600,000 signing bonus as part of his contract package. Other signings would now follow quickly.

On the plane ride from South Carolina to Indiana, Chris and I discussed again our goals concerning this contract. We wanted a two-year deal with a good salary base, fair incentives and a decent signing bonus. We talked about the lowest base salary for which he would sign, his "goal" base salary and the seldom-attained "pie-in-the-sky" base salary. We reexamined the incentive clauses from his previous contract to determine which were worth argument and which he could live without. We then took the last three or four recent signing bonuses of other free agent punters and determined our asking price. Finally, we factored in the intangibles: the cost of living in Indiana would be much less than Chicago, playing in a dome could help Chris increase his chances for a longer career, good feelings about the people we knew at the Colts, namely Mr. Tobin, Jim Harbaugh, and our new friend Hank Kuhlman, and Chris had heard great things about head coach Ted Marchibroda.

Hank greeted us at the airport, and we briefly toured Indianapolis and some of the neighborhoods where other players lived before going to the Colts' training complex. At the complex, we were introduced to Coach Marchibroda, Jim Irsay, and Bob Terpening, who handled most of the Colts' player contract negotiations. Mr. Tobin and Steve, our partner who had flown down that morning from Chicago in case Chris' visit led to any offers, were also there.

After the introductions, Chris was whisked away to undergo physicals intended to detect injuries or potential medical problems, while Steve and I went into a large conference room with Mr. Irsay. For the first forty-five minutes, the three of us just talked about normal things, and got to know each other. Mr. Irsay was a fascinating man. Certainly the most down-to-earth owner I had ever met, he told us that one of his greatest passions was music and shared with us his hobby of song writing. He had been involved with the team since his early twenties and because they were close in age, he was good friends with Rohn Stark, the Colts' current punter. He told us what the team and the people of Indianapolis meant to him, and I immediately recognized that Mr. Irsay was genuine. I was enjoying myself so much that I almost forgot we were there to discuss Chris' future.

"Well, it is obvious we are interested in Chris, and provided his medical exam is all right, we would like to sign him today, if possible," Mr. Irsay began the negotiations.

Gulp. Thank God Steve had flown in to meet us. If it had just been me, by myself, to negotiate this deal, I would have frozen right there in that expensive leather chair with my feet tucked neatly under the expansive conference table. I hate math and numbers. My brain paralyzes itself when it hears them, and refuses to compute the information.

When Mr. Irsay started talking numbers, Steve explained what would satisfy us. For the next hour, we hammered out a few details. They wanted a five year deal; we wanted two or three; we all settled on four. We wanted incentive clauses; they didn't. However, they were willing to pay more up front, as a signing bonus, which decreased the importance of the incentives. We were in agreement upon the base salary, although we originally had wanted a little more the last two years of the deal. But considering the "intangible factors" Chris and I had discussed, Steve and I felt this point wasn't as important. Mr. Irsay left the room to speak with his dad on the phone regarding the negotiations, and Steve and I waited for an ordered-in lunch.

As soon as the door closed behind Mr. Irsay, I took off my boots and laid on top of the conference table. Thank God this thing was going well! Mr. Irsay was such a gentleman and understood the art of negotiation. I had expected treatment like we were accustomed to receiving from the Bears, and I was euphorically surprised. I had been prepared for a knock-down-drag-out fight and was so relieved to be treated fairly.

Steve turned around, saw me, and said, laughing, "Get off that table! What if Mr. Irsay comes back in?"

"I don't care. I am just so tired from thinking I have to lie here a minute." We were laughing when there was a knock at the door. I scrambled off the table and shoved my boots on the wrong feet as Steve cracked the door open. It was just the delivery man with two Subway sandwiches and two sodas. Whew!

Steve and I needed a comedic diversion from the number-crunching of the negotiation and I decided to tease him about the kind of sandwich he had ordered. "I know you didn't get tuna fish. Please tell me you didn't get the fish. Because if you did, if that is Charlie the Tuna in that bag, I'm not letting you eat it!"

Steve and I had a running joke about his eating tuna fish sandwiches. He could and did eat them at all hours of the day — 8 a.m. or 11 p.m. — the time did not matter. He loved tuna. In New York at the Toy fair, where we had just spent the last week together, crammed into a space the size of a king-sized bed, Steve ate tuna sandwiches from sun-up until sun-down from the down-stairs deli. I told Steve that if he brought one more tuna sand-wich back into our foxhole, I was going to have to buy Stick-ups. People would walk through our booth after he had just eaten and I could visibly see their noses *wither*! I teased Steve he was responsible for the loss of sales.

As Steve unwrapped his tuna fish sandwich in the conference room and began licking his lips, I told him I was going to throw up. It smelled so bad. I didn't even eat my lunch. I had a pack of Cinnaburst gum in my purse and I spent the whole hour chewing that pack and blowing the cinnamon smell out of my mouth in different corners of that large room. I did *not* want that room to smell like *tuna* when Mr. Irsay came back to finish the contract! Steve was laughing hysterically because I was about to hyperventilate.

"Can you imagine what you must sound like on the other side of the door?! Stoppit before they think something is going on in here! What if this room is bugged with a video camera and they can see you? They will think you are a lunatic!" he teased.

After the quick lunch we regrouped and were ready to finish our negotiations. I went to look for Chris, since he was the only one who could obligate himself to the contract and was told by one of the trainers that he wouldn't be back for "a while." I returned to the conference room where Mr. Irsay, Mr. Tobin and Mr. Terpening were with Steve. The only thing the deal lacked was Chris' signature. The accountant was even staying late to cut

Chris' signing bonus check. We all talked as we waited for Chris to arrive.

Steve decided that while waiting for Chris, we should call Ted Phillips to let him know what was transpiring in Indianapolis. I agreed, for Ted to hear of Chris' signing through the grapevine was unprofessional on our part. I hadn't even told Ted that Chris was going to visit Indianapolis. After the Bears first offer, I knew they weren't serious about keeping Chris, so I felt that playing a "leverage game" with Ted was pointless.

Steve placed the call. He had barely gotten out, "Hi, Ted. Steve Mandell, here. Look I am with Chris and Sally in Indianapolis and we are pretty sure that Chris is going to sign here and we just wanted to let you know..."

From where I was sitting, the rest of the conversation sounded something like this: "Look, Ted, there is no need to get upset...you had your chance to sign him...well, you should have thought of that earlier...yes, Bill Tobin and Jim Irsay are here...there is no need to be insulting, Ted...look, I don't think that even if you *beat* the Colts offer, Chris would sign with the Bears because of the way he's been treated...okay, sure, we'll give you ten minutes... I'll call you back then."

Steve was so mad I could count the veins in his neck. In all of the years I had known Steve and in all of the stressful business situations we had been through together, I had *never* seen him angry. *Never* had he been this upset.

"Steve don't worry about Ted. The Bears have been treating everybody poorly recently. Screw 'em. Don't even give it a second thought. They had a chance to sign Chris and didn't. If Ted is mad that Chris is going to sign somewhere else, that's his problem."

By now, Chris had returned and we had only five minutes to educate him before we had to call Ted back. Chris decided to sign with Indianapolis no matter *what* the Bears offered. Steve called Ted and told him of Chris' decision.

The phone call was a repeat performance of the earlier conversation. If George Halas was everything I had been led to believe, I know he would have been embarrassed.

Chris signed the contract. We were thrilled! I felt like I had come home. I knew I would like Indiana and this team. I could feel sincerity in Mr. Tobin's smile, in Coach Marchibroda's handshake and in Mr. Terpening's eyes. Mr. Tobin asked us to meet him for dinner at the Eagle's Nest, a revolving restaurant at the top of the Hyatt in downtown Indianapolis. We left to go back to our hotel and change clothes before dinner.

It is hard to describe how Steve, Chris and I felt when the doors of our rental car closed in the Colts parking lot. As we pulled away from the complex, we looked at each other and screamed! We had done it! We had found a place for Chris where he would be happy and the team was happy to have him! We got the salary we wanted and Chris would have an awesome head coach. It truly was one of the happiest moments of my life. Chris had put his career in my hands, and I hadn't let him down. At that moment, Steve and Eldon became permanent members of our family. They had just shared stress, worry, work, frustration, sadness and now extreme joy with us. They were friends for life.

We arrived at the restaurant and met Mr. Tobin and his wife, Duschene and Hank Kuhlman and his wife, Donna. The four of them made us feel welcome in this new town and Mr. Tobin even had the pianist at Eagle's Nest play a song about Indiana for us. The lights of beautiful downtown shimmered, welcoming us to our new city.

The only "downer" of the evening concerned Rohn Stark, the punter Chris was replacing. He was on a cruise with his wife and Mr. Tobin was trying to place a shore-to-ship phone call during dinner to let Rohn know the Colts had signed Chris. He didn't want Rohn to read it in the paper or hear it from anybody else. He also wanted Rohn to be able to catch on with a new team quickly. Many people wouldn't have made that extra effort. I thought this spoke volumes about Mr. Tobin's character. Everybody is going to be cut one day, but the fact that Mr. Tobin was trying so hard to do it "the right way" impressed me. I knew that one day Chris would be cut too, but if it was after a long, healthy career like Rohn's, and by someone who had the nerve to tell Chris before the media was alerted, it would be easier. Not easy, but easier. Besides, Rohn was still one of the best punters in the league. He had been to the Pro Bowl four times in his long career, and I knew he would be picked up immediately. (He was. Three years after the fact, he is still playing and doing well. He and Chris have even golfed together on occasion.)

Chris called from the Eagle's Nest to check our phone messages at home and was shocked that some of the Bears personnel had already heard about his signing and had left congratulatory messages on our recorder. It meant a lot to Chris and to me. There *were* some good people in Chicago and I would miss them.

After dinner, we bade the Tobins and Kuhlmans "goodbye" and went to the bar in Union Station with Steve. We all drank until we were blind. After months of sleepless nights, countless prayers, ten-hour work days and pouring over statistics, we allowed ourselves that luxury.

I think that I had one hand in my purse, clutching that check, all night long. People desire money for many different reasons. Some think it will bring them happiness and others think it will bring them fame. I don't think that it can do either of those things, but I respect money because it can bring security. Not security of your health, but it can enable you to stay at home and raise your children with the knowledge that you can send them to college; that you can pay off your home and car mortgages; that you can provide health-care for elderly parents; that you can donate to worthy charities and make a difference in someone's life. Money can't make you moral or give you character, but in the hands of someone with character, it can be a force for good.

I kept pinching myself all night. I just couldn't believe free agency was over and we had been successful. I felt like we had won the Lotto. And now, after three years of being associated with the Colts organization and the good people of Indianapolis, I know we did.

We were so happy and excited when Chris and Cary Blanchard both made the Pro Bowl for the Colts — obviously, they enjoyed the experience too.

Move Over, Don Ho

Nice work if you can get it,
And you can get it if you try.
                    — Ira Gershwin, *A Damsel in Distress*

At the conclusion of every football season, coaches, players and fans pick the top players by position to represent the "best of the best" in a football game between the AFC and NFC. The event is the NFL Pro Bowl, and it takes place in Hawaii every February. It is a great honor to be named to the team and all players strive to make this post-season roster.

Much to our joy, Chris was selected to represent the punter position for the AFC in the '97 Pro Bowl. During the season, he and I didn't discuss the possibility of his first-time election, although it was mentioned frequently in the media. I didn't want to jinx him, and even though he was leading the league in most punting categories throughout the season, one bad game can shoot your chances all to hell. So I just kept my fingers crossed during every game and drank a whiskey sour for luck. The drink became my pre-game ritual, and I took much ribbing from the other wives.

When Chris called to tell me that he and Cary Blanchard, the Colts' kicker, had both been awarded the honor in December of 1996, I was thrilled. Only three previous times had a punter and kicker from the same team been elected to the Pro Bowl, and I was glad that Chris and Cary would be going together. It was gratifying to see their many years of hard work rewarded.

"How'd you find out?" I excitedly asked Chris.

He started to laugh and said, "Well, actually the linemen told us."

This seemed odd. I thought that either the head coach, Lindy Infante, or Chris and Cary's special teams coach, Hank Kuhlman, would reveal the good news. "Why didn't Hank or Lindy tell y'all?" I asked.

"Well, they tried to," was Chris' only response.

"What do you mean 'they tried to?'"

Chris told me that Coach Infante had called an impromptu team meeting — one reason being the announcement of their selection — but he and Cary hadn't heard about it because they were pursuing one of their daily morning rituals.

"And which ritual would that be, Chris?" I asked.

"Well, we were in the bathroom," he replied.

"At the *same time*?" I asked incredulously. I knew that Chris and Cary, as the punter and kicker, were close, but even I didn't know they were *that* close!

Chris then explained that they were in the habit of sitting next to each other in the bathroom stalls so they could talk as they used the facilities each morning. Only men will be able to understand this, because I know I don't.

Anyway, they were in the bathroom doin' their thing when the linemen barged into their stalls and said, "Where have you guys been? They just announced at the team meeting that you both made the Pro Bowl! We were clapping and looking around and you guys weren't even in there. What the *hell* are you two doing in *here* together?"

I laughed so hard when Chris told me this story. And I also knew that he and Cary would never live it down.

Since this was Chris' first time to be selected, we took everybody — Cole, my mom and dad, Chris' mom, the snapper from the team, Bradford Banta, and his wife. The whole "Fam Damily" as they say, but we wanted everybody to share the success of Chris' hard work. We had heard that the Pro Bowl was a lot of fun and was family oriented.

After a ten-hour flight and losing all of our luggage, we arrived at the beautiful Ihilani Resort and Spa in Oahu, Hawaii. The grounds were lush and the white marble lobby featured oversized urns with fresh Hawaiian flowers in every little nook. Each guest room was at least 800 square feet, which was about the size of our first apartment in Chicago! Upon going to the Front Desk to ask a question, I encountered one of the players whining to the clerk that his room wasn't large enough! He was demanding a *suite* in a rather loud voice. I wanted to grab his ears and say, "Your room *is* a suite, you ungrateful boob!"

I then realized that most of the players at the Pro Bowl were the NFL elite, the mega-millionaires, and a few of them were probably so accustomed to star treatment that they had forgotten how to be grateful. The NFL had so graciously footed the bill for these beautiful rooms. My mama had always told me, "Don't look a gift horse in the mouth," and I wanted to yell the cliché at the obnoxious player.

Most of the players and their families though, were friendly and nice, and it was fun meeting people from other teams and renewing friendships with previous teammates and their families. The NFL staff was great and offered everyone special tours of the island. One such tour was of the USS Pentada, a nuclear submarine that was stationed at the naval base on Oahu.

The itinerary consisted of a guided tour of the sub followed by an autograph and picture session with the hundred-plus men on board. Chris and I thought this would be fun, so we rounded up our clan and decided to participate. I had never been on a nuclear submarine, nor any submarine for that matter, and I had imagined all of the men would look like Alec Baldwin in his "navy whites" in *Hunt for Red October*! So, I was looking more forward to the tour than the game!

We arrived to much fanfare. Sailors and their families were lined up along the street to greet the large buses of players and their families. Our group stepped from the bus with one the base's officers and walked to the Pentada submarine which we were to board.

Now, I don't know how much *you* know about submarines, but I thought they were all like the children's ride, "20,000 Leagues Under the Sea," at Disneyworld. I expected a roomy luxury liner that could be boarded from the *side*. Imagine my surprise when there was no large door and we began *scaling* the side of the slick vessel for who-knew-what reason. I just followed everybody else.

"What the *hell* are we doing?" I wondered, but didn't ask any questions for fear of looking "foo-foo wifey." At this point, Mama was forced to head back to the bus with Cole because it was just too dangerous for us to try to hold him and walk on the slippery convex surface.

Ahead of us, there were about fifty men standing at attention on top of the sub. It was such a unique experience and I put my fears aside for one moment. My heart swelled with pride that I was an American and that these men were willing to lay down their lives to protect our country every day. It was inspiring and I was lost in admiration...until I saw the "door" we had to enter to get inside the sub.

I couldn't possibly be expected to enter this way! The opening was a mere hole on top of the ship. No, I needed to go back to the bus, too. I kept thinking, "No one will care if I leave now. These sailors are definitely not here to see me, anyway. I can just turn and leave."

But I couldn't because there was a *line* of people behind me and the surface wasn't wide enough for two people to stand abreast. If I got off now, I would have to be *passed* down the line like a hot potato. *Oh, hell!* I kept eyeing the entry. I finally looked at it long enough to see that it was only about three feet in diameter, round like a steel tube and went down so far you couldn't see the bottom. @#&*! *What was I going to do??* As I kept observing, I noticed an officer on the other side of the tube to whom you had to jump, and he then helped to lower you into the tube until your foot hit the first rung. From where I was standing, it looked like the rungs were about four feet apart! Besides thinking this really wasn't a good day to have worn a short, lycra dress and a large-brimmed straw hat, I could feel my claustrophobia squeezing me like a boa constrictor! I panicked!

I looked at Chris, who isn't scared of anything, and said, "There is no way I am going down in that hole."

Chris just sort of laughed.

"No, you don't understand. I can't do this," I tried to tell him.

He looked at me and said, "Sally, this is no time to be dramatic. You can't insult these people by not going down there. They invited us here. This is where they live and you are my wife. You are going in that hole. Just follow your dad and don't think about it."

And my dad chimed in, saying, "Oh, it's no big deal. Just watch me." And I knew then that I was going to have to go on this tour if it killed me.

My dad jumped across the portal, and as he began his descent, he turned to me and said, "See..its no big deeeeeeaaaaalllll"...and he was gone. He had slipped and fallen at least ten feet down into the bottom of the sub. I could then faintly hear my dad saying to one of the officers, "No, I'm okay...really, I'm fine...really, I can get a bandage when we get back on the bus..."

*@!&! was my only thought. My dad didn't even bother yelling up further words of encouragement to me. I just said a prayer, jumped across the tube and held on to the officer's legs who was lowering me. He looked me straight in the eye, smiling and said, "Nervous?"

With all of the strength in my voice that I could muster, I said, "Nah. This is a piece of cake. We may have to take my dad to the hospital after the tour, but no, I'm not nervous at all." Ha! What a lie! But I was determined conquer my fear and enjoy this tour.

Cognizant of the numerous men looking up the tube from below, the same officer looked at me again and said, laughing this time as he lowered me into the tube, "It wasn't really a good day for you to wear a dress, was it?"

"No, but at least I remembered to wear my underwear," I replied.

It Wasn't the Hershey's Kick for a Million Smackers, But Twenty Thousand is Still Pretty Good Pay for a Day's Work...

Like the playoff game between the Chiefs and the Colts in 1995, the 1997 Pro Bowl would also be determined by a field goal. I hadn't even thought about the importance of an AFC victory... until I heard what were to be the victor's spoils. Prior to hearing

what was at stake, I had thought the Pro Bowl outcome wasn't *that* important because unlike the regular season, a player's *job* wasn't on the line. But when I heard what we could win, I felt like a high-roller on the Vegas strip, yelling, "Come on, twenty! Show me twenty! Come home to Mama!"

If the AFC won the game, Chris would receive a check for twenty thousand dollars. If the NFC won the game, he would be awarded ten thousand dollars, which still isn't bad for one game's pay, but ten doesn't seem so great when you think you could have had twenty! Money can make people crazy, and I don't even like to gamble, but the game seemed more vibrant and intense knowing the ante. Ten thousand dollars wouldn't pay for all of the extra plane tickets we had bought to take our family and friends with us to Hawaii. Twenty thousand dollars, however, would not only pay for the extra tickets, but I would have enough left over to buy an oil painting of English Whippet dogs that I had been eyeing. Come on, twenty!

It was the fourth quarter, with only minutes to go, and we had been at Aloha Stadium for *seven* hours. I was exhausted and Cole was getting antsy. It looked like the AFC was going to lose the damn game, so my family packed all of our stadium paraphernalia and began the long trek to the car. We were in the "nosebleed" seats of the stadium and had four long sets of stairs to descend. The journey seemed longer going down than it had coming up since we were losing with only minutes to go. About halfway down the stairs, I realized Cole needed his diaper changed, so with him standing on a step, I changed his pants. I was just too tired to find the bathroom.

Not at any point during law school did I think I would be changing diapers, *especially* not in public. It also had never crossed my mind that I would lug fifty pounds of child crap with me wherever I went. I had always pictured myself as a female Clarence Darrow, dressed in Armani with every hair in place, arguing in front of the Supreme Court so persuasively that the Justices didn't even bother listening to the other counsel. The closest I get to a closing argument now, however, is with Cole. I argue that it is not nice to slap people in the face, and as he slaps me across the bridge of the nose, I realize that I have lost the "case." I just thank God that I couldn't see myself now when I was in law school. I know I would have quit. My education in Torts 101 did not enlighten me in the art of reasoning with a toddler, and I could have understood Barney without my law degree.

As I was applying Desitin to Cole's heiney, I heard the roar of the crowd. Since we were under the stadium, we couldn't see the field. My dad quickly ran back to the portal to see what was happening. He excitedly yelled to us that the AFC had just scored to tie the game! I had thought we were going to lose, but now it looked like we had a chance. Slim. But that fat Hawaiian lady hadn't sung yet. The game went into overtime, and our clan settled ourselves against a chain-link fence through which we could peer. I was not about to mount those stairs again. I didn't care how much good it would do my cellulite.

I could only see about thirty feet of the field, a small slice, but just enough to see the faces of Chris and Cary. If this game were going to be determined by a field goal, which most overtime games were, I wouldn't be able to see if the ball had gone through the uprights. But I would know by the expression on Chris and Cary's faces if the field goal was good.

As both sides fought for field position, I noticed out of the corner of my eye that a young woman was staring at me.

I turned to look at her. "Are you married to one of the players?" smiling, she asked.

"Yes," I answered, not in the mood to encourage a long conver-sation, especially when I was trying to concentrate on the game.

She then told me that she identified me as a player's wife because of the back-pack I carried. She knew that only players had been issued that particular kind. "I'll bet you don't like games like this, do you?"

"No, I hate it when games come down to the wire. It's great for the fans but hard on the families." Standard pat answer. I had repeated it a thousand times.

Hoping she would ask no more questions, I turned to my slice of reality. Our field goal unit was taking the field. We were attempting a forty-yard field goal. It would be decided now if those Whippets would be chasing their tails on my stairwell wall or if they would remain in that cramped art gallery.

The snap was good. The hold was good. But the ball went wide left. I could see it on Chris and Cary's faces before the fan reaction roared in my ears. Shit! Now the NFC would get the ball back on the forty and they would only have to make two first downs before they were in scoring range. We were screwed. I just felt it.

The NFC quickly executed the plays and moved downfield. They couldn't score in the red zone, so they sent in John Kasey, the kicker for the NFC, to finish the job. I closed my eyes. He is so good. I *knew* he would make this. Damn, so close, I could hear those Whippets barking. "Don't make it. Don't make it," I whispered to myself.

He missed it!! Yeah! I liked John Kasey and his wife, but I wanted those dogs! Now we would get the pigskin back.

We moved the ball downfield, but couldn't get past the thirty-five yard line. Chris and Cary jogged out, nonchalantly, as every eye in the stadium was on them. The fans were so quiet that I could hear the traffic on H-1, Hawaii's only interstate, a few hundred yards away. Again, if Cary made this, we won. If he missed it this time, we were sure to lose because Kasey would not miss again if given the opportunity.

I once more felt the bystander's eyes on me. She said, "You don't look nervous. I would be nervous. Does this not bother you?"

Why couldn't this woman shut up? I was *very* nervous. My God, I had chewed the French Manicure off of my thumbnail. I didn't want to be explaining myself when this game was being decided. "Look, I'm really sorry, but I *am* nervous. I have to watch this field goal, okay?"

She said, "Oh, sure. Have you had fun in Hawaii, this week? I know a great..."

I didn't hear her last comment. Chris was grabbing the ball from the air, spinning it on the ground, turning it with the laces pointed out so Cary could kick it. Cary's foot hit the ball and it travelled, straight, going, going, going... The ball moved in slow motion. I glanced at their faces and knew the ball was true. Chris and Cary had started to jump up as I pictured the ball hitting the net behind the goal posts. We won! We won! The Whippets were mine!

The bystander was on me before I could high-five my dad. She was hugging me around the neck and screaming. I hugged her, also. What the hell, she seemed just as excited as we were.

I looked for Cary's wife, but couldn't find her. She was the only one I really wanted to see because she would understand what else that kick meant. She knew that his success today would eventually help him obtain an even better contract when he became a free agent in two years. She knew that each kick paid for bricks in her new house. She knew that this kick was seen by millions. She just *knew*.

The bystander didn't know. She just understood what she saw. So much of football transpires in an unseen world. Behind closed doors, within the four walls of team offices, careers are started, put on hold, and ended without a bang. Only a fellow wife would ever understand the importance of one play. Only a kicker's wife would understand the importance of one kick. I couldn't explain all of this to the bystander.

I looked high into the clouds and thanked God for one more game. I looked a little further down, around the top of the stadium, and smilingly shook my head at those kicking gods for teasing me yet again.

That's me, Chris and our son Cole at the 1997 Pro Bowl

Kickers

I get no kick from champagne.
Mere alcohol doesn't thrill me at all,
So tell me why should it be true
That I get a kick out of you.
— Cole Porter, *Anything Goes*

Heroes or goats? Every time a kicker or punter takes the field, the football gods above the stadium flip a giant coin. If the coin face pictures Zeus, the kick is successful and the player becomes the laurel-wreathed hero. If the coin face portrays Medusa, the kick is shanked and the player becomes the curly-tailed goat. The kicker's world is one of black and white, no wavering gray. He either gets the job done or he doesn't and *everybody* in the stadium knows it. There is no one else to whom the blame can be shuffled or reassigned. Solitaire is the *real* game of a kicker.

Kickers' wives have the thickest skin of the "professional athlete wife" species. We endure all, unflinchingly. Boos, stares, paper missiles and curses. We are popular when our husbands have just won the game or placed the enemy deep within home territory, and we are avoided like the black plague when our husbands lose a game or have a punt run back. The wives of kickoff specialists and punters also endure, "Did he *mean* to do that?" from people who do not understand the politics of place-

ment. At least with field goal kickers, the intention of ball place-
ment is clear: up and through.

The kicking gods know me well. I pray to them before, during
and after each game. My humility is my sacrifice, laid at their altar.
My wishes are chanted during the game, hoping that the gods will
answer my pleas. Chris takes the field, lines up to kick the ball,
makes contact with the pigskin, and I hiss silently, "Go ball, go
ball, go ball, go ball!" until it is captured and in enemy hands. "Get
him, get him, get him, get him dammit!" is my next chant, repeated
in a whisper, until a bone-crunching tackle is made, hopefully not
by Chris. (If Chris clobbers the runner, somebody screwed up.
Punters and kickers are the last line of defense and if they are
forced to make the tackle... it is not good. These tackles are always
followed by a silent dinner after the game.)

Of all players, kickers live the closest to the lunatic fringe. If
the kicker has one bad game, he gets spooked. If the kicker has
two bad games, the coach gets spooked. If the kicker has three
bad games, management sprinkles voodoo powder in the kicker's
locker to clean out the evil spirits so the new kicker doesn't get
spooked! Kickers often are teased for having the "easiest" job on
the team. And, as far as physical exertion goes, the ribbing may
be well deserved. But *nobody* on the team has to be as mentally
tough as the kickers. They must believe in themselves at all
times, *even when nobody else does.*

The Ambrosia Must Have Been Sour

One kick determined the outcome of the Chiefs v. Colts playoff
game in 1995. Thank God I didn't know it would come to that when
the game began. No, at kickoff, all I knew was that the wind was
going to be a factor. I just didn't know that it would be a $12,500
factor.

Chris called with the bad news about the wind five or six hours
before the evening game began. The wind had been swirling in
Arrowhead Stadium that morning during walk-throughs and the
weather experts were expecting negative temperatures, possibly
snow, by kickoff. Chris explained that every field goal attempt of
more than thirty yards would be a "crap-shoot." And I knew that in
weather like that, *all* of the balls would be frozen, not just those of

the players! There is nothing a kicker hates more than cold, hard balls that feel and move like a block of concrete when kicked. The football gods were getting their Bark-o-loungers and master remote controls ready, because in weather like this, they would control the outcome of the game.

The Colts were predicted to lose. This was the battle between David and Goliath. The Chiefs had only lost a few regular season games and had enjoyed a bye week while we were getting banged up and injured beating San Diego. We had been nicknamed the "Cinderella Colts," blessed with an unbelievably successful season and winning when we had to, but most football analysts felt like our lucky streak was going to end with the Chiefs game. The prognosticators had the Chiefs shattering our glass slipper and leaving us in the hovel of defeat with our ugly stepsister, the Jets. I wanted the Colts to do well because they had been labelled "losers" for the majority of the past ten years. If we could keep the carriage from turning into a pumpkin and beat the Chiefs, maybe the losing spell would be broken and we would garner an invitation to *The Dance*: The Super Bowl.

As the game started, I settled into my chair in front of the television. I was eight and one-half months pregnant and I was watching the game alone — sort of. During the televised away games, I always "watch" the game with my mom and dad through intermittent phone calls. But by the beginning of the fourth quarter, the game was so intense that we just stayed on the line. The tension had also affected Cole, my then-unborn son, because he had begun his *own* kicking campaign in my stomach.

The Colts missed field goals and the Chiefs missed field goals: wide left, wide right, not enough distance... Both coaches were dismayed because they were having to "go for it" on fourth down if they were even remotely close to the ten-yard marker since no long field goal could be attempted. It became clear with minutes to go that the game's outcome was going to be determined by wind velocity and the leg strength of two players: Lin Elliott of the Chiefs and Cary Blanchard of the Colts.

As the game came to a close, and with every players' jaw clenched, Lin Elliott lined up for the final field goal attempt. If he made it, we would lose and be knocked out of the playoffs. If he missed it, we would win and play Pittsburgh for the AFC Championship. Every eye was on Elliott. The tension of the moment filled the stands like cheap cigar smoke in an old pool hall.

I've always felt that to pray for the outcome of a game bordered on sacrilege. I mean, God needs to be worrying about floods and wars and disease and asteroids, not football games and which team would get an extra twelve thousand dollars on their next paycheck because of a kick. So, I just prayed to let *His* will be done.

As Lin Elliot stood on my screen, his warm breaths causing cumulus-like clouds to form around his face, I realized that he probably had a wife, just like me, watching this game. She was most likely praying and feeling a vise-like grip on her stomach too. Suddenly, I felt for her. I felt for him. After the key misses he had suffered tonight, his job was on the line. If he *made* this field goal and won the game, his earlier mistakes would be forgiven and he could eat free barbeque for life in Kansas City. He would be the laurel-wreathed hero. If he *missed* it, he would probably be looking for a job.

Abruptly, I was pulled in two directions. I had been pulling for us to win, for the Chiefs to miss all of their field goals. But now, when I realized that "the Chief" had a face, it was hard to pull against one person's career. As Elliot paced off his mark, I rode the fence. I wanted the Colts to go to the Super Bowl because they *deserved* to go. But I didn't want it to be at the expense of one person.

The kick was wide left. He missed. My phone began ringing. Friends called in congratulations that we would be going to the Championship game. We were one step closer to The Dance. I thanked them for calling, but for hours and even days after the game, I couldn't erase the image of Lin Elliott, head down, tears streaming down his face, walking off the field. No one had to tell me that he felt the weight of Arrowhead Stadium on his shoulders. No one had to tell me that his wife or significant other had cried as she watched the game unfold, but *I* knew that she would have dried her tears long before she saw him. I was sure that she knew her job, now. She would have to be his sponge.

Those football gods are SOBs. They laugh at us. They mock us when we think we have them beaten. The next weekend, when the Colts played Pittsburgh for the AFC Championship, the football gods allowed us to believe that *we* would win until the *last second* of the game. But we lost. I had never, ever been so devastated over a game in my entire life. It was heartbreaking to have come that far, proving so many wrong, only to lose in the last second. The football gods enjoy teasing us in that way. It serves as a constant reminder that the game is *always* bigger than the players. Especially the kickers.

And You Can Score Three Points From A Good Punt?

When I met Chris through his first agent, I didn't really know the difference between punting and kicking. I thought the punter *was* the kicker. And I became even more confused when Chris told me that he handled both duties in college. What the hell did that mean? Like most of my female peers, the only thing I had watched in college at home games were players' butts. The nuances of the kicking game were as foreign to me as heterosexuality was to Liberace.

I didn't even try to lie to Chris about my ignorance. My mama always taught me that if you lie, you'll get caught with your pants down, so I told Chris that I really didn't have a clue why he did what he did on the field. He laughed and said that a lot of people didn't understand punting and was glad that I had at least been honest. He said that most girls had lied to him about their unfamiliarities with special teams play.

The next week, Chris called and asked if I was free for lunch, that he had something to show me. I told him when to pick me up from my law firm and I looked forward to our rendezvous. Instead of a romantic dejeuner for two as I had imagined, we dined on Church's drive-thru greasy fried chicken. And instead of eating beside a lake or at a picnic area with a scenic view, Chris took me to the practice fields at Clemson University, where we snarfed down lunch while he explained the objectives of offense, defense and special teams.

By the end of the day, I knew three things. First, punting was a defensive play, designed to pin the opposition deep within home territory; that there were coffin corner punts, the intent of which was to kick the ball out of bounds, keeping the opposition inside the twenty yard-line; that there were high, floating punts, aimed at giving the coverage unit time to run downfield and tackle; and there were short, pooch punts that were devised to keep the opposition pinned inside the twenty yard-line, but not necessarily out of bounds. A punt, even if it is perfectly kicked, will not score any points.

Second, field goal kicking was an offensive play, called to score points. The kicker and the holder of the ball position themselves behind the line of scrimmage, where they wait for the snap of the ball. After the snap, the holder catches the ball and spins it to the ground so the kicker can kick the ball through the uprights. This was more simple to follow because the ball either went through and the team scored three points, or it didn't and the kicker sat by himself on the team bus. Kickoffs, where the kicker lines up at the thirty yard-line and kicks the ball straight downfield, were designed to restart the game after a score by your own team or to start a half.

Third, I realized that I was going to break my dating taboo of seeing someone younger than myself. Chris was twenty-one and I was a whopping twenty-five. But in actuality, Chris was more mentally mature than I. After leaping the age hurdle, it didn't take me long to realize that Chris was good for me because he kept my feet on the ground, and I was good for Chris because I encouraged him to reach for the stars.

There was so much more to Chris than I had originally imagined. Quiet, easy-going and gentle-natured, it took him months to reveal one of his deepest secrets to me. He suffered from dyslexia, a learning disorder, which had caused him great pain as a child and had almost prevented him from being accepted to college. But instead of letting the disorder beat him, he fought it every day, learning how to read and write without hindrance. His success in the classroom was hard-earned, and from this experience he cultivated the patience, determination and mental toughness that had enabled him to become a great punter and kicker.

The obstacles Chris managed to overcome were staggering. He remains my daily inspiration because he never gives up in his quest to be the best. He approaches every season with the same drive and enthusiasm that motivated him as a child. And he represents well the stoicism needed to be a successful kicker. He will always be my hero.

Charlie Sheen could have told us all about the public eye...

Goldfish

To create a public scandal is what's wicked;
To sin in private is not a sin.
— Moliere

"One fish, two fish, red fish, blue fish!" (Dr. Seuss) Living your life in a fishbowl means *always* having to wear clean underwear! Literally *and* figuratively. Of all the challenges a player's family faces, this is one of the toughest. From learning to hold your head high in the face of defeat to shielding a child's ears when fans scream obscenities at its father, dealing with fame and a scrutinizing public is oftentimes more of a burden than a joy. No one is perfect, and from DUIs to spousal abuse and infidelity, players in the NFL are no different than the rest of society. It's just a bigger deal when they are caught.

Unfortunately, there are no "shorthand" courses in *Dodging Paparazzi 101* or *Winning Public Favor 202*. Most NFL families, therefore, learn about the cruel double-edged sword of publicity by making mistakes. NFL bad news is a tabloid's good news and nothing boosts sales like a good ol' public scandal, or an insignificant incident that has been whipped to slanderous status by an unscrupulous spin doctor. And as long as the public remains fascinated with the everyday goings on of their athletic heroes, reporters are more than willing to provide the jolting headlines. Unfortunately, the *entire* NFL is sometimes judged by the actions of just a *few* of its members.

Most NFL families lead relatively normal lives, and experience the trappings of fame on a much smaller scale than would be expected. The following stories exemplify the more humorous side of being caught by that ever-roaming public eye. And they represent the one maxim about publicity that always rings true: You are *never* recognized when you need to be, and you are *always* recognized when you don't want to be!

Would You Like a Bun with that Wienie?

Parents love to take pictures of their babies and I am no exception to the rule. I have taken so many pictures of Cole that I was forced to take a second job, writing this book, to pay for photo development costs! Recently when I was trying to finish a roll of film, Chris was giving Cole a bath. Since one of my favorite places to capture him is lathered and splashing in the bathtub, strapped into "Toby the Tub Turtle," I quickly snapped the photos of Cole. I really focused on framing his face and trying to shoot the pictures when he was showing the most gum.

We spend our off-seasons on a small island off the coast of South Carolina and there are not many places to develop one-hour pictures or shop for household sundries. The Hilton Head Wal-Mart, allowing its shoppers to do both, is the most *happening* place on the island, and I am there so often I notice when the Kathie Lee Gifford display changes from leotards to cruisewear. Chris jokes that I could apply for the job of "Wal-Mart Greeter," the person who stands at the entrance and says, "Hello. Welcome to Wal-Mart. Here is a shopping cart for your convenience."

I filled out the film processing form and we proceeded to shop and browse. The hour passed quickly and Chris went to pick up the pictures while I waited in the check-out line. When Chris didn't appear, I checked-out without him and waited outside. Finally, he came out and said the photo developer had recognized him and had spent almost ten minutes getting his autograph and asking him about the Colts, the playoffs, and the Pro Bowl.

We got home, shelved our purchases and I sat down to look at the pictures of Cole. As always, I counted them to see how many hadn't been processed because of my ineptitude with lighting, focus, and film removal, and I was happy because only one hadn't been printed. All of the pictures were really cute, especially the ones of Cole in the tub.

As I was putting the photos back in their vinyl container, a small piece of paper fell to the floor. Curious, I picked it up. It read, "We are returning your processed negatives without certain prints. We have established guidelines in our one-hour photo labs prohibiting us from printing those negatives which we have classified as unsuitable. We regret any inconvenience this may have caused you and trust that you will understand our position."

"What is this?" I thought.

My next thought was that maybe they couldn't process some of the tub pictures of Cole because he was naked. I could understand if that were the case. There are so many sickos in our society, and there was no telling what people had probably tried to get developed in there.

With my curiosity piqued, I removed the negatives and held them to my kitchen stove light. I just couldn't remember any picture of Cole that would be "questionable," but there must have *been something* borderline in my pictures for the photo people to include the disclaimer with my prints.

At first, I didn't see anything. Then, I saw it.

I found the questionable picture.

Oh, God! Chris was going to *kill* me! *Why* did they have to pick *this* time to recognize him? I couldn't believe this. We were *ruined! Ruined* at Wal-Mart! We would be driving an hour away to shop for sundries!

As I looked at the picture again, though, I started to laugh. The picture was so innocent on the surface. Chris and Cole were in the tub, laughing and having fun. They were both "cheesing" for the camera, hair wet, looking like identical twins having the time of their lives, except that an albino water snake was stalking Chris! His *personal* tub toy was *floating* on the *surface* of the water! Laughter was now *snorting* through my nose!

Chris, who was completely unaware of the whole situation and was in the other room watching television, yelled, "What is so funny? Are you alright? You sound like you are having a seizure in there."

I couldn't respond except with hoots of laughter. I looked at the picture again, without focusing on Chris' penis, which was difficult because it was the *piece de resistance*, and noticed that otherwise, the picture was great.

By this time, Chris walked into the kitchen to see what was wrong with me. He started smiling because my face was so contorted from laughing and said, "What is so funny?"

Finally, I managed to get a breath in between laughs and said, "You know, you may not want to go back in Wal-Mart for a while."

Chris was completely baffled and said, "*What* are you talking about?"

"An identifiable object of yours may be posted on the wanted board of the photo lab, just like in that movie *Porky's!*" I responded. Chris was completely lost, so I showed him the negative.

"Oh my God! This is a picture of my dick!" Chris screamed at me. This made me laugh even harder. I was now writhing on the kitchen floor. I couldn't even stand up. Chris' second reaction was one of embarrassment. "That man *knew who I was*. I can *never* go in there again." His third thought was, of course, to blame me because I was the one who took the picture. "How could you not have seen that?" and "This is *not* funny. This is *terrible*."

I just kept laughing. I was married to the "Wal-Mart Wienie." Then I started singing it like a child, "Wal-Mart Wie-nie, Wal-Mart Wie-nie," which only served to make him angrier.

He didn't see the humor in this situation. Of course, I probably wouldn't have either if it had been me in the picture, but it wasn't. The more I thought about the situation, the funnier it became. The man that Chris had spent ten minutes talking to was the *only* person running the photo booth, which meant that he was the one who had to *develop* the negative to decide its inappropriateness! Which further meant that he had seen Chris' wienie and had *still* carried on a conversation with Chris! For ten minutes! I would have been so embarrassed had I been that man I would have left our pictures on the counter with a note, stating no amount was owed, that I had to leave because of a sudden emergency. I could *not* have made small talk and looked a stranger in the eye after seeing his wienie on film! Oh, this made the story even funnier.

If we live to be one hundred and fifty-four, I will never let Chris forget the wienie story. It has become one of my favorites because it shows that players are just people and, above all, they are human. That roving public eye! It caught Chris where he least wanted it to!

Raise Your Hands and Drop that Dollar Bill!

It was a Saturday night in November of 1991. I was slathering gobs of Retin-A on my face in preparation for bed, looking forward to *Saturday Night Live*, when I heard the sports news anchor excitedly say, "Stay tuned to see what the Bears *really* do the night before a big game." I quickly settled in my bed and turned up the television volume in anticipation of the report.

The news returned from break with a shot of two rookies stealthily entering a stretch limo. I thought to myself, "They just rented a limo to grab dinner. This sportscaster is really stretching to make a story out of this." The next scene, however, turned my blood cold. It was a shot of the same two guys, plus a few more players, inside a smoky, hazy strip bar. It was obvious that the camera had been hidden under the reporter's jacket because the picture was skewed and the images were black-green. The faces were fuzzy, but I recognized immediately which players were going to be permanent residents of The Dog House. They had been *busted*!

The camera then showed a small stage, around which this group of Bears sat, with a large pole in the middle. I only picked up the reporters words in flashes, this scene striking me like a thunderbolt, unable to process everything my eyes were seeing.

"...and these players' curfews are in minutes, folks....but the players certainly don't seem to care...if the Bears lose against the Vikings tomorrow, maybe we will know the underlying reason...so much drinking...our undercover reporter following the players...unaware they are on film...Ditka will surely be upset over this blatant infraction of the rules..." the reporter went on and on, digging player graves with every word.

On the screen, the players were carefully placing rolled-up dollar bills in a cheap-looking girl's g-string as she unwrapped her pretzel-like self momentarily from her disco pole to collect her earnings. "Oh my God," I thought, "She is more nimble than my old rubber Gumby from childhood." The guys, completely un-aware of the camera, were laughing abundantly, swilling beer and leering.

After making sure that neither Chris nor any of my closest friends' husbands were in the jovial group of voyeurs, I called Kim Willis and we finished watching the three- or four-minute piece together. "Oh my God, is the *shit* gonna hit the fan now!" was our first response. The punishment that these players would receive from the team wouldn't be *close* to the freeze-out they would experience at home.

Kim and I couldn't believe two things. First, that some of these guys were *stupid enough* to be doing this the night before a game. I didn't really care that they were in a skin dive, but they should have exercised discretion. These men were so big and some of them were really famous. They should have realized they would be recognized immediately. Stupid, stupid, stupid, they were and obviously thinking with the wrong head. Second, we couldn't believe that a news station found *this* a newsworthy report. This was more like tabloid trash, not major network news. The only people who probably cared about this report were the girlfriends and wives of Bear players.

Across town, also watching the news, was the girlfriend of one of the dollar-stuffers. When she saw her boyfriend laughing, drinking and feeling, she decided she had endured plenty. It was bad enough that he had not yet asked her to marry him after years of dating, but this type of public humiliation was intoler-able. By 3:00 a.m. she was packed and on her way back to the west coast.

Since the Bears game was in Minnesota, neither the team nor the players were aware of the Chicago broadcast. Often, as was the case in this hotel, the front desk operators were instructed to hold players' incoming calls after 11:00 p.m. This meant that all of the wives and significant others of the outed men had all night long to stew and simmer without hearing an explanation or excuse from their loving companions.

Chris has a routine of calling me before breakfast on game days and when he called that next morning and I relayed the news of the broadcast, he was *stunned*. *None* of the players were aware of the report and he knew that the ones who had been caught would *die* when they heard.

When Chris returned home, he told me the reporter who leaked the story was a marked man. The outed players were ready to kill him! I teased him that he was lucky *he* hadn't been in that bar and he responded that he had been in the bathroom when the camera had been filming the scene. "Ha ha. Very funny," I told him. We laughed, but I knew this wasn't funny for many other people.

The rookie with the girlfriend from the west coast returned to an empty apartment. His girlfriend and all of her clothes were gone. So was their future.

One of the other rookies, who had been a relative unknown on the field, was now known for the "Rebel Yell" he had given in the middle of his star performance.

I don't really know if any of the players were fined for missing curfew. I think the public outrage in the aftermath of the report was worse than any monetary loss they could have suffered. And being labeled as "pigs" to all of the women in Chicago was worse than any tongue lashing Ditka could have given them.

That darn public eye. It can find you in even the darkest of night. In the tackiest corners of the world. With your true colors shining brightly.

There are some perks to being in the NFL: Chris and friends with Bruce Willis at Planet Hollywood in Chicago

Lessons

*Draw from others the lesson that may
profit yourself.*
        — Terence, 190 B.C.

"I hate you! I hate you! Why did you cut him? He was my *friend*," sobbed twelve year old Justin as he ran, red-faced and teary-eyed, from the old dorm room. Slam! He was gone, disappearing behind the shaking door.

"Why do I have this job?" Tom Drapak asked himself. "*Why?*" He usually contemplated his position as Vice President of Player Personnel of the Arizona Cardinals when red-faced *men* questioned his decisions, not his own son.

He *hated* firing players. Hated it. It stunk. No matter how many times he had done it, in all of the years he had worked for various teams, he never became comfortable with his duty. No doubt about it, he had the worst job in management. Oh, he had a handsome salary, drove a nice car and had a great house, but he never grew accustomed to cashing the checks that the coaching staff wrote. *They* didn't have to look these men in the eyes and tell them it was finished, that the fat lady was singing.

Worse than the firings, though, was the fact that Tom had to hide his real feelings. Inside, he was a compassionate man, but in order to do his job well he had to maintain a gruff exterior. Only his secretary of many years knew how hard it was on Tom to end someone's career. Only she had heard the many phone calls he had placed over the years asking local companies to offer a job to a newly-released player. Tom cared about these men and their futures and some of them who had seemed to slide into the business world so easily had done so because of Tom's calling in of favors. The former players would never know it, but that was all right with Tom.

Other than his secretary, the rest of the office was scared of him because of his hiring and firing power. "Don't piss Tom off," he could just hear people whisper, "He might fire you." Everybody feared him, everybody except his family and that ended exactly three minutes ago when his son, Justin, painfully realized what his daddy did for a living.

"How did I let this happen? I should have explained my job to him before we came," Tom thought miserably. "Why did I even bring Justin to camp?" Tom had thought training camp would be a great experience for Justin. Most young boys in Phoenix only dreamed about being ball boys at the Cardinals' five-week training camp. Justin had begged to go for the last two years and Tom had finally relented.

"How can I explain this to Justin?" Tom sighed deeply and rubbed his forehead. He sat, emotionally spent and dejected, on the edge of the twin bed, elbows on knees, thinking. Tom felt like the armor of their father-son union had just been pierced, sustaining its first real chink. Tom's mind was racing. He did the unthinkable. He picked up the old-fashioned rotary phone and he dialed Tony Talbot's room.

◆ ◆ ◆ ◆ ◆

Tony Talbot was thirty-one years old. He was a League survivor of nine years. Although he had bounced between several teams in those years and had rarely played for more than minimum salary plus incentives, he was a steady kicker and had made a decent living for his wife and two kids. His wife had been a trooper through all of the moves. She never griped about not being in one place long enough to become familiar with the neighbors, and she could parallel park the hell out of a U-Haul truck.

Tony wanted to play just one more year. An even ten-year career would be respectable. That was his goal.

This was his first camp with the Cardinals. He only knew a couple of players on the team, but once camp started, he was in his natural habitat. Attending a new team's training camp was similar to being at a Wendy's in a city different than your hometown: same food, just a different place to stand in line. Most training camps were held at deserted college campuses. They all featured the same lackluster dorm rooms, same humdrum cardboard food, same asinine rookie pranks, same lumpy, standard-issue college bed, and the same practice drills. Tony was "home" even though he had yet to meet all of the members of his new family.

The other kicker in camp had kicked for the Cards the previous season. He literally had the leg up. It would be tough for Tony to beat him out of a job, but it could be done. Tony had done it before. Cap management personnel *loved* Tony because he was bargain-basement cheap. If the other booter was a high-priced, Neiman-Marcus kicker, the roster spot was usually Tony's if his legs and feet didn't lie.

Tony was a likable guy. With his wide, affable grin, he resembled actor Billy Crystal, and like Crystal in "City Slickers," he was unsinkable. Always happy, he was a camp favorite, especially with the ball boys.

The ball boys worked more closely with the kickers than any other players during camp. The boys fielded punts, kickoffs and field goals and from one end of the field, they quickly shuttled the balls back to the other end, to the kicker's feet, arming them with new balls to perform their drills, over and over and over, all day long. It was one of the most tiring and unglamourous jobs of camp, but most appreciated by the kickers. Especially since the kickers had at one time fielded their own balls in the time-consuming routine.

Ball boys were usually in junior high or high school and worked for pennies, plus room and board. They didn't care about the money. They just wanted to be close to the players. They wanted to return to school in August and tell their peers they had spent *their* summer with an NFL team. That was the coolest! *That* was a summer job, not cutting grass and lifeguarding.

The kickers, spending a lot of time with the boys, really got to know them well. "Good ball," the boy would breathlessly utter as he dropped a retrieved ball at the kicker's feet.

"Yeah, but its gotta be about five yards further if I want to get this job. But thanks," the kicker would respond. Small words of encouragement. Small appreciative replies. By the end of a five-week camp, the boys knew where the balls were going to land even before the kickers did. At dusk, when the players went to dinner, the boys stayed on the fields, mimicking the closely-observed techniques of their mentors.

Justin Drapak and Tony Talbot bonded instantly. The tow-headed kid with a spray of freckles across his nose immediately liked Tony's friendly, wide smile. One camp tandem had been decided.

Camp was going well for Tony. His mind was clear, his legs were limber, and he had performed well in the specialist drills (the drills performed with the entire offense, watched closely by the head coach). With an accuracy rate of about ninety percent, he felt like ten years would be his lucky career number.

And Tony was enjoying working with Justin. Quick to return the balls, Justin was a fast learner, and he didn't chatter excessively during the drills, unlike some of the ball boys. Tony appreciated Justin's taking his job seriously because some of the boys didn't understand that practice wasn't just practice, that a job was at stake. But Justin understood the importance of every kick and the reverential attitude he needed to adopt when his feet hit the practice field.

Off the field, Justin and Tony established early in camp a nightly after-dinner ritual of playing Nintendo and watching *Gilligan's Island* re-runs until curfew. Tony had a big-screen television in his cramped dorm room, and he and Justin sat on the floor and golfed, snow-boarded, and played football. They even double-teamed the other kicker and his ball boy and played boisterously until lights-out at 11:00 p.m. Justin was having the time of his life.

Justin thought Tony was the coolest player he had ever met. He was a great kicker, but more importantly, he treated Justin like an equal, not a kid. Justin had even talked to Tony's wife on the phone. And when Tony had introduced him as his "Little Buddy," Justin swelled with pride. The two had adopted nicknames for each other after their many nights of watching *Gilligan's Island*. One day when Tony was attempting a fifty-yarder, he said, "Little Buddy, do you think I can make it from here?"

Justin responded with, "Aye, aye, Skipper."

It was then settled. Justin was the Skipper's Little Buddy.

The phone reverberated in Tony's brain three or four times before he actually heard it. Mentally, he had been miles away from his room. The steady noise brought him back to the dorm. He was packing and had paused at his wife's picture before the phone rang. He was studying it so closely that her face had dissolved into individual color pixels. He wanted to occupy his mind so he wouldn't rehash the last hour's events.

He had been cut. It was the last day of camp and he had been cut. He thought he had done so well, that he had won the job. Now, he somehow had to call his wife and break the bad news. The ringing phone had broken his reverie.

"Tony?" asked the nervous-sounding voice as Tony put the receiver to his ear. It was Tom. He'd had enough of Tom for one day. Tom had just been in this room an hour ago, firing Tony. It wasn't that Tony disliked Tom. Actually, Tony thought Tom was a great guy, the kind of guy he'd like to have a Martini with under other circumstances. Tom just had a shitty *job*. He was the grim reaper, the ax-man. But Tony knew that his firing probably wasn't Tom's call. It had just been Tom's job to tell him.

"Yeah, Tom. What can I do you for?" Tony tried to sound upbeat, masking his discouragement.

"Tony, have you seen Justin?" Tom asked with a hint of fear in his voice.

"No Tom, I haven't. Not since last night. Why?"

"You have kids don't you?" Tom asked.

The question threw Tony. He had expected an inquiry about

his social security number or permanent home address, information needed to process his last check.

"Yeah, why Tom?" Tom then told Tony about Justin's emotional reaction to the news of Tony's firing.

"I'll go find him, Tom. Don't worry. I'll find him and talk to him." Tony replaced the receiver on the phone cradle, tossed his wife's picture into his duffel bag, and left his room.

Tony didn't even have to think to know where Justin would be. He knew he would find the kid at the practice field, which would be empty on an early Sunday morning.

Tony never, during the five-week camp, really thought about Justin being Tom's son. Now he understood that, for Justin's sake, he probably shouldn't have gotten so close to the kid. His "Little Buddy" now hated his dad for firing Tony. And that wasn't fair to Tom.

Tony was thankful he didn't have Tom's job. Firing people would suck. Since *no* player in the NFL wanted to be fired, and hardly anybody ever quit, Tom was forced to constantly levy bad news. What in the world was he going to say to Justin to make this situation better?

The sun was high and bright over the practice fields. In the distance, he could see Justin from behind, kicking balls off a tee, trying to hit the net behind the goal posts. Justin killed one down the middle as Tony approached, and as it found its mark, Tony yelled, "Nothin' but net!"

Justin spun around and Tony saw the child's swollen eyes. Justin had obviously been crying, crying because of Tony's loss, crying because his dad was the causal domino in the chain.

Justin tried to be strong, but when he saw Tony's smiling face, the tears came again. He ran to Tony and hugged him. "I'm so sorry, Tony. I'm so sorry. My dad is an asshole. You're the best kicker! I can't believe he cut you," choked Justin.

Tony pushed Justin away, gently, looking into his eyes. "Wait a minute, Little Buddy. Wait a minute. Your dad is not the bad guy here. It wasn't his decision to cut me. Your dad just had to *tell* me. Don't blame him. Its not *his* fault. *I'm* the one who didn't play well enough to make this team. And neither your dad or the coach can help that."

"Yeah, but he could have told them not to cut you. He could have made them keep you. He should have told them how nice you are and that you played Nintendo with me," Justin said, unaware yet of the harsh realities of the business of football.

Tony was touched by the naivete and emotion pouring from the child's heart. This little boy really cared about Tony, and he didn't understand that this game, this business, doesn't care if you are a rapist or a saint. It only matters that you can play and that you're in the right place at the right time. But how would he make a twelve year old, full of ideals, understand this without telling him that Santa Claus didn't exist? That life can be star-crossed sometimes, that good people can fail? This was harder than Tony thought. Maybe he shouldn't have come. Maybe it would have been better if Tom and Justin had this discussion, not he and Justin. But he had to try because he had told Tom that he would.

"Justin, what I'm going to tell you isn't easy, okay? You may not understand all of this, but I want you to try and to listen, okay? Your dad isn't a bad person because of what he did to me. I choose to play this game and being cut is part of it. I've been cut before and hopefully this won't be the last time. Later on in life you'll learn that there is good and bad in everything and today you're seeing the bad, sadder side of my job. But there's been lots of good for me, kid, lots of it. It's not your dad's fault that there isn't a roster spot for me. Your dad and I, we didn't invent this game or the rules we play by. We're just here, both doin' our best to hold on for as long as we can.

"Don't be hard on your dad, Little Buddy. He's probably feelin' pretty rotten about now, probably even worse than me. I know that it was hard for him to cut me today because he knew we had gotten to be buddies during camp. But the bottom line is that he had to do his job. If he didn't, somebody else would have done it for him and then he would have been in trouble. Either way, I'd have still been cut. You understand, kid?"

"Yeah, I guess," Justin replied, wiping his face with the back of his hand. "It's still not fair. I want *you* to be the Cards kicker."

"I want to be the Cards kicker, too, but what I want wasn't meant to be. But it's not your dad's fault. You've got a great dad, Justin. Don't hold this against him, okay?"

"Yeah, I understand now. He was just doin' his job like you said. I guess I better go back and tell him I'm sorry, huh?"

"I think you'd better. He needs to know that you don't blame him for this, and that you still love him."

Justin turned to leave, but turned back to Tony one last time. "Hey, Skipper?" he asked, looking like the little boy that he was, "Can I write you sometimes? So you won't forget me?"

"Little Buddy, I'll never forget you. You're a good kid and one day you're gonna' be a great kicker. You *better* write me or I'll find you and kick your butt!" Tony mussed Justin's hair playfully.

Justin smiled, turned and jogged back toward the dorms. Tony looked at the field goal posts, the net and the field. It didn't seem like so long ago that he had been Justin's age, with a dream of playing in the NFL. He realized that his ticket for this ferris wheel ride of highs and lows had probably been punched for the last time, used up, but it had sure been one hell of a ride. The depressing lows had been worth it for the experience of the euphoric highs. And as he watched Justin's image growing smaller and smaller against the sun, Tony realized that his dream may be ending, but maybe Justin's was just beginning.

McKenna's Story

Do not follow where the path may lead. Go
instead where there is no path and leave a trail.
— Muriel Strode

As I was watching my second game from the Bears' Wives' Room in 1991, it became obvious to me that a woman named McKenna was the warm center around whom the room orbited. Like the sun, her bright smile drew the other wives to her. All of the women made it a point to gain her attention, as if her acknowledgment was a public approval of their worthiness, and as I watched wives jockey for position within her circle, it became apparent that obtaining a word with her was more important than watching the game. She was the one to know. She could make or break a rookie wife's acceptance into the room. She was the one I needed to meet in order to endure this ordeal and to make friends in this room.

McKenna's beauty was not breathtaking compared to the standards of perfection in the wives' room. Instead, she blended into the crowded room like pale cream melts into chocolate espresso, leaving it a light shade of taupe. Her brunette hair framed her features well, highlighting her bright golden-brown eyes and smiling mouth. Her peals of laughter rang up the scale and back down again like the trill of someone's fingers on piano keys. It was obvious that she enjoyed life and all of these women's friendships.

McKenna flitted around the wives' room like a butterfly, landing here and there, handing out compliments like pieces of candy. She told wives that their husbands were playing well, that she had enjoyed dinner with them the other night and that there was a meeting on Tuesday for a charity of which I had never heard. Her confidence and wisdom connected her to every identifiable "clique," yet I couldn't categorize her as belonging to any one of them. She moved with ease between them all like a Washington lobbyist in search of political support.

When I finally heard someone call her last name, I quickly glanced at my program's roster to see who her husband was. Winslow, Beau. Kicker. NFL 10 years. Oklahoma. Of course, now I understood. So *this* was Beau's wife. Chris had already told me so much about Beau I felt like I had known him for years even though I had yet to meet him. Chris enjoyed working with Beau, the prankster of the special teams unit. He was funny, friendly and didn't give Chris the usual grief that comes with being a rookie. He had quickly become one of Chris' favorite teammates.

Chris had met McKenna at camp and told me she was the wife I most needed to meet. He said she knew *everybody* and she had offered to introduce me to the other wives. The Winslows were practically an institution in Chicago, having been with the Bears for years, and McKenna was one of the oldest and most-respected wives on the team. Chris said the other players spoke highly of her, playfully calling her the leader of the "Kotex Mafia!"

He told me that she and Beau were very close, that she was the only wife to drive two and a half hours twice a week during the six-week camp for a mere two-hour visit. Evermore the perfect wife, she even brought the special teams unit home-baked cookies.

As I watched her, I kept thinking, "Should I just go up and introduce myself? Or do I wait for her to look at me?" Maybe she would notice that I was sitting by myself and come over to rescue me. I couldn't decide what was appropriate and after all, I didn't know if she had *really* meant that she would introduce me to everyone. Maybe she was just trying to be nice. I was sure that she didn't need an albatross around her neck for the '91 season, the desperate rookie wife seeking friends and encouragement.

The longer I questioned what I should do, the more nervous I became. This was ridiculous! Why was I so concerned with *how* I met her? "Oh, what the hell, just introduce yourself," was my last thought as I left the safety buoy of my seat and walked toward her in the choppy, frightening sea of the crowded room.

"McKenna? McKenna Winslow?" I asked, hoping she would be as nice to me, the newcomer, as she was to everyone else in the wives' room. "Hi, I'm Sally Gardocki," I began, extending my right hand, "My husband is Chris, the rookie punter and holder. He told me I should introduce myself to you, that he had met you at camp," I smiled, hoping I wasn't putting her on the spot.

"Oh, hi! Yes, I know exactly who you are. Your husband is so sweet. Beau really likes him. He is so glad that Chris is going to be the holder this year. He told me that Chris knew exactly how to spin the laces the way he liked and they worked well together in camp. Since they have to be together so much of the time, you know, that whole "kicker" thing, I'm glad they get along so well," she kindly said.

"Yeah, Chris told me that he liked holding Beau's balls, I mean...you know what I mean, that uhm, they have a good rhythm as holder and kicker," I was thinking what an idiot, a *twit* I was for saying that! This was not the time or place for a *stupid* verbal faux pas that would label me a goof.

Instead though, she laughed, kindly relieved me of my embar-rassment, and said, "I just hope Chris' hands aren't calloused! Those balls have to last *me* a lifetime!"

It was my turn to laugh. She was funny, kind, had been in my shoes before, and made me feel welcome in this room of strangers. We watched the rest of the game sporadically, talking during the offensive and defensive plays. We were the only two women in the room who focused in on special team plays and it was great to have found an ally. As her husband kicked the game-winner with forty-three seconds left, she invited me to an organizational meeting of the charity function she had annually headed for the past eight years, the Bears' Wives' Cancer Foundation. I gratefully accepted, hoping I could be a part of this new group of women. I was glad McKenna Winslow was becoming my friend.

I followed McKenna's intricate directions carefully, and as I pulled into the driveway I hoped was hers, in the beautiful North Shore subdivision of Hawthorn Hills, I saw the strangest sight. I couldn't suppress my laughter as I exited my car. A beautiful little girl with long dark hair flew past me on her tricycle in the sprawling front yard. She waved, a blur, and said, "Hi!" in her baby-child voice. I laughed because the child was completely naked! With her perfectly rounded, little baby-butt perched on the tricycle seat, she had no inhibition whatsoever. In her own world with no concerns, she was enjoying a fast ride, as the wind whipped against her delicate skin.

"Hi, there," I said, smiling at her innocence. "Is your mommy inside?"

"Un-huh," she replied, bobbing her head up and down. "She's takin' a shower. She told me that I could ride my trike if I stayed in the yard. Do you have a trike?" she asked, turning her pert little nose towards me. She had one of the smallest, prettiest faces I had ever seen. Long, long lashes framing midnight-black eyes. One day, this little girl would break many hearts.

"No. I don't have a trike. But ya' know what? I used to. When I was a little girl about your age. I named mine Trixie. Does yours have a name?" I asked on bended knee, enjoying the company of the child.

"No, but I'm gonna' name it now! What would be a good name? I'll hafta think of one," and with that she was gone, making her wide circle around the house.

I rang the bell and McKenna appeared, harried-looking, and said, "I can't find Savannah! I swear that child is going to be the end of me. I told Billy to watch her outside and he said she came back in with him but she is nowhere to be found! I've looked under every bed and in every closet. Come on in and help me find her, then we'll go."

"I think she's out here riding her tricycle," I cautiously said, thinking McKenna probably didn't know the child was naked. I didn't want to make a big deal of it in case they were practicing nudists, thinking that au naturel was the way to go, and I was the odd square. But I didn't have to tell her.

As Savannah breezed by, McKenna let out a shriek. "OhmiGod! _Savannah get your butt in this house now!_ What in the world are you thinking? Our neighbors! They are going to think we live like heathens!"

I was laughing hysterically because I didn't have children at the time and had no idea that laughing only encouraged a disobedient child. The longer I laughed, the more Savannah evaded her eventual capture by McKenna. McKenna had to chase her a good three minutes before stopping the tricycle. Winded, she said, "Just wait until you have kids. The grey hairs I have covered every month were hard-earned! That Savannah is a little monkey! If she weren't so funny, she'd get whipped every day! Lord, but she does make me laugh. I mean, why in the world would the child even think to come out here at high noon, with no clothes on, and ride that tricycle? Beau and I are in for it when she turns fifteen. You know when your mom says 'I hope your child does to you what you did to me?' Savannah is going to be my 'payback' child!"

After roping Savannah in and persuading her to go upstairs and put on some clothes, McKenna gave the babysitter instructions. The tranquility didn't last for long, however, because Savannah came running back downstairs wearing her favorite pajamas. "Savannah! Why did you put those on? Those are your 'nighties.' You can't wear those during the day!" McKenna was exasperated. "Eventually," she began, turning to me, "we'll get out of here. The meeting is at a restaurant not far from here. We won't be late. I plan for things like this to occur!"

On the way to DaNicci's, McKenna chronicled the year of the Bears' last Super Bowl victory. She told me how incredible it had been and how everyone in Chicago had embraced the team. The city even threw the players a ticker-tape parade in downtown Chicago. The diamond encrusted pendant she wore on her necklace was an exact replica of the players' Super Bowl rings. It was beautiful. She told me that year had been one of Beau's best, as he kicked twenty-one field goals in a row and was rewarded with his first trip to the Pro Bowl. McKenna made it all sound so exciting. I just hoped that Chris would make it through the first year. Then I would hope for things like the Super Bowl and Pro Bowl.

The Winslows led the life most people imagined of professional football players. They had a beautiful home, drove nice cars, wore expensive clothes, and were friends with every celebrity I could name. But there was such a down-to-earth quality about both of them that their lifestyle wasn't the least bit intimidating. For all of the stories McKenna would tell me about meeting movie stars and dining with politicians, she told just as many that bespoke her firm tether to the real world, the world of raising her own children instead of having a nanny, of painting her own fingernails instead of getting a weekly manicure at an expensive salon, and of taking sewing lessons to make her own curtains instead of hiring a costly decorator.

McKenna began one of these stories as she and I finally arrived at DeNicci's.

"A few years ago, the Bears were playing a Monday Night Football game. Beau was going to be highlighted at halftime because he had broken some old records. I was supposed to meet Frank Gifford before kickoff for a thirty-second interview, really just a sound bite saying that I was proud of Beau. Typical supportive wife stuff.

"I was eight months pregnant and nothing in my closet looked good on me anymore. I felt fat, unattractive, and the last thing I wanted to do was be on national television. But I had already agreed to the interview, so I had to find something to wear. I searched high and low for a decent maternity outfit. For a week I looked in the malls but everything I liked was a size 4. *Nothing* that I could comfortably wear looked good, much less great, and I got really frustrated before I found a cool, high-waisted, swingy suede dress that cost more than I will ever admit. But it was the only thing I liked, so I bought it, rationalizing that I could have it re-cut after I had the baby! Don't ever make that mistake when you're pregnant, Sally, because you will not want to wear *anything* post-pregnancy that you wore when you were pregnant! But anyway, I convinced myself that its life expectancy was longer than two months. So I bought it, laid it out on the guest bed, put some heeled boots with it and thought it looked pretty good.

"Just hours before the game, I was taking a shower when Billy, then three and a half, came into the bathroom with an empty maple syrup bottle. I didn't really pay him much attention, thinking he must have gotten the bottle out of the trash. He had a habit of rummaging through the garbage, collecting various objects to haul in his G.I. Joe truck. I thought he was just building a fort or something, but as I was combing my wet hair in the mirror, I asked, 'Billy, where did you get that syrup bottle?'

"And he said, 'Out of the pantry, mommy.' It was then that I realized the bottle was the same bottle that had been full at breakfast.

"'Billy, what happened to the syrup inside the bottle?' I asked, trying to be calm, and praying that he would say that he just poured it in the sink or the commode. Instead, he looked at me and said proudly, 'Mommy while you've been in the shower, I've been making pretty pictures on the floor and on your dress in there. I think you'll really like 'em.'

"I almost died. I ran into the guest room and the dress I was planning to wear was *ruined*. Billy had tried to write his name in big, syrupy capital letters on the entire front. I was too stunned to be mad.

"'Where else did you decorate, Billy?' I asked, not really wanting to know the answer.

"'On the rug in the big room downstairs, Mommy. You can *really* see my name down there!' I ran downstairs and was mortified. He was right. In big letters, he had used almost the whole bottle of syrup on my silk rug. I started to cry. That rug had been the first expensive gift Beau had ever bought me. He had picked it out himself and was so proud of it. It was my most cherished possession. And as I got down on my knees in my dining room and began to scrub the syrup off of the white rug, my towel fell off. As I went to retrieve it, I caught a glimpse of myself in the big mirror hanging over our buffet. I was on my hands and knees, as big as a house, my hair clung wetly to my head, I had on no make-up, Lauren was picking me up in less than thirty minutes, I was supposed to be on national television in an hour and a half and I now had nothing to wear that fit me except for leggings and a big, old hairy sweater that I wore to clean house. I cried and cried until I started laughing. I knew that I would remember that moment forever. It was then that I realized what being a mom was all about.

"I was just putting on my make-up and had curlers in my hair when Lauren pulled into the driveway. I got ready in such a hurry. As I was hefting myself into her convertible Rolls Royce, looking at her perfect hair and skinny body, I wanted to cry again. My *Limited* stretch pants didn't quite measure up to her twenty-five hundred dollar Versace ensemble. I looked ridiculous next to her! We looked like Mutt and Jeff as we drove down the highway. She was the beautiful friend who was bringing the "sweet" friend along. I decided to make the best of it, though. I mean I couldn't have the baby and lose the weight before the game, so there was no sense in worrying about not being svelte! Lauren cheered me up by telling me funny stories and pushed that Rolls to 110 to get us to the stadium in time for me to do the interview. I'll never forget that game, though!"

I was laughing so hard at McKenna. She made me feel so comfortable, made me forget my own insecurities, and helped me through that first year. Eventually, she became one of my best friends, the wisest of our group, the one we younger wives looked to for guidance and support. Her patience with us was inexhaustible.

She spent many an hour counseling us younger wives when we had stupid questions, like "What do you do if somebody's mistress strikes up a conversation at a game? Do you walk away or answer her?" or "What should we wear to the Christmas party?" or "What is the best way to get to Soldier Field?" We drove her crazy, I'm sure, but she never acted like we were a bother.

We all aspired to one day to have the grace of McKenna Winslow. She *was* the perfect wife, perfect mother, and the perfect friend. As we became closer friends, she revealed her life-before-football to me one lazy afternoon over ocean-side margaritas in Sanibel, Florida at a charity golf tournament. And I learned about her Midwestern childhood and relationship with Beau, as well as her feelings about their family and football.

McKenna Morrisey was born in Oklahoma City, Oklahoma in 1959. She lived on the upper-middle-class North Side, where her neighbors were Oklahoma City's rich factory owners. In a town where your address determined your social standing, and a North

Side salary could buy the best house, the best clothes and the best food Oklahoma had to offer, McKenna's family prospered.

Oklahoma life was a simple existence, but the differences were many between the north and south sides of town. The factory workers lived on the poorer south side where people lived in cookie-cutter tract homes, drove pick-up trucks and wore Wrangler jeans.

North and southside teenagers even partied differently on the weekends. Southsiders line danced to Kenny Rogers and Dolly Parton in their shiny, not-yet-broken-in leather boots, while Northsiders gathered en masse at newly paved pre-construction subdivisions on the outskirts of town, drinking cold ones and listening to the music of U2 and Rush. Southside girls proudly flaunted their bodies, wearing short denim skirts and tight blouses tied at their waists, while northside girls wore preppy shirts, designer jeans and tied long silk ribbons in their hair. Materialism and lifestyle differences between the north and southsiders were endless, but the basic societal mores of Oklahoma were shared between the two.

Church activities were a central feature in the routine of all good Oklahomans. Children attending church on Sundays and Wednesday nights became entrenched in the routine of Sunday school and church services. They were taught not to question their parents, to do as they were told, to be honest, loyal and hard-working. Boys were taught as young men to protect women, to respect and honor them as life-givers, but at the same time to keep them on a short leash. Men, as sole providers, were seen as the disciplinarians of the household.

Girls were taught that their primary role in life was to support their husbands, to be worthy mothers, a stay-at-home mom being the pinnacle of self-sacrifice. Women who chose to work were frowned upon, unless they became teachers. Teaching was an ideal job, a middle-of-the-road compromise between men who wanted their wives home and women who wanted to work. Teaching enabled mothers to spend quality time during the summers with their children. And during the school year, they were finished by 3:30 p.m., which meant they would have time to take their children home and fix a full meal for their hard-working husband.

McKenna represented the ideal of a young Oklahoma girl. Always striving to do what she was told, she wanted to be a teacher. She was popular with everyone, made good grades, was an acolyte in her church, and a candy-striper at the local hospital. She dated, but never, ever had sex, even with her steady boyfriend, because she believed in saving herself for her dream husband. She believed in everything she had been taught, living a "Simon-says" life, until she went to college.

McKenna first saw Beau their freshman year on OU's campus in 1978 while she was studying late one night in the library. Beau had come over and put his books on the end of her table and asked if he could share the space with her. She didn't know it then, but Beau had already spotted her on campus, and thinking she was beautiful, had been too nervous to approach her. He felt he needed an angle to meet her, and he had been planning on "running into" her at the library for two days.

Instead of studying, Beau and McKenna struck up a conversation and McKenna found herself immediately drawn to him. She sensed that Beau was different and was intrigued by his sad eyes that betrayed his cheerful voice. Later, they left the library and went to McKenna's apartment where they stayed up until dawn. The sunlight creeping through her window shade was the signal that Beau should go back to his dorm room. But even after he had left, McKenna couldn't stop thinking about him.

By the end of McKenna's freshman year, she and Beau were *the* couple on campus. The sorority girl and the football player. They were completely devoted to each other, and McKenna became one of the few people in Beau's life that he allowed himself to trust and love. McKenna told me that it took a long time for Beau to reveal his past and explain to her why he and his mother weren't close.

McKenna and I hadn't realized we had been talking in the sun for so long. I was now a ripe shade of pink and freckles had blossomed on her legs. The time had slipped away because I had been so engrossed in her story. I was glad her childhood had been normal and somewhat similar to my own. So many of our other friends had suffered atrocities as children, and I remarked to her that I was glad to hear she had no skeletons.

"I know. It's really sad that so many of our friends had such difficult pasts. The longer Beau plays, the more I am convinced that one spouse out of every couple has had a dysfunctional past. That is certainly the case with us. You wouldn't believe the things that happened to Beau as a child. What really amazes me is that he's normal today," she said to me. "I'll tell you all about it tomor-row. It'd take too long now, and if we sit our here any longer, your skin's gonna' fall off!" So, we packed our belongings and headed back to the air-conditioned hotel.

I've always been a glutton for punishment when it comes to the sun, and that next day was no exception. I had parked myself in a beach chair by 10:00 a.m., this time with a little more sunscreen, and was joined by McKenna, daiquiris in hand, by 11:00. We chatted about the previous night's dinner and wondered if our husbands were having fun at the annual "Bears in Florida" golf tournament in which they were playing. This was our third year to attend the event and I enjoyed it because the wives had an opportunity to lounge by the ocean and talk. We weren't hurried for time like we were in the wives' room at the games and it was a much more relaxed environment. McKenna started talking about Beau's childhood before the sun had hit its apex.

It was the summer of 1965, a dark, warm night and the loud music pulsating from Joe's Juke House woke the sleeping child on the back seat of the car. The little boy rubbed his eyes, con-fused with his surroundings having fallen asleep in his small bed at home, and wailed, "Mama, Mama, where are you?" The scared youth began to cry when his mother didn't appear to comfort him. He didn't know what to do. The five and a half year old was as afraid of leaving the car to find his mother as he was of staying in the dark back seat. He began to sob.

By the time Margaret Winslow staggered out of the bar at 3:30 a.m., with her feet aching from dancing, little Beau had already cried himself back to sleep in the car's back seat. It hadn't even crossed Margaret's mind that leaving her child, alone and asleep in the car while she got drunk and danced with strangers, was irresponsible. No, with the tenacity of a professional tracker, Margaret was consumed with finding another husband, and Beau was getting in the way of her hunt. Like tonight, when she wanted to get a drink and dance a little, she couldn't because Beau was already asleep in his room. That's when she decided to just take him with her. "What difference would it make if he slept in the car instead of his bed? He is so young, he won't remember this," she reasoned to herself.

This scenario was typical of Margaret's treatment of the child. Beau had been a mistake, unplanned and unwanted by Margaret. There were only two people who truly loved little Beau Winslow, and one of them, his father, William, was scared off by Margaret by the time Beau was a year old. The other was his grandmother Savannah Winslow, and if it weren't for her love and guidance in rearing Beau, he would have never made it past high school, much less been named an academic All-American at Oklahoma.

Grandmother Winslow loved baby Beau and it pained her to witness Margaret's neglect of the infant. But William begged her not to interfere, as if he were scared of Margaret. But when the baby was one year old and Margaret had driven William out of her life, Savannah tried to convince Margaret that Beau would be better off in a stable environment. But Margaret wouldn't listen.

So for the first six years of Beau's life, Grandmother Winslow was on the outside, helping Beau when she could and visiting him every time Margaret would allow. Grandmother Winslow cared for Beau when her good-for-nothing daughter-in-law disappeared and left Beau alone in an empty house with no food, or was too drunk to pick him up from school.

In 1966, with Beau in the car, Margaret was arrested for speeding while under the influence of alcohol. After hearing all of the evidence which proved Margaret an unfit mother, the court legally made Savannah Winslow Beau's guardian. She took him under her wing, and for the first time in his life Beau felt the warmth and safety of a loving home. The insecurities Margaret had created in the seven year old took time to heal, but with the strong love of "Granny 'Lo," as Beau lovingly referred to Savannah, he recovered. She taught him everything he learned from the second to the twelfth grade. She taught him what it meant to love selflessly, was there from the time he kicked his first football, made his favorite foods daily and washed his dirty clothes. She *was* his mother in his eyes.

Beau had a good life with Savannah. Margaret left them alone much of the time, sending post cards infrequently from the different places she drifted. He saw his mother once or twice a year. However, his dad visited often from his home about thirty miles away, and they developed a good if distant relationship.

Beau's love of football began with the gift of a ball from his dad. He and his dad played endlessly with that ball in Savannah's back yard on Sundays, and the two adults had held countless balls for Beau as he practiced kicking over the power lines in the yard. He was a natural athlete with a special feel for the ball. He knew where to kick it, how hard to kick into the wind, and how to put a spin on it to make it go where he wanted. It didn't take a genius to see that the child had a knack for kicking field goals. With years of practice, Beau went from being one of the best kickers in the county to one of the best kickers in the country.

By the time Beau was in the tenth grade, college football scouts from all four corners of the United States began recruiting him. By the end of his eleventh grade year, Beau had set and broken most of the kicking records in the state of Oklahoma. And William and Savannah had been at every game and rejoiced over every record attained. Beau was on his way to earning a full ride at the college of his choice, and Savannah couldn't have been more proud of him. When Beau finally made his decision to attend Oklahoma University, he couldn't wait to tell Savannah that he was staying close to home, so he could be close to her.

Beau opened his grandmother's back door like he had thou-sands of times before, but never with this much excitement. Beau knew that Savannah would be so happy that he had chosen a nearby school. She had been afraid he would go far away, making it difficult for her to visit frequently. But since OU was only a thirty-minute drive away, he could see her anytime. He wanted to share his moment of success with the one person who had made it happen. Savannah was the person who taught Beau to strive to be the best, but to temper his competitiveness with compassion. She was the one person who would understood how far he had come.

"Granny 'Lo" he began calling as his feet hit the well-trod back step. When he didn't see her downstairs, he yelled up the old staircase. "Granny 'Lo, come on down here. I have something important to tell you!" He was so excited he could hardly contain himself. He was so eager to share this moment with his grandmother.

"Oh, there you are. I thought you were upstairs. Why didn't you answer?" he asked his grandmother, who was sitting in her rocker, back to the door, facing the television set.

As Beau rounded the side of her favorite knitting chair with the biggest, proudest smile on his face and looked into her tranquil face and closed eyes, he knew immediately that she had passed into another world.

"No, no, no, no, noooooooooo. NNNNNOOOOOO!" he screamed as he shook her as if to wake her up. When she didn't stir, he knew his worst nightmare had come true. In this strange world of opposites, he had experienced extreme happiness and extreme sorrow almost concurrently. Sobbing and falling to his knees, he clasped her tired, worn and calloused hands.

"Oh Granny 'Lo, why today? Why? This isn't fair, God! Do you hear me? This isn't fair! She had a right to know that I made it! That everything she taught me made a difference. That I got the scholarship I wanted. That I am going to make it because of her. Why did you have to take her now?" Beau cried over and over, harder and harder.

After what seemed like a very long time, he composed himself. Looking at her sweet, peaceful face, he said, "Granny 'Lo, I know that you can hear me. I want you to know that I love you more than anything in this world. I want to thank you, Granny, for all of the sacrifices you made for me. You loved me when nobody else wanted me, and you made me feel safe and warm when nobody else cared. You taught me well. You were the best mother anyone could have. And I'll never let you down, ever. Everything I do from now on will be to honor your memory. I got the scholarship to Oklahoma today and I am going to make you proud," and with that said, Beau Winslow, straightening his youthful body from the floor beside his grandmother, walked as a man to place the 911 call.

McKenna finished her story by saying that Beau still had a hole in his heart over the death of Savannah. She told me she had held him many nights after a game-winning kick in an attempt to comfort his sorrow that his grandmother hadn't been there to share the victory.

"But she was there, Beau," McKenna would whisper to him, "she saw everything and I know she is proud of you. You know, I'll bet 'ole Granny was the one who blew that short-kicked ball through those uprights!" McKenna told me she would try to tease Beau out of his dark mood. And I knew that she probably did because McKenna could charm a snake out of its skin.

McKenna told me that by the time she and Beau were seniors, they had become engaged and dedicated their lives to making each other happy. McKenna had grown into a free-thinking woman, sifting through her childhood teachings and only keeping the ones she felt applied to the mature McKenna. She had learned it was okay to be something other than a teacher, just as she had realized she didn't have to go to church every day to love and respect God. She appreciated people for what they were and no longer worried about being judged by others. She and Beau drew their strength from each other, and their marriage in 1981, which was just prior to their move to Chicago and Beau's first year with the Bears, was the happiest day of their lives.

I now had even more respect for Beau. To survive what he did was a miracle. I asked, "Does he even talk to his mom, now?"

"Not really," McKenna responded. "He hasn't seen her in a long time. It's best for everybody if they keep their distance. Margaret had to be the worst mother-in-law on the face of this earth. She was so mean to me and was always complaining about something. Whenever I hear somebody griping about their mother-in-law, I just laugh because Beau's mother would make *anybody's* look like Mother Theresa. You wouldn't believe how it all ended between them..."

In November of 1983, the telephone rang loudly, interrupting the Winslow's dinner and *Miami Vice.*

"Oh, McKenna, I was hoping Beau would answer," Beau's mother said rudely.

Instead of responding "Yeah, well I wish he would have answered, too," which is what she really wanted to say, McKenna said, "Hold on just a sec, Margaret, I'll get Beau." Without any further conversation, she handed the phone to her husband.

"Hi, Mom. How are you?" Beau asked, rolling his eyes, anticipating the question before it was even asked. "Sure, how much do you need this time? I'll overnight you five hundred tomorrow. That should cover the rest that you owe on the rent and the two hundred for your car insurance." There was a pause, then, "Yeah, sure. No problem. Yeah, I'm glad I play football too, mom. But one day you're gonna' hafta learn to stand on your own two feet. What if I wasn't here to bail you out?" Pause. "Sure, I'll send you a ticket. Okay. McKenna will pick you up from the airport. No, remember to bring the coat that we bought you last year. It's cold here now. Alright. 'Bye," and as Beau hung up the receiver his appetite was gone.

Turning to McKenna, he said, "Which do you want first? The bad news or the good news?"

McKenna groaned because there was never any good news from Margaret Simmons, Beau's three-time married mom. But she managed, "Tell me the bad first."

"Well, she's coming in for this weekend's game and you have to pick her up at the airport, which means you have to tolerate her by yourself until I get home from practice. However, the good news is that she only needed five hundred dollars this time, not her usual thousand," Beau said, smiling comically, rustling McKenna's hair, trying to make light of the situation.

"Uuuuugggggghhhh," McKenna said. "You know Beau, it's not so much the money as it is the fact that she *never* calls you just to tell you that she loves you or to wish you luck before a game. She only calls you when she needs something or when she wants money. I just don't get that. How can she treat her only child that way? I doubt that she even feels bad about asking for the money."

"I know. I know. I don't understand why I feel obligated to her. I just do. I guess I just do what she wants because she's my mother. But, I promise I'm going to talk to her about the money. This weekend. I promise." And Beau Winslow meant it. This weekend, his mother was going to have to answer some tough questions about his past if she wanted to stay in their future.

McKenna patiently waited for Margaret Mason Winslow Randolph Simmons at Chicago's O'Hare airport in November of 1983. She finally saw Margaret in the distance, purposely dragging her two pieces of luggage in an attempt to solicit McKenna's assistance. McKenna left the warm refuge of her car to help her mother-in-law manage the bags and shivered as the cold, blustery wind forced itself into her pores.

"Hello, Margaret. How are you?" McKenna kindly asked as she lightly embraced her mother-in-law.

"Oh, alright, I guess, considering my new job stinks. I don't want to work anymore. You know, I thought when Beau was drafted and started making so much money, he would take care of me," she said, already starting her usual tirade. McKenna had to bite her tongue in an attempt to control her anger at Margaret's attitude.

Margaret continued, "You know, I saw his salary the other day in the newspaper and I can't believe he makes so much money. You'd think he'd have bought me a new house by now. I mean the car he got me last year was nice and all, but I would really like a new house. I'm going to talk to him about it tomorrow."

McKenna wanted to tell Margaret that the newspaper salary was pre-tax, that Beau really only pocketed half of what was printed. But instead, McKenna remained silent and tried to tune out Margaret like a bad song on the radio.

McKenna wished that she could kick Margaret's ass right back to Oklahoma. When Beau had needed her the most, during his childhood and even after Savannah died, Margaret had remained absent, not even showing up for Savannah's funeral. She didn't even try to contact Beau until every newspaper in the country predicted him to be a first-round pick and celebrated him as one of the most talented kickers to ever enter the NFL draft. As soon as Margaret sniffed the money trail, she reared her ugly head in her son's life. Poor Beau had been so confused by her new-found affection he didn't allow himself to see her underlying reasons.

And for the last two years, she had been milking Beau. The more he gave her, the more she wanted. In the last year, Beau had bought her a car, sent her more than ten thousand dollars in cash and had bailed her out of jail twice.

McKenna wanted to be supportive of Beau's relationship with his mother, and could have even tolerated some of the money-giving, but it was so obvious that Margaret didn't really care about Beau's needs or his feelings. She didn't care about mending the wounds of the past or trying to make up for lost time and love. It was painfully obvious to McKenna that Margaret didn't care about anybody or anything but herself. She even had the audacity to still remind Beau of what an inconvenience he had been to her. McKenna had never met a more vile person in her entire life. She had just recently started voicing her opinion about Margaret, trying to help Beau see the truth. But McKenna knew that it was going to get a lot worse before it got better.

When Beau walked in the door from practice, he expected to hear the incessant chatter of his estranged mother. But instead, there was silence. He found McKenna upstairs, crying in their bedroom.

"I can't take any more of your mother, Beau. You won't believe what she wants now. Her greed is getting out of control. I think that she needs to be the one to tell you what she told me. She's in her room. Please resolve this mess one way or another. You know I will support you in whatever you decide," McKenna told him, swollen-eyed.

Beau's mother had been prepared for this meeting. She even had the copy of the newspaper that had published his salary. "Beau, I came here this weekend because I want something from you," she began. "You make a lot of money and there is no reason that I can't share in that wealth. I want *you* to buy me a new house. I have already picked one out and I just need the downpayment. The house is $235,000 which I don't think is that expensive considering what you made last year. If you'll write me the check, I can leave now. I don't need to stay for the game."

Beau had always kept the rage he felt toward his mother safely tucked away. He didn't want to remember the horrible feelings of abandonment and unworthiness. Those insecurities had taken years of Savannah's love to heal, and he wasn't going to let Margaret What-ever-her-last-name-was-now do this to him again. When he confessed to McKenna months ago that he felt guilty for feeling no love toward his mother and for wanting to deny her never-ending requests, she had uttered a phrase that Beau now repeated to his mother.

"Mom, you can pick your friends, but you can't pick your family. I sure as hell wouldn't have picked you to give birth to me, because that is all you did. And the act of giving birth doesn't make you a mother. A mother earns that title through years of love and caring for her child. You never lifted a finger for me. You didn't raise me, were never there for me, were taken to jail because of what you did to me, and if it hadn't been for the love of Granny 'Lo, I would probably be in jail myself. You have never done anything for me that didn't have a string attached. So I'm going to make this real simple. I'm cutting all ties between us. Pack your bags. You are going back to the airport. Do not ever call me, write me or bother me again. It's time I made you feel like you've always made me feel. Unwanted. You have five minutes to meet me in the car."

As Beau turned to leave, Margaret screamed, "Oh, I'll show you, mister. You *owe* me! I'm your mother! I'm calling *Geraldo* when I get home. I'll bet he'd love to have a show on rich boys who treat their mothers like dirt! I'll expose you. I'll call the *Tribune* and the *Sun-Times*. I know they'd like to hear what I have to say. You'll never be able to hold your head up again in this town for leaving me to starve on the street!"

"You know what? You do just that! I don't care anymore. I have never done anything to you but treat you with undeserved respect and give you money! If you think I'm bad because I won't buy you a house and tolerate your shit anymore, then you go right ahead and call the *President* for all I care! Get out of my house this instant! You are no longer welcome here. And you can wait for your cab outside on the sidewalk. If you're lucky, the next time I see you will be at your grave!"

Beau called the cab company and within thirty minutes, Margaret Simmons was out of his life forever. She never tried to "expose" him because there was nothing bad to reveal. McKenna and Beau's lives were finally tranquil and they could move ahead without emotional turmoil. Beau was at peace with himself because he had tried. He had bent over backwards trying to please his ungrateful mother, wanting nothing from her in return but love. She just didn't have any to give.

But McKenna had plenty to give, and during the next eight years, she and Beau increased their family by two. In 1984, William Beau Winslow took his first breath, and in 1988, Savannah Katherine Winslow, named for her much-loved great-grandmother, made her worldly appearance. And Beau and McKenna established themselves in Chicago's prominent society. They headed charities, joined the school PTO, went to every game and recital of which Billy and Savannah were a part, and fell even more deeply in love. They had both finally found what they deserved in life.

As McKenna finished their story, I was yet again amazed at some of my friends' inner strength. Thank God Beau had found McKenna. She was the backbone he needed and filled the void that Grandmother Winslow's death had caused. But most importantly, McKenna would never allow anyone to treat Beau poorly again.

♦♦♦♦♦

"I'm sorry to tell you this, William, but it really doesn't look good. The cancer has spread to your pancreas. The experimental treatment didn't stop the growth like we had hoped. It only slowed it. I am so sorry," the white-coated doctor gently broke the news to his friend, William Winslow, Beau's father. The two friends embraced in their sorrow, not as doctor and patient, but as mortal men realizing the frailty of the human condition.

It was October of 1992, and as William stared out the office window at the cold Pacific Ocean, choppy and white-capped, he had but one thought. "I don't want to die in the winter. I want to live to see the birth of spring with the sun beaming brightly and children playing on the beach, feeling sand between their toes for the first time. I want to smell my roses from the garden at the

Claybourne and feel the soft, new grass under my feet just one more time."

"How long do I have? I want to know," William asked the most difficult question of his fifty-eight years.

"These things are never certain, William. Just last week, a patient who I thought wouldn't make it three months, passed two years after I had told her the parameters of her illness. So I don't want you to treat this like it's an absolute. But, it's my estimation that you have six months to a year. With medication and blood transfusions, you should be comfortable. However, if you want to do any travelling or take any kind of trips, do it now before you become too weak. Again, I'm sorry William."

As William Winslow left the medical center, he knew where his final trip would take him. He would go to Chicago and watch his only child play football. How could he have let so much time come between them? Even though they spoke weekly on the phone, it had been so long since he had put his arms around his son and told him that he loved him and was proud of his accomplishments. He also realized that now was the time to confront the past, and explain to Beau why he had left so many years ago. He needed to answer Beau's unasked questions about his childhood and his mother, William's ex-wife. William Winslow had spent the better part of his life hiding these facts from his son, but it was time to face the truth because his life-clock was pealing.

"Son? Hi! How was practice this week? I caught the Buffalo game on satellite last weekend. Great game! I was really proud of that forty-five yarder you kicked. And into the wind!" William wanted to sound happy. He had decided not to break the horrible news of his pancreatic cancer over the phone.

"Dad, it's so good to hear your voice. I've been thinking about you lately. How's the inn doing?" Beau asked.

"It's doing well, Beau. I wish that you and McKenna could come out here with Savannah and Billy. They would love it," William said, knowing he would never live to see his grandchildren playing in the halls of the prosperous bed-and-breakfast he had worked so hard to restore.

"Hey, do you think you can come out for a game this year? I'd really like to see you. And you need a break from that great weather," Beau said, laughing. He always teased his dad about the move from Oklahoma to California. But Beau was glad for his dad's happiness.

"You know, that's why I called. Is it okay if I come this week-end? I know it's short notice, but I really want to see you."

"We'd love to have you come this weekend, dad. It should be a good game to see, too. The Lions have been playing really well this year. Did you know they have a new quarterback? Hey, if you come on Thursday, we can make a whole weekend of it," Beau said excitedly. His enthusiasm warmed William's heart.

"That would be wonderful, Beau. Thanks son. And tell Savannah and Billy that I'll have surprises for them."

When William hung up the phone, his shoulders closed in around his chest. He hung his head and sobbed. Everything that he had found so late in life was soon to be gone. He didn't want to leave his son or the inn he had grown to love. There was so much more that he wanted to do with his son and grandchildren. There were so many memories he wouldn't live to see. Life didn't seem fair as William looked out at his rose garden, but those were the cards he had been dealt. He willed himself to make the best of it.

By the time Beau kicked off, starting Sunday's game, William still hadn't disclosed his illness. He had always been a proud, strong man, and even though he had tried several times, he just couldn't find the right words to reveal his cancer or express his emotions. Maybe his loss for words stemmed from the fact that the weekend had been so glorious, so laughter-filled and light-hearted. He didn't want to spoil the mood. How do you tell some-one you love that you are going to die? How do you tell your only son that his birth and life made yours worth living?

By the fourth quarter, as McKenna passed him popcorn and a soda, he decided that his death would be a solitary affair. He didn't want to pain his son's beautiful family any more than he had to. There was nothing they could do to help him anyway, and he didn't want them to feel an obligation to come west to be with him. He resolved to explain everything to Beau in a conclusive, explanatory letter. Beau would then understand how much he was loved, that he hadn't been abandoned willingly long ago, and that the inn must live on through him. It was going to take all of the strength William had left in his quickly weakening body to accomplish this most important task. But at least now he had decided how it would all end.

Content with his decision, he now focused on the game, breathing the cold, invigorating lake air of Soldier Field. As he watched his son approach the middle of the dirt terrain for the last time, he was overcome with pride in what a fine gentleman Beau had become. And as Beau kicked the last field goal, and turned to wave victoriously to his dad in the stands, William Winslow knew that his life *had* been for something and was now complete.

McKenna called me early one morning in late July of 1993. She was crying and asked if I would ride with her to Platteville, to training camp, because she had to break the news of William's death to Beau. She knew his death would be such a shock to Beau that she didn't want to do it over the phone. During our two-hour ride, she told me that neither she nor Beau even knew William had been sick.

"I have no idea how I'm going to tell him this, Sally, because it will come as such a surprise. I've never had to do anything like this before, and I am so scared. I want to cry, but I know that I have to be strong for Beau," McKenna said, looking pale and worried.

"McKenna, I don't really know what to tell you, because I've never had to break that kind of news to anybody either. But I do know one thing: you *always* know how to do things the right way and you are one of the most compassionate and caring individuals I have ever known. So, I know that when the time comes, you'll find the fitting words," I said, trying to give her the confidence for which she was searching.

Beau looked forward to each day of the Bear's training camp in July of 1993. Whereas the days of the previous twelve camps Beau had participated in had been long and tiring, he felt invigorated by his thirteenth camp. Beau knew that every camp from now on could be his last, and instead of feeling relief at his accomplishments and looking forward to the day he would retire, Beau instead worked harder, desiring that roster spot more than ever. He was the first one on the practice fields in the morning and usually the last player to head for the dining hall. He had even worked out almost every day of the off-season, feeling stronger and more healthy than when he had been a rookie.

Beau knew the odds were finally catching up with him, but he wasn't ready to give it up and be a mere number in the crowd. He needed this job to ensure his family's security. Even though he had been a successful kicker for twelve years, kickers weren't the highest paid starters, and he needed this last year to meet his financial goals.

Beau was practicing field goals with the special teams unit when his coach whistled practice to a stop and called him to the sidelines. McKenna was standing to the coach's side and looked distraught.

"God please don't let it be one of the kids," Beau thought as he approached her.

"What's wrong McKenna?" he asked as they walked away from the crowd of players and coaches.

"Oh, Beau, I'm so sorry, but something terrible has happened. I think we better go to your room," McKenna gently told him.

"Is it one of the kids?" he quickly asked.

"No, they're fine. I have a sitter watching them for the day."

"Well, what is it then, McKenna? Just tell me out here," Beau desperately wanted answers.

"It's your dad, Beau. He passed away this morning. I got a call from the doctor who had been treating his cancer," McKenna began.

"His *cancer?* There must be some mistake, McKenna, because *dad* doesn't have cancer. My God, he would have *told* us. There has to be a mistake! I mean, I just talked to him four days ago and he was fine," Beau was confused, hoping McKenna was somehow wrong.

"I said the same thing to the doctor, Beau. He had told your dad to tell us months ago, but your dad just couldn't. He said your dad didn't want to upset us. Apparently he had known that he was dying for eight months. I'm sorry, Beau. I don't know what to say. I know you really loved your dad," McKenna opened her mouth to speak but couldn't utter another sound.

"I can't believe he's really dead. Why didn't he tell us? There are so many things I wanted to ask him, and so many things I wanted to tell him. And now I'll never have the chance. I just can't believe this! Why would he leave this way?" Beau was confused almost to the point of anger, and shocked.

By the time they mounted the stairs in front of Beau's dorm, the finality of the truth had settled in and Beau's attention turned to the funeral arrangements.

"Did the doctor mention any wishes my dad had for his funeral? I mean, I don't even know if he wants to be buried out there or in Oklahoma. What are we supposed to do?" Beau asked McKenna, wiping tears from his eyes.

"The doctor told me that your dad made all of the funeral arrangements months ago, when he found out he was sick, and he planned everything down to the type of casket he wanted. He didn't want us to worry over those details. He wants to be buried in some small cemetery overlooking the ocean near Monterey. He told the doctor that his last wish was for you to attend his funeral. You need to call the doctor yourself because he can tell you much more than I. As soon as he told me the sketchy facts, I stopped him so I could drive up here to tell you. Here's his number," explained McKenna as she dug through her purse in search of the long distance number.

Beau called William's doctor and received confirmation of the horrible news. The doctor told Beau that the cancer had been incurable, but his dad had put up a good fight. When he finally succumbed to the illness, he had peacefully passed in his sleep at the hospital with the doctor by his side.

"It was your dad's last wish that you come here to see him buried. He will be interred in two days, on Sunday. He made all of the arrangements himself, so you don't need to worry about any of the details," the doctor told him.

"I'll be there. I just can't believe he's gone. We hadn't always been close, but I always loved him."

"He loved you too, Beau. He used to talk about you a lot. He gave me something he wanted you to have. An envelope. I'll give it to you on Sunday. Your father and I had been friends for years and I will miss him tremendously. He was a good man. Again, I'm sorry."

Beau hung up, sad and bewildered. Why hadn't his dad told him about the cancer? And why had he made it his last wish for Beau to come to the funeral?

Chris and I kept the Winslow children while McKenna and Beau flew out to California for William's funeral. McKenna was hopeful that the trip would answer many of the questions still surrounding his sickness and death. When she called that first night to check on the children, she filled me in on the details.

A limo had picked Beau and McKenna up from the airport. Winding along the highway heading toward Monterey, Beau felt the allure that had drawn his father here from Oklahoma. It was simply the most beautiful land he had ever seen. The powerful ocean crashing against the jagged, asymmetric rocks stirred Beau's emotions, and he was immediately sorry that he and McKenna had never made time in their busy schedules to visit William here while he was still alive.

The older limo driver told them that the Claybourne Inn was the pride of Monterey and indicated that William had done a wonderful job as its most recent proprietor.

"The finest, fanciest retreat along this strip of the California coast, the Claybourne Inn accommodated every major starlet and leading man during its heyday in the late fifties. And before the construction of high-rise luxury hotels in the sixties, the Claybourne had been *the* "in" place. It was the *only* place a well-heeled Romeo would take his Juliet for a romantic sojourn. The walls of that place held more passion, love and secrets than the old backlots at MGM," the driver informed Beau and McKenna.

He then told them that like everything else in California, the novelty and popularity of the Claybourne eventually waned. When the new luxury hotels became *en vogue*, the reservation list at the Claybourne dwindled — until Beau's dad had rebuilt it to its former splendor.

But nothing the driver said could have prepared them for the huge mansion which spilled over the top of a high bluff. It was simply the most magnificent structure either one of them had ever seen, and the location was incredible. The views from the wide porches had to be the best for miles.

"Oh my God!" was all McKenna could say, "Is *this* the inn?"

"Yes ma'am, sure is. Never seen it before?" he asked.

"No, we've never been here. I had no idea it was so big or beautiful," McKenna told the driver.

Beau was in awe. "No wonder dad loved this place so much," he said to McKenna. "He was just so modest. You know, when he talked about the inn, I thought it was a small place, sort of old. I would have never guessed it was this."

And at that moment, Beau felt a swell of pride. His dad had obviously worked his fingers to the bone for this place, but how it did show! Beau only wished now that he had shared this moment with his dad.

McKenna couldn't wait to go inside and wander from room to room. One of William's long-time borders took her on a "grand tour" while Beau met with William's doctor, who had been waiting for their arrival. McKenna couldn't believe the elegance and opulence of the old inn. There were at least ten immense suites decorated with no expense having been spared. Ocean views were visible from every upstairs window. And the five bathrooms were all marble and mirrors.

The downstairs provided the common areas of the inn. There was a carved, stately library, an ornate smoking room, a ball-room, a kitchen complete with a hearth, three ovens and two stoves, a dining room that could easily accommodate thirty and the most glorious sun porch McKenna had ever seen. It wrapped all the way around the house, leading to the well-manicured grounds and rose garden in back.

As McKenna strolled through the well-tended rose garden, she wondered how William had held this place together by himself. There were only a couple of people who had helped him with chores like grass-cutting and laundry. He had prepared all of the meals, did most of the housekeeping duties and still had time to nurture this lovely garden. McKenna thought to herself that William Winslow had been quite a man.

Beau postponed his tour of the inn when William's doctor introduced himself. Telling McKenna to go without him, he and the doctor chatted for a few minutes before the doctor gave Beau the envelope to which he had referred on the phone. The doctor then left Beau alone to read its contents.

The envelope was large and contained several pieces of paper. The first document was a letter, scrawled in William's handwriting, which Beau hoped would answer some of his questions. His eyes misted as he imagined William's hands were the last to touch the paper before sealing the envelope. He began reading....

Dear Beau,

*As I write this letter, I know you will be reading it only upon my death. Please forgive me Beau, for not telling you about the cancer. I tried when I came to see you play in October, but when I saw how happy you were with your children and your beautiful wife, I couldn't find the necessary words. I didn't want to make your life miserable, for you to wake up every morning wondering if today was **the** day. There was nothing you could do to change my fate, and I didn't want to burden you with the knowledge. I will die knowing that you love me. I only hope you know how much I love you.*

There are so many things I want and need to tell you as only a father can tell a son. And there is something that I want to give you. But first, I want to start with why I left you with your mother so many years ago. My leaving you was the biggest regret of my life and a pain I had to live with every day of my fifty-eight years, but perhaps I can try to set it right now.

I never told you this before because I didn't want you to realize what kind of person your mother really was. But since you are now a grown man, and I will be gone, you need to know the truth, even though it is hurtful.

Your mother was beautiful and kind when I met her. She captured my heart the first time I saw her, and I quickly came to love her. We married soon thereafter, and I was very happy. We made plans for the future, and I fell in love with her more each day.

But I didn't know who she really was until I came home from work one day and found her sitting in our kitchen with another man — there was just something about the way they were sitting together, so intimate. I knew then that she was in love with him, not me.

There was a scene, I won't describe it, but it turned out that the man was her long-time love, and together they had planned to scam a fool-in-love out of his money. She told me that she never loved me. I was crushed. I realized that I had never meant anything to Margaret. Our whole relationship had just been a game to her.

She told me that she would give me a quick divorce if I paid her ten thousand dollars. Her original scheme had been to steal money from our checking account in small amounts over a year and a half's time, sending it to her waiting "friend". But when I caught them together, she just wanted out. I had planned to give her the money just to get her out of my life, and she planned to go back to her first love. But then she discovered she was pregnant with my child, you, and he wouldn't take her back.

He was outraged — sleeping with me had obviously not been part of his plan, at least. He told her to stay with me, that he didn't love her anymore. She was devastated, and I didn't know what to do. I almost felt sorry for her. I knew she didn't love me, but I felt an obligation to her because of you. So I stayed with her until your birth.

I wanted so badly to be a part of your life and growing up years. You will never know, son. But she told me that she wanted me to leave, that if I didn't go away and let her live her life, she would disappear and take you with her. She was so crazy that I believed her. I knew if she left I would never see you again, so I went. Leaving you was the hardest thing I ever had to do.

I stayed in Oklahoma all those years just so I could be near you. She would let me see you as long as I gave her money, and that continued for seven years until she was arrested, thank

God, and my mother took you to raise. It was a wonderful privilege to be able to visit you whenever I wanted.

I guess I should have then taken you with me, but I knew that Granny 'Lo would be a better parent than I could ever be. And I knew that if I had you, your mother would never leave us alone. But always know that I loved you and thought of you every waking moment I was away from you. I only did what I thought was right. Your safety was the most important thing to me. Please forgive me, son.

Because I love you, I want to give you my most prized possession — the only other love of my life. I want you to have the Claybourne. It helped to heal the scars of my past. Repairing it room by room, floor by floor, and shingle by shingle was my therapy. I did it for you, so that I would have something worthy to give you after all of these years. I wanted to give you something to have after football, something that will last forever. I wanted you to be able to leave the game with no trepidation about the future. I wanted to provide you with the security I couldn't when you were a child.

That's why my last wish was that you would come to Monterey for my funeral. Since you had never been here, I was afraid you would just sell the inn without ever seeing it. It is my hope that you and McKenna will keep it, run it, and pass it to Billy when he is a man.

I hope this letter has answered most of your questions. I'm sorry I didn't have the courage to tell you all of this face to face. Take care of McKenna, Savannah and Billy. And be assured I will always look over you, and will always be there in your heart. All you have to do is think of me. I love you.

> Dad

When Beau finished the letter, thirty-three years of sadness swept over him. So many thoughts and emotions tumbled in his mind. He felt a burning hatred toward the woman who had given birth to him. She had been more horrible than he even imagined, and he was thankful that she was already out of his life. Now, he felt even more justified in her exclusion.

And he felt an intense love for his father. He had suffered more than Beau had ever imagined. Beau wished that he had an opportunity to tell his father that he understood, and that he didn't blame William for the choices he had made. But somehow Beau knew his father understood this.

As he looked through the rest of the envelope, he found the deed to the Claybourne Inn, and worn, yellow pictures of himself as a baby that his father must have carried for years in his wallet. Also in the envelope was a recent appraisal of the inn's value. Attached to the top of it was a note from William, telling Beau that the appraisal had been made in case Beau wanted to sell the inn.

But regardless of the monetary value, Beau knew he would never sell the Claybourne. His dad was right. The inn was something that could live on from generation to generation. It could pass from father to son, keeping the Winslow lineage alive. This was Beau's tribute to his father. It would be his legacy. He couldn't wait to find McKenna and tell her...

When McKenna got home she showed me all of their pictures of the Claybourne Inn. What an incredible place it was! She had photos of every room and of the many beautiful views. The Pacific Ocean was truly magnificent. McKenna had already told me about the letter and Beau's inheritance, but she had one piece of news that she wanted to tell me face to face. The recent events surrounding the death of Beau's father had been so sad, but when she told me her big news, my tears were of joy.

Beau wasn't the first NFL kicker to retire. But he was one of the few to retire willingly. He still couldn't believe he was leaving the game, especially not since he had worked so hard for this thirteenth camp, and his thirteenth year. But his father's gift had changed his perspective of life. He would always love the game, but his family needed him more than he needed to play football. The inn would allow them all to work together, and Beau and Billy could make the memories that had escaped Beau and William. Because Beau didn't want to miss one more precious minute of his children's lives, he left the sport that had been a comfort and a pleasure to him for so many years. He wished his father were there so he could thank him. His dad had enabled Beau to leave the NFL after twelve years with no regrets, no remorse, and only blue skies ahead.

◆ ◆ ◆ ◆ ◆

I awoke to the sun shining through the cracks of the wooden Plantation shutters. The rays formed a pattern on the quilt that adorned my mahogany rice bed. I stretched, smelled the coffee percolating downstairs and put on my robe. I had come for a couple of days to visit McKenna. It had been too long since she and I had gotten together to catch up on old times.

In the four years since Beau's retirement, the Winslows had made the Claybourne Inn one of the most popular bed-and-breakfasts on the West Coast. Prospective guests had to book rooms three to four months in advance and *Traveler* placed the Claybourne Inn on its "must stay" list.

Beau and McKenna had adjusted to life-after-football without batting an eyelash. Having the time of their lives, McKenna played hostess to all of the unique guests, preparing scrumptious meals for them every night, and Beau loved being the handyman and dinner storyteller. In finding their way to the real world, the world to which all player families must eventually adjust, they had once again set the example we all hoped to follow.

The Last Game

No athlete is crowned but in the sweat of his brow.
— Saint Jerome

I hope your journey behind the NFL curtain has been interesting and entertaining. While writing, I couldn't decide the most appropriate place to end this book. I thought about ending it in Hawaii, with the AFC's victory at the 1997 Pro Bowl. And I also thought of ending it in Anderson, Indiana, where Chris is beginning his seventh training camp. But finally, I decided it was more appropriate to end it in the room where it all began, the Wives' Room in Soldier Field.

♦♦♦♦♦

"Memories, light the corners of my mind; misty, water-colored memories, of the way we were...." Barbra crooned as I entered the Kennedy Expressway from Lake Bluff, two hours before kickoff of the last Bears game of the '94 season. Her words perfectly reflected my mood. I knew Chris would never wear the orange and blue after today, never run through the canvassed tunnel to the expanse of painted green dirt, and never look at Soldier Field through the space between Jay Leeuwenburg's legs from which the punts were snapped. I knew my experiences in the big-shouldered town of Chicago were dimming, closing around me, and Barbra's plaintive voice pulled at the strings of my heart.

On this last trip to the hundred yards of turf beside the mighty lake, I had no fears of getting lost or missing the game or finding the safe harbour of my parking space under Soldier Field. Nor did I have any naked, smiling escorts on Interstate 94 to divert my attention and make me laugh. No, my only companion in the car was my memory, and during the long forty-five minute drive from Lake Bluff to downtown, I thought about other people's "last games." I thought about friends who hadn't made the team, friends who had made the team but were later cut, friends who were forced to retire because of injuries, and the women behind all of these men. And as each of their faces popped into my mind, I was forced to acknowledge their legacies once more.

◆◆◆◆◆

Chris' college roommate and fellow draft pick in 1991 was one of the first to occupy the front seat of the car with me. "Tony" had been one of the best offensive linemen to enter the NFL draft in 1991. Winning many college honors, including the Jacobs Blocking Trophy, a roster spot on the All-American squad, and appearing with Bob Hope on television, Tony was a sure bet for the NFL. He was a workhorse who was good-natured and big-hearted, and he and Chris had been elated when they were drafted together by Coach Ditka.

I'll never forget the day they left South Carolina to follow their NFL dream. It was raining, a typical April morning, and as I stood waving goodbye to them, watching their packed cars drive away from me to begin the twelve-hour trip to Chicago, I wanted so much for both of them. They were everything that was young and good in this world, and they deserved to succeed. No longer under the protective umbrella of Clemson's athletic program, they were entering the world as men, leaving their boyish ideals behind. They could feel the brass ring tickling their fingertips.

Tony's first practice with the Bears his rookie year, however, would be his last. He suited up and took the field with the other offensive linemen. Under the seasoned eye of line coach Dick Stanfel, Tony wanted to perform well, to impress upon Stanfel and Ditka that he was worthy of their consideration. On the first snap of practice, however, another player accidentally rolled into Tony's knee.

That was the end of Tony's career.

Tony re-habbed during the '91 season, but was never able to don the uniform of the Bears. His dream ended before it had even started. I felt his presence in the car, forcing me to remember his game that never was.

♦♦♦♦♦

"Steve" was also along for the ride that day. Steve and his wife, "Lynne," were two of our best friends in Chicago and we were excited when Steve had an opportunity to finally start at his position in 1993. No one ever wants to see a starter injured, but unfortunately, injury is the most common way a second-stringer is afforded a chance to play. Steve was coming into a situation less than perfect because he had not had as much practice as the starter, and it would be tricky getting snap counts and signal calling in rhythm with only one week's practice. But that is the story of every second-stringer. The conditions are never going to be perfect, but perfection is nonetheless expected.

On game-day Sunday, it was raining and as nasty as I had seen it in two years. The field looked like it had just hosted a Monster truck drag-racing exhibition. After the first series by both teams, the white ten-yard lines were sucked into the brown muck, leaving first downs to the guesswork of the field officials. The game stunk. No matter how hard Steve tried, he had to throw off his back foot, or worse, his back, into traffic. Steve had no protection and was driven into the snowy, wet mush over and over again. Even though he almost cut off the tip of his finger on a defender's helmet, he didn't stop trying. I could hear his voice getting raspier with every snap count, full of frustration and exasperation. Nothing worked. We lost. And I could feel his disappointment radiating into the stands.

There is nothing a wife can say to comfort another wife whose husband has suffered a bad game. Any time Chris has an "off game," I try to speak to people before they can speak to me and let them know I am okay. But because one bad game can be a player's last, wives don't feel the necessity to chatter after a game. No, after a bad game, a thin, pressed-lip smile is the common speaking courtesy.

The day after the game, I called Lynne. "I'm sorry, Lynne. He'll get another chance. *Nobody* could have played any better in that shitty weather. And the field was a joke. Further, it's not Steve's fault that he had what, one and a half seconds to drop back and throw the ball? Surely, they'll start him again."

My friend, who had shared with me the laughter and tears of this two-year roller coaster ride responded, "That *was* his chance, Sally. It's gone now. It doesn't matter how everyone else played. *You* know that. And you know that he probably won't get another chance."

No words came to my mouth because there wasn't anything else to say. I knew that she was right.

The Bears cut Steve after that season and Chris and I lost some of the best friends we ever had in football. I was driving in my car, back from my health club, listening to the radio when I heard they had released him. I pulled off the road, into the nearest parking lot, and cried. Hard. "Sonofabitch, sonofabitch, sonofabitch" was all that ran through my head. Steve and Lynne were good people. She was pregnant with their first child. Why was this happening? Never again would we go to their house for Thanksgiving or Christmas dinners. Never again would everybody sit around their kitchen table playing "Balderdash" or "Taboo." The group of wives who watched away games together would never again be complete, because the circle had been irreparably broken. In our group of wives, this was the first cut, and it was too close to home.

My mind raced in the parking lot. I couldn't understand why it seemed like *everybody* got spit out of this system, kicked hard in the ass, after giving it their all. Why couldn't life freeze in time, when we were on the top of the world, young and strong, and stay there indefinitely? Why *must* all good things come to an end?

◆ ◆ ◆ ◆ ◆

As I thought about Steve's departure, I was at least thankful that he hadn't left on a stretcher like "Erik." Erik suddenly squeezed Steve out of the car as I remembered his last game in Soldier Field. It would be the last of his NFL career. Erik was a star running back, in his first season with the Bears, and was having a great year. He had previously been with a contending AFC team and was an integral part of their offense. He was the ripest plum picked from the free agency crop in 1994.

It had been a normal play. No tricks. No gimmicks. The ball was handed off to Erik and the pigskin disappeared under his strong arm. He ran upfield and then vanished into a pack of men. One by one, the men clambered off the pile. Erik didn't move. Seconds passed. Erik still didn't move. "Marla," his beautiful wife, sat directly behind me.

"Is he okay?" I asked her, knowing that some couples have signals, like a hand wave, when a player goes down to let his wife know that he isn't badly injured.

"I don't know. He's still down. Get up, Erik. Get up. Come on, get up!" she was whispering, willing her husband to move.

The team doctor ran onto the field. After working with Erik for what seemed like an eternity, Erik came off the field by stretcher, and was taken immediately into the locker room.

"I'm sure he'll be fine, Marla. The doctor is with him. He'll be okay." I tried to reassure her.

About five minutes later, one of the trainers came to my seat. "Sally, where does Marla sit? We need her down in the locker room. It doesn't look good." The trainer, who was usually jovial and fun, was very solemn.

"Umm, she's right behind me." I responded, knowing that Marla had heard the whole exchange.

He looked up at her and said, "Sorry. You need to come with me, Marla."

She left her seat and followed him. We all knew it must be bad. In the four years I had been in Chicago, personnel had *never* come to the wives' section to retrieve a wife after a player injury. All of the wives anxiously watched the tunnel after Marla left, hoping to catch a glimpse of her face, and praying she would smile and give us a "thumbs up." We all swallowed hard as we saw the hospital ambulance back into the tunnel and carry Erik away, Marla climbing into the back with him. Oh God, it *was* bad.

After the game, I tried calling Marla several times. No answer. I called other wives. Nobody knew anything yet. The next day we found out Erik had suffered another concussion, the third of his career, and it looked grim. He didn't know who Marla was nor could he recognize their toddler daughter. He didn't even remember that he played for the Bears or that he lived in Lake Bluff.

The situation was terrible. He would be forced to retire, in the prime of his career. One more blow to his head could kill him or disable his mental capabilities permanently. The only saving grace was that he had disability insurance.

For weeks, when any wives would call Marla to tell her something or drop by their townhouse during a walk, Erik was confused and didn't know who we were. It was scary to think that it would take a month or maybe longer for him to recover, and even then the doctor's weren't sure that it would be complete. All of us were shaken by his accident and reminded once again of the dangers our husbands faced daily. Thankfully, Erik recovered fully and currently enjoys a healthy career in broadcasting. But I'll never forget his last play. It is a strong and constant reminder of the ferocity of this game.

♦♦♦♦♦

"Tommy" was the next player to invade my car. In the whole of Chris' career, Tommy is one of the few players we have known who left the game of his own volition and retired at the top, while he was still respected and feared by his opponents. Although I was never personally close to Tommy or his wife "Sandi," I regarded them with admiration from afar. They were such a wonderful example for the rest of us to follow. They had a good marriage, strong family values and a handle on their life in the NFL. Always a benchmark of professionalism and class, Tommy touched the lives not only of fans but also of his peers and their families.

Soldier Field was somber the day he played his last game. During Tommy's retirement ceremony, there wasn't a dry eye in the stadium. He was recognized for all of his accomplishments on and off the field, and it was staggering to think one man had singlehandedly achieved so much. The mood would have turned even more dismal if fans had known then that this game would be

Mike Ditka's last home game as the Bears' head coach. But looking back, it somehow now seems fitting that two great Bears shared their last walk from Soldier Field to the locker room together.

As the clock ticked down the last seconds of the third quarter, I left the stands to use the restroom in the wives' room. The retirement ceremony had been touching and I kept thinking that Tommy's exit must be the dream of all NFL players. Chris had only played for two years and the ways of the NFL were still fresh to me, but even then I understood the importance of being able to leave the game when you were on top. I wondered how Tommy's wife felt. Because Sandi was one of the most regarded veteran wives, I had never felt comfortable enough to engage her in deep conversation, so I didn't really know her that well. But I was thinking about her when I heard the sound of someone softly crying.

I walked into the main television area and there sat Sandi, alone, with tears coursing her cheeks. I didn't really know what to say to her since we had never been close. I just sort of smiled. But as our eyes met, I think I understood her tears. She wasn't crying tears of sorrow. She was crying because a chapter in her life had just come to a close. She was bidding the wives' room goodbye just as a homeowner walks through his home for the last time collecting his memories, before the moving truck pulls away from the curb. The wives' room was her home, and the curb of Soldier Field was her comfort zone. Outside the stadium, in the real world, was a new territory. And new territory meant an adjustment.

All of these thoughts passed between us in the instant that I pressed my lips together in that "I understand you" look. The moment may have been unremarkable for her, but it will never leave me.

Her grace in their departure was her gift to me, an example to be followed at the end of Chris' career. After that brief exchange, I became a true veteran's wife. My initiation was complete.

◆◆◆◆◆

As I pulled underneath Soldier Field to park, all of these memories left my car, one by one, and I felt drained, even before the game had begun. So much had happened here. So much of what I had learned about life and about myself was within the parameters of this field. It was strange to think I would never be back here as a Chicago Bears' wife with that pass to the wives' room clutched in my hand.

An hour before kickoff, I walked through the tunnel, around the perimeter of the field, to the portal below the wives' room. As I looked into the sparsely-seated stands, I thought about a strange scene I had witnessed just weeks ago. Before the game against Tampa Bay, I had seen a Bucs player walking through the stadium in his uniform. In his arms he had carried delicate roses ever-so-carefully. I was mesmerized by this odd sight, a warrior dressed for combat carrying exquisite roses. I looked around and noticed Jack, an Andy Frain security guard and friend who patrolled the wives' section during the games. He was also watching the player.

I said, "Well, this is really strange. What do you think that guy is doing?"

Jack replied, "Actually, I know what he's doing. He does this every time Tampa Bay plays in Soldier Field. A few years ago, his mom was sitting in the stands over there, watching him play, and she had a heart attack. She died right there in her seat before the paramedics could get to her. I was there when they told him after the game. Every time he plays here, before the fans arrive, he comes out to the stands, to her exact seat, and in honor of her memory leaves those roses where she was sitting. Kind of touching, isn't it?"

I was stunned. I felt like an intruder on the most private moments of this player's personal life. I felt so sorry for him. How terrible it must have been for him to find out after the game that his mom had died while watching him play. I watched as he carefully placed the flowers, said a prayer and then looked heavenward. My eyes filled with tears as I prayed that he would have a good game.

Oh, the things I had seen and felt in that stadium! It was the Tilt-O-Whirl of life. And even though I knew it was time for Chris to move on, there were a lot of things I would miss. Of my friends, I would miss Stacy Mangum and Cathy Butler the most. I would miss holding their hands during punts. I would miss hugging them during victories, and I would miss their encouragement after defeats. I would miss their friendships which bordered on sister-hood.

The game seemed to pass in a millisecond of life. During the last minutes, I forced myself to memorize every detail of the stadium. Every smell in the air. Every second ticking down off the game clock. Every wives' face in the stands around me. Cara Waddle. Carla Woolford. Stacy and Cathy. They are all frozen in my mind's eye, young, laughing and carefree.

I entered the wives' room of Soldier Field and silently bade it "goodbye." Goodbye television with the rabbit ears that never worked. Goodbye sofa torn ragged with holes. Goodbye oddly-placed urinals in the women's restroom. Goodbye worn-through carpet. Goodbye. The room was my friend because it wouldn't be my final stop. I was moving on to a new city, and a new team. I had a new wives' room to enter, and a new group to meet. The system hadn't defeated us. Not yet. And even though I was leaving a lot behind, I would take with me the lessons I had learned in the Wives' Room of the Chicago Bears.

*No matter what challenges lie ahead —
I know we can face them together.*